Being Gay,
Being Christian

Being Gay,
Being Christian

You can be both

Dr Stuart Edser

EXISLE
PUBLISHING

First published 2012

Exisle Publishing Limited,
'Moonrising', Narone Creek Road, Wollombi, NSW 2325, Australia.
P.O. Box 60-490, Titirangi, Auckland 0642, New Zealand.
www.exislepublishing.com

National Library of Australia Cataloguing-in-Publication entry
Author: Edser, Stuart.
Title: Being gay, being Christian : you can be both /
Stuart Edser.
ISBN: 9781921497070 (pbk.)
Notes: Includes bibliographical references and index.
Subjects: Homosexuality—Religious aspect—Christianity.
Christian life. Bible and homosexuality.
Dewey Number: 241.664

ISBN 978-1-921497-07-0

10 9 8 7 6 5 4 3 2 1

Text design and production by IslandBridge
Cover design by Katy Yiakmis
Printed in Singapore by KHL Printing Co Pte Ltd
This book uses paper sourced under ISO 14001 guidelines
from well-managed forests and other controlled sources.

To the late Rev. Fred Warton,
Uniting Church minister and founding minister
of the Covenant Community Church,
now the Hunter Christian Community Church,
my friend, mentor and fellow musician,
the only clergyman in over 30 years
who ever told me I was okay.

And to my parents Bill and Betty Edser,
for their amazing lived example of
unconditional love.

Contents

Foreword   9

Preface   15

1 Why Another Book?   19

2 Two Kinds of Knowledge   29

3 Being Gay or Lesbian Today   38

4 Important Background Research   43

5 The Biology of Being Gay   49

6 The Psychology of Being Gay   58

7 Coming Out   71

8 Sound People, Sick Therapy   81

9 The Bible and Christianity   105

10 The Evangelical View of Homosexuality   124

11 The Catholic View of Homosexuality   157

12 Final Thoughts   199

Notes   231

Index   243

Index of Biblical References   247

Foreword

The struggle for the soul
of contemporary Christianity

The Hon Michael Kirby AC CMG

I hope that this book will gain a large readership among people of diverse sexualities: heterosexual, homosexual, bisexual, transgender and intersexual.

There was a time, not so long ago, when sexual minorities comprised people who were expected to be thoroughly ashamed of themselves and keep their sexuality a deep, dark, hidden secret – hidden from their families and communities life-long, hidden from their neighbours and, above all, hidden from their religious friends. Did not the scriptures, from the ancient Book of Leviticus,[1] condemn homosexual practice as an 'abomination'? The punishment prescribed by the holiness code of the Old Testament was death. And so it was for centuries in the criminal laws of England, from whose books of law we in Australia inherited our criminal codes and statutes.[2]

This was the situation when I was growing up in Australia. The Crimes Act of New South Wales,[3] in traditional language, imposed severe criminal punishments upon same-sex attracted men (women were ignored). These were the 'unnatural offences', involving the 'abominable crime'. The fact that the acts were performed between consenting adults in private was no defence. For, so it was said, the Bible condemned these crimes because they brought an infection of sin into the body politic of the entire nation, which was polluted by them.

Little wonder that generations of sexual minorities felt deeply alienated from themselves. Often they told no one, not even close friends, about their state. They were expected to go through life celibate, denying themselves the loving relationships and tender companionships (not to say, sexual fulfilment) that heterosexuals enjoyed as of right. This was a very big ask. But being backed up with criminal sanctions, many responded with shame and self-denial.

Some homosexuals married, against the order of their natures, plunging another human being into the burdens of their life. Furtive, unstable, fleeting encounters were all that was generally available to them. Not a few sought release in suicide. Many were the victims of violence and humiliation. Could this really have been the imposition that a loving religion imposed upon people whose sexual orientation was slightly different from the majority? Was it really so impossible to be both Christian and gay?

I was brought up in a loving Christian home, attended the local Anglican Church and learned its familiar and welcoming ways, so it seemed unlikely to me, at puberty, that I was truly 'intrinsically evil', condemned to a life beyond the pale and denied fulfilling love with other human beings and empathy with the society around me. Yet there are still good church people today who are still of that mind.[4] Things are changing, slowly, in my country. But globally, in most places, religion, even the Christian religion, seems pitched in a battle with the minority of individuals who discover that their sexuality does not conform strictly to the norm.

Then came the enlightenment. Substantially, it came first in the research and writings of scientists. Great writers in the psychological discipline, which the author Stuart Edser shares, began to question whether there was anything particularly 'unnatural', 'evil' or 'abominable' about sexual minorities and their sexual expression: Richard Krafft-Ebing, Havelock Ellis, Sigmund Freud, Evelyn Hooker and other psychologists dared to question the rationality of the hatred that was visited on sexual minorities. Their writings, in turn, stimulated an empirical search for evidence by the noted Professor of Zoology at Indiana University, Alfred Kinsey. Writing in the 1940s and 1950s, Kinsey detailed his investigations into sexual behaviour among human males and females. These appeared to establish that the sexual minorities were not insignificant in number; that they conformed to an apparently universal pattern; and that they reflected variations among human beings which were similar to other natural variations, such as skin colour, height, left-handedness and astigmatism. In short, the variations, scientifically speaking, were no big deal.[5] So why did the churches keep on propounding their message of hatred?

Be in no doubt that to this day the churches frequently continue to promote this message with vehemence and profound disrespect, not to say irrationality. Writing in the journal of the Sydney diocese of the Anglican Church of Australia (my own denomination), the Archbishop of Sydney, Dr Peter Jensen, recently declared that denying rights to fellow citizens in same-sex unions was 'not unjust – it is not even discrimination in the current sense of the word – but a refusal to call different things by the same name.'[6]

He asserted that same-sex marriage would result in the 'undermining of the family unit' and lead to 'the normalisation of homosexuality'. He went on:

> This claim for a right to be married could open the way for other forms, such as polygamous marriages or perhaps even marriage between immediate family members.[7]

These remarkable assertions were written without any apparent reference to what has actually happened in those countries which have begun to drop the exclusion of this group of citizens from the legal and civic rights enjoyed by others. There is no evidence whatsoever that polygamy or incest have increased, let alone been legalised, in The Netherlands, Belgium, Spain, Portugal, Argentina, Canada or any of the other countries that have opened up marriage to same-sex attracted couples.

Analogising adult long-term loving relationships to polygamy and incest was simply an unworthy attempt by Archbishop Jensen to continue the denigration of same-sex citizens, just as the church and religions have been trying to do for centuries.[8] It is shocking that such statements should be made today in the face of what is now a huge body of evidence that denies the assertion. Science and empirical evidence are the friends of reform and rationality. Little wonder that the enemies within the churches do not want to trouble themselves with research and evidence. Little wonder that they do not wish to hear the voices of their congregants who happen to be gay or the families and friends of those congregants.

Still, time is on the side of changing attitudes, at least in countries like Australia. The self-same news item that reported the dire predictions of Archbishop Jensen contained reports of a recent Galaxy Poll which found that three in four Australians believe that it is 'inevitable' that same-sex couples will be allowed to marry.[9] If this poll is even partly accurate, it shows that there has been a huge swing-around in Australian opinions about the rights and dignity of gay people, which could certainly not have been predicted 60 years ago when Alfred Kinsey was writing and when I was growing up.

The contrast between Archbishop Jensen's message and the message of the opinion poll could not have been more stark. Ordinary folks are simply no longer buying the stigma against same-sex people and the insistence that they are in some way unworthy, undeserving of civic equality and needful of humiliation and a permanent second-class status. That this change has happened so comparatively swiftly is itself an indication of the thirst of informed humanity for rational and scientific responses to assertions of injustice. Where holy scripture appears to be contradicted by scientific knowledge, it is necessary for people like Archbishop Jensen to use their considerable intelligence, knowledge and power to return to the scriptures and to read them afresh, in the light of the growing body of factual materials now available – including the simple personal stories of gay people themselves.[10]

Beyond these shores, other changes are taking place. In June 2011, there were two very important developments at the United Nations. For the first time, at the High Level Meeting on the HIV epidemic held in the General Assembly in New York, that body accepted, by consensus, the need to acknowledge by name sexual minorities (specifically 'men who have sex with men') if the world was to get on top of the HIV/Aids crisis and to help prevent the further spread of this deadly virus. Other relevant vulnerable groups were also given a name for the first time: 'sex workers' and 'injecting drug users'. The previous denigration, wrapped up in anonymising descriptions, was dropped.[11] Science and reality won the day. Sadly, much of the opposition to this move in the General Assembly came from countries that pretend to religious adherence: Christian countries in Africa, the Caribbean and the Pacific, Islamic countries in the Arab lands, Iran and Asia, and the Holy See.

The week following this resolution of the General Assembly came a decision by the Human Rights Council of the United Nations in Geneva. Once again, this time by majority, the Council agreed to condemn discrimination, stigmatisation and violence against sexual minorities through a resolution proposed by two great Christian countries of the future: South Africa and Brazil. These developments show the gradual acceptance of the world we live in that the religious game of shame that we inherited from the past is coming to its natural close.[12] It is religion, not science, that will have to adapt.[13]

Of course, great struggles remain to be fought. There is an inherent resistance on the part of rigid minds to revisit the texts of 'inerrant' scripture and to reconsider what those texts were trying to convey, by way of instruction, from earlier millennia to our current much better informed world. Unless the process of reconciliation of text and science can be expedited, and can succeed, the outcome of the conflict will be a continuing erosion in the numbers of believers, an ongoing decline in attendances at traditional houses of worship and a rising schizophrenia amongst congregants who love the fundamental messages and familiar forms of worship of their religions but cannot take seriously their 'out of touch' instruction on contemporary ethics affecting minorities in the human family.[14]

Some gay people, faced with continuing evidence of what they see as irrational and unloving attitudes towards them, their families and their friends, simply turn their backs on those who are currently in charge. My partner, Johan, is of this view: 'I cannot understand how you can take these nasty people seriously,' he says to me. 'They have always been horrible to women, to people of colour and to gays.' Sadly, there is some truth in what he says.

Others, like Stuart Edser and myself, ascribe the errors that they see to the small-mindedness of those who are presently in charge of our religion.[15] We have no doubt that, in the end, the loving kindness of the God of our beliefs and the spirit of reconciliation of the New Covenant will see the Christian church, or most of it, through to a new resolution. It will be a resolution informed by science and enlivened by love for one another, not misinformation, hatred and disdain.

So the subjects of this book are timely, important and interesting. They represent nothing less than the story of the present struggle for the soul of Christianity. Will the formalists win? Will the essentialists win? How will the struggle reach its conclusion? One thing is sure: the present unhappy compromise is untenable. Christian churches cannot feel obliged by science to denounce 'discrimination' against people on the grounds of their sexual orientation, but still condemn those people (so newly released from abomination) to a lifetime of celibacy, loneliness and shame. A moment's rational thought suggests what the eventual outcome will be. The speed of change in the past

60 years indicates that a new accommodation will be reached. It will probably be much earlier than many present religious leaders appear to think.[16]

For his thoughtful and informed contributions to this process of change, I thank Stuart Edser. I congratulate him on his book. Another pebble is thrown into the waters of life. The ripples are growing in strength. Their message is reaching the four corners of the earth.

Michael Kirby
Sydney
22 June 2011

Preface

On Wednesday 8 April 2009, former British Prime Minister and recent Catholic convert Tony Blair told gay magazine *Attitude* that he thought Roman Catholic church leaders were 'out of step with ordinary believers in their attitude toward homosexuals'. He believed there was a big generational difference on the issue, and that ordinary Catholics were more liberal-minded than their leaders. 'Actually,' he said, 'we need an attitude of mind where rethinking and the concept of evolving attitudes becomes part of the discipline with which you approach your religious faith.' Amen to that, Tony Blair. I hope yours is not a voice crying in the wilderness.

The Christian church worldwide is wrong about gays. It has been wrong from the start and it still is. This book is my attempt to use Blair's 'concept of evolving attitudes', the fact that knowledge develops and changes and, as it does so, we need to make allowances and adjustments. We must make a better world based on more sophisticated understandings, not on old worn-out themes or prejudices and 'rusted on' dogma that is no longer tenable. This is the basic premise from which I write this book and I do so in the hope that it will help both gay and non-gay people, clergy and laity, towards a better and more humane understanding of human sexuality, and gay sexuality in particular, as it intersects with the message of Jesus. Tony Blair's call to 'rethink' is an apt and an urgent one.

I first had the idea of writing this book in October 2007 while driving from Sydney to Newcastle just after completing two days of further professional development in trauma training. We had examined in great detail the triggers and emotional responses that often result in Acute Stress Disorder and Post-Traumatic Stress Disorder and how to work with such people according to the world's best evidence-based practice. It was a powerful workshop and I learned a lot, but I was tired and happy to be going home. As I listened to a Beethoven piano concerto on the CD player I pondered how incredible it was that the human mind can go through such horrible suffering and still move itself toward healing. This thought led me to suffering in general and to my own history and I realised that I was well prepared to write about being gay and being Christian. With my life history, plus my training, I reasoned, if I can't write that book, then nobody can.

I thought back to my meeting with out-of-the-closet former High Court judge, Justice Michael Kirby, a man I had greatly admired from afar for many years. It was August 2003 and I had journeyed to Christchurch Cathedral to hear him deliver the annual Morpeth Lecture. I had heard him speak on television and radio countless times, but never live. I was interested in his place in the community, his religious faith, his out status as a partnered gay man and his topic for the evening, the human genome. As he drew his lecture to a close I joined the queue waiting to speak to him. When it was my turn, I walked forward, shook his hand and introduced myself. I felt nervous but began by saying that I wanted to thank him for what he had been doing regarding gay issues in the community. He smiled immediately and I relaxed a little.

'I'm a psychologist in private practice and an out gay man too. I think it's so important to be out there unashamed and I just wanted to thank you again for being such a tremendous role model for us all. I really do appreciate it.'

He drew in closer and said, 'Look, you know, science will come through for us in the end, Stuart. It has in other areas where we've changed our thinking, and it will here too eventually. I have great faith in the science. We'll get there in the end.'

I was surprised that he looked to science first, rather than the law, but the more I thought it through, the more it made sense. We need the truth and objectivity of science to deal with this issue. Since it engenders so much emotion and so much heated rhetoric from all quarters, it would be wonderful if science could dispassionately say, 'Well, that's not right, this is how it works – and we have studies to show it.' The science is where the change will happen first. And psychology, as the science of being human, would be right at the forefront of any such resolution. I always knew that my own profession had a great part to play in the release of thought regarding gay and lesbian people. And I often wondered whether I might somehow play a role in that.

And so, driving home alone with my Beethoven blaring, I began to get excited as thoughts, ideas, chapters, psychologists, research and Bible verses all came flooding into my mind. I told my partner that night that I was going to write a book and that it was going to be about what I knew best: religion, sexuality and psychology. I began writing in January 2008 and I have written most nights and every weekend since. It has been a wonderful experience. I have so enjoyed the process and it has helped me, also, to grow as a person.

In the book's title I have deliberately put the word 'gay' before the word 'Christian'. A gay sexuality is part of the fabric of the self, whereas a particular religious affiliation is a belief that one can adhere to today and eschew tomorrow. Although I am very drawn to the Christian faith for what it offers and how it can change the world, I can discard my religion tomorrow but I can never discard my sexuality.

Because language is so important, making our innermost thoughts external and real and giving shape to what we believe, I prefer to use self-descriptive inclusive terms to describe same-sex attracted people, rather than 'homosexual' and 'homosexuality', which were coined by opposite-sex attracted people, most likely mid 19th-century lawyers decrying appalling treatment of same-sex attracted men under the Prussian penal code. Because it is not a word created by gay people about gay people, 'homosexual' can be described as heteronormative, the term used by sociologists and social psychologists to describe the point of view that regards opposite-sex attraction as normal and same-sex attraction as aberrant or abnormal. So, as often as possible, I will use the terms gay and lesbian sexual orientation or, more briefly, gay and lesbian orientation.

For ease, when I refer to God in the text, I usually use the masculine form, although I do not understand God as being either masculine or feminine. God is not human. I hope I do not offend here. The Bible verses in the text are all taken from the New International Version Study Bible, unless otherwise indicated.

I want to make plain that this is not a scholarly work. In other words, while it relies heavily on scholarship, it is written for the everyday educated person. I am not inviting academics to dissect this material, although they may do so if they wish. The whole idea has been to speak to intelligent non-experts, but in an educated style that does not dumb down. It will become increasingly apparent that I believe the church to be wrong in its attitude to gay and lesbian people. In fact, I go so far as to suggest that the church does violence in its rejection of gay and lesbian people and is causing untold damage both to good people and to the reputation of the Gospel. I speak very plainly about the church's mistreatment of gay and lesbian people. To do anything less is to collude with it, 'and in my own oppression', to use the words of Sister Jeannine Gramick. I value the church greatly and know it can offer much to the world. I just think it can do a whole lot better in so many ways. We are all children of a loving God. The Spirit of God is alive today in the lived experiences of people, both gay and straight, relentlessly inviting us towards greater intimacy with our creator and each other and entering more fully into our own humanity. If you are struggling as a gay person and wanting to retain your faith, then I hope and pray these pages will encourage you to find your own way through this rocky terrain. I know that God's Spirit will be with you as you do, just as He was with me.

Finally, there are some people I would like to thank. It is no small thing to ask someone not only to read a manuscript, but to offer remarks and suggestions for change and refinement. My friend Mark Toohey read the much longer first draft in this way. My heartfelt thanks to you, Mark, for your energy and enthusiasm. You were an enormous help. My partner Christopher May, who has been a tower of intellectual and emotional support in this endeavour, has my heartfelt gratitude. His meticulous efforts at creating the index to this book were sterling, and his incisive reading, notation and comments helped me immeasurably. Without his support, and his suggestions for refocusing and tightening, I would perhaps have doubted myself and the direction in which I felt I needed to take the book. Thanks, babe, you are awesome. Finally, a huge thank you to Benny and Gareth St John Thomas of Exisle Publishing for their belief in me and in this project, and an enormous merci to Exisle's structural editor Ian Watt, whose incisive comments and friendship were a great help to me in the preparation of the final draft and the development of the concept. Thank you, Ian.

And to my parents, Bill and Betty Edser, both now in their 80s, my heartfelt thanks for all your support, love and acceptance over the course of my long journey. I could not have wished for better parents.

Why Another Book?

There are many books about homosexuality and Christianity. Some are written by clergymen, some by lay people who have left the church because of its stance toward homosexuality, some by theologians, and even some by gay clergy who have been forced to resign or leave their vocation by their various ecclesiastical hierarchies. Some of these books are written with a great deal of scholarship; some are personal accounts. Some are enveloped by a deep sense of humanity and compassion, while others preach chapter and verse as though the authors themselves are blameless in all things. Some advocate pro-gay reform in the church, while more strident opponents tend to take a vociferous anti-gay position. A quick Amazon search with the words 'homosexuality AND Christianity' typed into the search box will obtain for you just under 50 titles. So why another one?

This book represents my efforts at easing the pain and diminishing the shame of being gay and being Christian. It is my attempt to bring you up to date with the latest science, theology and scholarship regarding gay and lesbian sexuality and the Christian life. It is written from the point of view of a psychologist who has a long-held deep faith and who has studied to understand the interface between psychology and science with spirituality and theology. Daily in my consulting room, I see individuals struggling with these issues and searching for a way forward. As a therapist, it is my duty to help such people to come to terms with their sexual orientation in a healthy, whole and educated way, to help them to accept themselves and their sexual identity and to assist them as they deal with family, friends, church or the workplace. I try to lead them away from self-hatred, self-loathing, guilt and shame and help those interested in the spiritual aspect, to see that, as much as anyone else, they are loved and accepted by God and that they can love and accept themselves as well.

I do not pretend to be a biologist, geneticist, sociologist, historian, biblical scholar or theologian. But these disciplines are not the sole monopolies of professionals: intelligent people can read their various discourses and offer opinion. Also, as a Christian man, I have no problem in sharing my own faith, such as it is, and discussing it openly in the hope that my small understanding of the things of God might offer encouragement to others and perhaps lessen their turmoil. However, I am a trained psychologist, registered in Australia with several degrees in psychology, plus a range of qualifications in other areas, such as hypnotherapy, the humanities, education and music, so I do claim expertise in the domain of my professional training and am prepared to argue a position.

My own story

I was born in Newcastle, Australia in 1959. I was a child in the 1960s, a teenager and youth in the 1970s and a young man starting out in a teaching career in the 1980s. After a successful teaching career, I returned to university to read psychology and went on into postgraduate education to research psychology and cancer for my doctorate. I have always been in private practice, although I continue to work for the medical faculty of my local university where I teach, tutor and examine Counselling Skills for Sexual Issues and lecture on the topic of homosexuality to third-year trainee doctors.

I am the third of four boys, the product of what the Catholic Church used to call a mixed marriage: Dad was Catholic and Mum was Anglican. In order for them to marry, Mum had to sign a declaration that all offspring would be educated and brought up as Catholics. From the time I was in primary school, I always had 'a heart after God', as many 'Bible-believing' people put it. I attended the local Catholic school, Holy Family, and was taught by the Sisters of St Joseph, some of whom were wonderful and some of whom put the fear of God into us with vivid stories of hellfire and God's judgement. Even as a little one, I would often go into the church during lunchtimes to pray and talk to God. When my mother came to pick me up after school, she would often have to wait until I had made my 'visit' in the church.

I felt the love of God very much in the kindly and gentle Fr Thomas Cronin, our parish priest. It was mostly due to his gentleness and beautiful spirit that I determined to become a priest myself. This thought was unshakeable and when, at the age of 13, the opportunity came for me to leave home and live in a minor seminary with a view to joining the Redemptorist Congregation of priests and brothers, I did so, having begged my parents to allow me to make the long journey to Galong.

Galong is a little village of a few hundred people nestled into the South Western Slopes of New South Wales, about an hour's drive from Young. The biggest thing in Galong is the Redemptorist monastery and in those days, 1973, it sat majestically amid hundreds of acres of prime farmland and alongside its heritage-listed cemetery. The monastery housed not only the priests and brothers of the order, the Reds as we called them, but also the Redemptorist Juvenate, a live-in high school for boys interested in the priesthood.

I lived in the juvenate for three years and most of the time found the experience rewarding and wonderful. I attended Mass daily at 6.30 am, said The Angelus at midday and at 6 pm to the call of the monastery bell, attended communal prayer daily after lunch and said communal night prayers every evening and Compline on Sundays. We went to the Our Lady of Perpetual Help novena every Saturday night, where I played the organ for the Redemptorist confreres and the local community. I walked the mile-long drive each evening saying the Rosary with others so inclined, sometimes in Latin, sometimes in English. We had regular retreats several times each year and we attended CD, or Christian Doctrine, each evening before dinner, which consisted of basic philosophy and theology. My faith grew in the structures that the juvenate provided, but my hormones were raging as I went through puberty and I knew, most assuredly, that I was attracted to other males. I was interested in other boys and had experimented with same-sex 'fooling around' *before* I went to the monastery, so it was not a case of my 'normal' heterosexual orientation being hijacked by living in an all-male monastic environment.

By my final year, 1975, I had decided against the priesthood. I had grown tired of the church's liturgies and wanted something more real so at fifteen and a half I returned to Newcastle, ready to complete my final year of high school. I fitted back into my former school, which was run by the Marist Brothers, and quickly took up again with old friends, who were all very welcoming.

At the same time, I became reacquainted with some very dear childhood friends who were involved with the local Anglican youth group. They were all very alive and energetic to their faith, reading the Bible privately and discussing it with great enthusiasm, something I had never experienced before. I was reminded of being with them back in 1971, when I had prayed the 'sinner's prayer' under a tree, not unlike the Buddha under the bodhi tree, at a Baptist youth camp beside Lake Macquarie and asked Jesus to be my personal Lord and Saviour. Catholics didn't really do such things, so I kept it quiet later at the monastery, but I always wondered somewhere deep down whether I was a true Christian and that my fellow juvenists, or at least most of them, were just going through the motions, never having received Jesus as an act of will outside their infant baptisms.

After reuniting with my Protestant friends, I decided it was time to leave the Catholic Church, which I did gradually, and join the other mob, much to my father's chagrin. Every Sunday, I would first go to early Mass, then walk up the hill to the Methodist service, where the Wesleyan music sent me into raptures, and then, in the evening, I would attend the Anglican service before walking around the corner to the little Baptist church for yet another service. I loved it; I couldn't get enough of church. I loved God. I believed He was real in my life and was helping me to live my life the way He wanted.

When I went to the local university I joined the Evangelical Union. With other like-minded students I would stand in the University Union handing out 'godly' tracts and inviting people to talks given by local pastors or visiting evangelical academics. I led camps for Christians all over the town and, with my academic proclivity, became a solid student of the scriptures and of evangelical scholars. I was a talented musician and speaker and led music in church and taught music camps to other churches. I became an elder in the Uniting Church and studied to become a lay preacher. I regularly taught the Word of God in my own local church and was invited to speak at other churches and groups both in Newcastle and around New South Wales.

With a group of other seriously spiritual people, I helped to found an independent 'Spirit-filled' church in Newcastle, which still exists, and became one of its principal leaders. I was invited on a six-week preaching, teaching and music tour of the United States, which I enjoyed immeasurably. I had discovered charismatic renewal and was 'baptised in the Spirit', immersing myself in the heady world of speaking with other tongues and using the gifts of the Spirit, such as prophecy, word of knowledge, word of wisdom, tongues and interpretation of tongues and the laying on of hands for healing. It was a wonderful time of spirituality and learning and I believed that God had great things in store for me. However, there was one giant fly in the ointment: I was gay.

I had steadfastly suppressed my desire. I believed the scripture to say that the flesh was evil and had to be crucified with Christ. I was in total denial about my sexual orientation and believed God was testing me to see how faithful I would be and how determined I was to live according to His ways. I was *convinced* that God would change me. When I was teaching in Texas, I even bought a gold ring as an act of faith that God would heal me or deliver me from my torment so that I could marry according to His natural design.

No matter what I did or tried, however, I could not stop, much less eradicate, my desire. I would regularly fast for a week, eating and drinking nothing at all. I would pray all night regularly. I went to all manner of holy men who might be able to speak the Word of God into my soul and set me free. They ministered to me healing of the body, healing of the mind, and healing of the memories. I took on the 'manhood of Christ'. I tried 'living in the Spirit', which consisted of speaking in tongues for hours and hours on end as I gave my life over to God. At home I would walk round and round in a circle praying 'in the Spirit' for hours at a time. I eventually came to believe that I was oppressed by a demon and requested deliverance, the Pentecostal version of exorcism, from a number of different 'spiritual warfare' experts. I began to learn about spiritual warfare myself and went on the attack against Satan and all his cohorts. Nothing worked. Year after year, I sought the Lord to deliver me from my great sin. And year after year, I remained exactly the same, apart from the fact that my sanity was deteriorating.

My sense of hypocrisy knew no bounds. Here I was, preaching and teaching the Lord's Word, leading His people in worship, and yet all the while convinced that I was the filthiest, most abject of sinners. Sometimes people with the same problem would come to me for help and I would recycle to them the same platitudes that I had been given, even though I knew in my heart that they were untrue and would offer them no solace. It would be better, I thought, not to be a Christian leader than to live like this. As a consequence of this hypocrisy, and a crushing loneliness, I became suicidal. I could not change my desire yet I had a genuine heart after God. In my mind, the two were mutually exclusive. The church life I had been leading would never countenance homosexuality. I could not be both a Christian *and* gay.

There was no deliverance. I felt so dirty, so filthy, so fleshly. One evening I aimed my car for the cliff overlooking one of our local beaches. I would smash myself on the rocks far below and let the ocean take me. I flattened the accelerator to the floor of the vehicle and sped toward the precipice. Three-quarters of the way to the edge, I slammed on the brakes. I flopped onto the steering wheel, frightened and distressed, and wept and wept. I lived this way until I could stand it no longer. In my early 30s, lonely, confused, celibate and angry, I went to the top of a hill in the middle of the city and shook my fist at God. I called Him a fucking bastard and told Him that I needed to put Him on the shelf for a few years. I was angry that He could have made me straight and yet chose to make me gay, and then condemn me for it. I was angry that He could have healed or delivered me from all same-sex desire, yet He chose to remain silent and immovable. I was angry that I had served Him so faithfully and yet He had let me down so blatantly. I would not discard Him forever, but I needed to find out some answers, and they had to be from someone who knew what they were talking about. I was done with seeing pastors, elders and teaching evangelists offering me prayer or so-called Christian counselling. God would have to wait for me because I was over waiting for Him.

It was then that I sought out the help of a local psychologist, Dr Sandra Pertot, whom I found in the phone book. I saw that she had expertise in sexual matters, but little did I suspect that she was one of

Australia's foremost sexologists and sex therapists, an author, a highly skilled clinician and a wonderful, down-to-earth woman. Later, many years after my therapy, we would become colleagues and firm friends. Driving to my first session, nervous and fighting church-ingrained instincts against looking for answers 'in the world' rather than in God, I decided I would finally get to the bottom of this, no matter what it took. Whether I was straight or gay, I would never again return to the terrible war in my being – what psychologists call cognitive dissonance – that I had lived with for 20 or so years. If I were straight, I would be straight. If I were gay, I would be gay and accept myself. It was a huge decision and one that I understand now much better from my experience as a clinician and scholar.

Sandra took me slowly through a deconstruction of my desire: its origins, how it manifested itself and what I had chosen to do with it over the years. She educated me on the scientific research about homosexuality and helped me to see that it was not pathological and that I was not sick or disordered. Sandra and I slowly and carefully discussed all my questions and concerns; nothing was taboo. I saw that the body was not evil or dirty or sleazy and I began to appreciate that desire itself was not my mortal enemy. I eventually began to accept that I was neither sick nor sinful and that I had an important choice to make: would I accept and learn to love who I was or would I go on fighting what was clearly my natural orientation? By the end of a few months of therapy, there was only one way I could answer that question. Should it cost me everything, my church, my friends, my faith, I could not go back to living an inauthentic life predicated on denial and mendacity. I needed to love myself. I needed to accept myself. I needed to love and be loved, just like the majority of the human race. I began to understand that my sexuality was part of who I always was, part of who I am, part of what makes me, me.

And what of my own faith? Did I ever return to it and find God waiting for me? The answer is yes, although it took me many years of learning how to become just plain human again rather than regarding myself as one of God's special messengers. Nowadays, I am very happy and comfortable just being one of us. I now have a greater appreciation of the human condition that I try to take into my clinical practice. And wonderfully, I discovered that even though I thought I had put God on the shelf for all those years, He had actually been with me all along, integral to every part of my journey.

And my personal life? I am very happy. Today, I am no longer alone. I am in a relationship with my life partner, which is the greatest blessing of all. We love each other dearly: we care for each other, look out for each other and want only the best for each other's life. He is a wonderful man with great gifts of intellect, music and humour, and we regularly enjoy scintillating conversations about every conceivable topic and indulge our mutual passion for music. He shows me the tenderness that I always craved and I him. And to top it all off, he's pretty easy on the eye too!

Being able to discard the old 'saved' versus 'unsaved' model has freed me. It was ultimately my lived experience, not dogma, which set me on the course to finding such freedom. We deny our lived experience at our great peril. As the Gestalt therapists say, it is our reality that is the only thing we can truly do anything with. All our desires, wishes and longings that life might be otherwise are insubstantial. It is only our reality that we can interact with and mould.

My faith now is very different, and this book is not the place to detail that journey, but I can say that I believe in a God who is infinitely compassionate and loving-kind, who understands and greatly esteems our human nature and who wants and desires us to enter into our humanity in the most complete way we can. And that includes our sexuality. As Jesus put it so succinctly, 'to have life and to have it more abundantly'.

Who this book is for

There is no more divisive an issue in the church today than the highly controversial topic of being gay and being Christian. Even the abortion debate has not caused so much hysteria, debate and nastiness or, as is happening in the worldwide Anglican Communion, edged the church so close to schism. Gay man Gene Robinson and lesbian Mary Glasspool were both consecrated bishops in the Episcopal Church in the United States in 2003 and 2010 respectively amid huge controversy.

I hope this book will meet the needs of a number of different groups. You may be a young person participating in the life of the church but, unknown to anyone there, including your closest friends, you are attracted to the same sex. These desires make you feel very uncomfortable because you're not supposed to be having them. You may feel dirty or sinful because of the thoughts that go through your mind and you may have even heard priests, pastors or youth pastors talk about homosexuality in a way that indicates that it is abnormal, sinful and deserving of God's punishment. You may have heard them preach that anyone leading a gay lifestyle needs to repent of their sin, turn away from their ungodly life and turn to God, that Jesus will save them and help them to live a godly life. To persist in that lifestyle is to turn their back on God and his love and power. Some may even say that, according to the Bible, gay and lesbian people will never ever see heaven, never feel God's presence or experience His radiance and will even burn in hell for eternity.

As a result, you may hate yourself and loathe the thoughts and emotions you have regarding another young man or woman to whom you might feel attracted. You may call yourself filthy, think of yourself as perverted or as a selfish sinner and find yourself constantly repenting and asking God for forgiveness for your desires, only to have them come back again and again relentlessly. You may even have thought, sometimes, that it might be better to die rather than be Christian and gay, for surely no one in church would accept you in this condition if they knew. I know how all this feels for I lived this life for many years – too many years. If, as I did, you love God and want to live a spiritual life in the midst of a greedy, acquisitive and often cruel world, then hearing that your same-sex attraction excludes you from the life of God's grace is unbelievably painful. Then take heart – not everybody thinks this way.

You may be a young gay or lesbian person participating in the life of the church, but not disclosing your orientation to others. You are out to yourself but not to anyone else. Your sexuality is a secret that you do not feel you can share with those whom you love in the church. This is a hard place to be. You feel isolated and lonely. You watch as all your straight friends pair up and their 'good wholesome behaviour' is sanctioned and blessed by the church. Resentment may have already begun to grow but you attempt to keep it at bay because you are trying to live the life that Jesus talked about. You go to weddings and secretly wonder, in your own private pain, if there will ever be anyone for you. 'Do I have to choose between loving God and loving someone else?' Friends joke about when it will be your turn, and you joke and laugh along with them, but inside you long to hold someone and be held in their arms. Then take heart, for there is a more fulfilling way to experience your life.

You may be an older person participating in the life of the church who is same-sex attracted. You have never been comfortable with the labels 'gay' or 'lesbian' and have never dared disclose your orientation to anyone in the church. Instead, you are content to be labelled the bachelor or spinster of the congregation. You know that people feel sorry for you or even pity you because you never married, but you feel it is easier to live with that prejudice than to disclose the truth. At your age, you feel that accepting the category gay or lesbian would be just too hard, and it's probably all too late now anyway. You may feel that your earlier decision not to live your life authentically was based on good scriptural grounds, that you're living the way God intended you to live. Or you may have a secret 'friend' that no one at church knows about. Or, sadly, you may even have denied your desire altogether and lived a life of never-satisfied longing. It's incredibly painful to allow those thoughts into your consciousness, so mostly, you try not to. But occasionally, it gets the better of you and you cry from the pain. Then please take heart: perhaps there can be change.

It is also possible that worried family or clergy are reading this book. I invite you to put aside your assumptions and read the work in its entirety. You will learn much and, if you have an open heart and mind, may grow in maturity yourself in this difficult area.

Two Kinds of Knowledge

Ultimately, this book is about epistemology. The dictionary defines this as 'a branch of philosophy that investigates the origin, nature, methods and limits of human knowledge'.[1] It refers to how we theorise about knowledge, how we obtain it, how we value it and what we do with it as a consequence of adhering to a particular intellectual position.

Conventionally, we tend to speak in terms of there being a debate between the Christian church and homosexuality. The problem with this type of language is that the church is an entity, an ideology, an established world religion, while there is no equivalent sense of meaning in the word homosexuality. There is no spokesperson for all gay people, no sacred text, no historic established institution and no set of gay beliefs that are considered orthodox. Yet there is a debate between the two and it is predicated on knowledge or, rather, types of knowledge. This is epistemology and it can best be seen in the way one sees the world – what philosophers usually call the worldview.

Two worldviews

There are many worldviews but the two basic ones often described are the classical and the modern.

Classical

The classical worldview sees the world as a finished product, not evolving or changing. Conserving the status quo or stability is seen as the main virtue; by implication, change is the main vice. This worldview describes phenomena as being natural or according to nature, it talks of the essence of things as though there is only one and it explains the world as being static and unchanging. Furthermore, its own views and pronouncements, once declared, are hard to change. The classical worldview places emphasis on truth, certainty and universal concepts; it does not concern itself with questioning or curiosity. Instead, it prefers dogma.

Modern

The modern worldview sees the world in a vastly different light – as dynamic and therefore constantly changing and evolving. It has much room in its discourse for the vast passage of time the world and humanity have experienced, for the history of phenomena and for how things alter and develop. It does not deal in unalterable truths but, rather, emphasises the growth and development of understanding as knowledge and human experience continue to evolve. There is much room for curiosity, questioning and even uncertainty. This worldview is the very underpinning of the Age of Enlightenment and birth of the modern era.

The debate over human sexuality, with the church firmly ensconced in one corner, and perhaps a whole group of others in the other corner, is primarily a disagreement over worldview. One kind of knowledge, based firmly in the classical worldview, relies on a set of texts written in the ancient world and adhered to today, to varying degrees, in a literal way, or ascribed as the Word of God and given the status of Holy Scripture. The other is a knowledge based within the modern worldview and on the conceptions of contemporary scholarship undertaken in a modern, post-Enlightenment, technological world where various academic disciplines can be brought to bear on all manner of questions, including that of human sexuality.

Without doubt, this second kind of knowledge is the dominant epistemological view today. It comes from the world of science, where knowledge is characterised as evolving, using observation, investigation, rigorous methodologies that can be repeated by others, and the notion of falsifiability – the capacity to discard something that has been shown to be wrong.

Within the sciences, this view of knowledge has itself become refined over the decades into the modern scientific method. Some other disciplines – archaeology, history, anthropology, sociology, gender studies, linguistics, biblical studies, critical literary theory and many others – have adopted a similar approach to the garnering of knowledge and use similar tenets to investigate their own points of inquiry.

In this book I argue that a modern understanding of knowledge is to be preferred over a blind, uncritical and literal acceptance of ancient texts, even if they are ascribed as God's Word, or over church dogma that was often synthesised and resolved in the mediaeval period and based on an interpretation of those even earlier ancient texts. I hold to an epistemology based in a modern worldview that deems nothing exempt from rigorous inquiry.

This is in stark contrast to accepting that ancient texts are appropriate for today's world, no matter what. Believing what the Bible tells us just because, as the fundamentalists will have it, 'it's in the Bible', is not how we generally deal with knowledge today. For example, we now have a different understanding about the solar system, the earth, war, sickness and disease, mental health, marriage and divorce, menstruation, food, animal sacrifice and gender relations, to name a few. Regarding the Bible as inerrant – without any error, and eternally true in all matters – or stating that 'thus it is because God said it in His Word', are notions that cannot be sustained in a modern world.

Such views are naive and ignorant at best and wilfully perverse at worst, especially when the church tells young people struggling with an emerging gay or lesbian sexual orientation that they are sinners, that if they pray hard enough, God will deliver them, or, worst of all, that they should live their lives alone and isolated from love. If the church wants to be part of the conversation, then it is going to have to get honest about what we now know about human desire and sexuality and stop pretending that its doctrines are excused from modern scholarship.

Two examples from history

In rejecting same-sex attraction as a legitimate form of human desire, the church, in its evangelical or its Catholic forms, looks to a certain mix of the scriptures and traditional teaching as its prime authority. In both 'wings' of the church there have been occasions where the church's prime authority has differed markedly from the findings of science. What has traditionally happened when the church says one thing and science says another? Let's look at the two greatest examples from the pages of history to see: the origins of the earth and humankind and, related to this, the experience of Galileo.

For centuries the church believed the biblical account of the creation of the earth as reported in the first chapter of Genesis, which stated that the earth was created some 6000 years ago in a period of six days. One 17th-century Anglican archbishop even analysed the genealogies in Genesis in great detail and concluded that the earth was created by God in 4004 BCE. Yet we now know, from the science of geology, that our planet is between four and five billion years old and that life on earth is around three and half billion years old. The church had no choice but to accede to this greater understanding that made the older biblical and traditional teachings obsolete. To hold fast obstinately to the error would only attract derision and mockery throughout a modern world, thereby subverting the cause of faith.

According to the biblical and teaching traditions, humanity was created on day six as two distinct, real individuals whom the Bible names Adam and Eve. Adam was formed out of the dust of the earth and Eve was created in response to God's realisation that Adam needed a partner: 'it is not good for the man to be alone' (Gen 2:18).[2] So He put Adam to sleep and took one of his ribs and made it into a woman, Eve. This was the human side to the story of creation. Yet we now know from the science of paleontology, the study of fossils and bone fragments, that modern man, Homo Sapiens, evolved from the apelike creatures scientists call Australopithecines, came into existence and walked out of Africa to populate the world somewhere

32

between half a million and two million years ago. Once again, the church has had no choice but to give ground on this most important of issues.

The case of Galileo Galilei (1564–1642) is a tragic one. A brilliant mathematician, physicist, empirical investigator and scientific philosopher, he added greatly to human knowledge by improving the telescope, studying motion, theorising and experimenting in the world of physics and investigating the heavens. Yet he died under house arrest by the church, whose Catholic faith he adhered to his whole life.

Galileo came undone with the church when he lent scientific support to the Copernican view of heliocentrism against the church's dogmatic position of geocentrism, which placed the earth as created by God at the centre of the universe and required all celestial bodies to revolve around it as if in deference to a superior heavenly star. Galileo, using his telescope, and making meticulous observations, found that Copernicus had been right: a heliocentric view, which had the sun at its centre with the planets of the solar system revolving around it, was the true state of the then-known heavens.

However, in 1616 the Inquisition of the Catholic Church directed that Galileo not 'hold or defend' such a view. In 1633 he was ordered to stand trial for heresy. The Inquisition, which wanted Galileo to recant his views publicly, be imprisoned and have his writing and future writings banned, won the day. Galileo lived out the remainder of his days in his own villa near Florence under house arrest where, although going blind, he continued to work until his death in 1642. It took the church until 1835 to completely drop its official position against heliocentrism by finally removing Galileo's and Copernicus's books from their index of banned books. On 31 October 1992, 350 years after Galileo's death, Pope John Paul II publicly apologised, expressing regret for the treatment that Galileo had received from the church. Better late than never, I suppose.

Neither facing up to the undeniable proposition that the Bible was not the inerrant Word of God nor admitting that its understandings of our world needed to be an evolving process came easily to the church. Nor did such ground-giving make everybody happy. The cosmological examples just discussed continue to cause heated debate and consternation among different groups of Christians. The creationists still insist that the earth is only 6000 years old and that Adam and Eve were two real people who ate an apple in a garden when they were expressly told not to, thereby condemning the entire human race to spiritual separation from God and some, even, to the everlasting fires of hell. Thank goodness that, throughout the ages, some in the church saw sense and placed value on the faculty of human reason. We certainly need such people today. Just as Galileo was asked to choose between church dogma and what he knew to be true, so the church today asks gay people to choose between church dogma and the authenticity of their natural sexual orientation, something they know to be true.

Examples of the two kinds of knowledge

The Gospel of Mark records two occasions where Jesus healed by commanding demons to part from the unfortunate person, Mark 5:1–20 and 9:17–29. In the first of these cases, there appears to be ample evidence of mental illness. The second example recounts the healing of a physical disorder.

In the Chapter 5 account, Jesus has crossed the lake and disembarked in the region of the Gerasenes. He is greeted by 'a man with an evil spirit' come down from the tombs where he lives among the graves. Fearing his condition, the townspeople had frequently bound his arms and upper body in chains and placed his legs in irons, and shunned him. The poor fellow, inconsolable and frantic to escape his torture, has broken open the chains, no doubt injuring himself significantly, and even lacerated himself with stones, just as people today sometimes cut themselves when undergoing a terrible psychological or emotional ordeal. The townspeople will not venture unnecessarily into the graveyard because doing so makes them ritually unclean, requiring cleansing rites to be performed. So the man has been left to his own devices as his mental illness grows worse and worse.

It is difficult to diagnose what is wrong, for not all his symptoms are clearly listed in the text, but it is possible that he had a form of schizophrenia. Perhaps a single psychotic episode has frightened the townsfolk and precipitated their severe 'treatment' of him. Maybe he has an ongoing psychosis in which he is unable to engage with reality much at all. Perhaps, in his delusional state, he has played along with the role because he cannot think things through clearly enough. Jesus completely breaks through and brings healing to the poor unfortunate. Yet the text states that the method he uses is to exorcise the demon possessing the man.

If we say 'it's in the Bible, therefore it must be true', then it follows that this is a legitimate way in which we might deal with individuals suffering from schizophrenia, schizoaffective disorder, bipolar disorder or any other mental illness that involves psychotic episodes. If it were your loved one, would you want exorcism to be the treatment of choice just because Jesus used it for the Gerasene man? Or would you think that maybe you need to interpret the text in a way that would allow you to have your loved one treated in a timely and compassionate manner according to the world's best-practice psychological and psychiatric standards and yet still to be able to walk in the path of Jesus? In the ancient world, mental illness was thought to be caused by the gods or by demonic possession. Today, we have a very different view.

In the Chapter 9 account listed above, Mark's Gospel recounts Jesus' healing of an epileptic boy. Not only does the boy get thrown to the ground, gnash his teeth, foam at the mouth and become rigid when he has a seizure, he is also unable to speak. The boy's father says he has been like this since childhood. Deafness has been identified as one of many symptoms of epilepsy. However, it is impossible to tell from the text whether the deafness is an epileptic symptom, whether the boy is also physically deaf and mute, whether he has an autistic spectrum disorder along with epilepsy that causes him to miss the usual cues from the outside world, or whether he is so traumatised by the violence of his epileptic attacks (the text says that sometimes he has been thrown in the water and in the fire when having a seizure) that he has withdrawn into himself and refuses to speak. I would suspect either the first or the last. Note, too, that the text does not refer to the boy speaking after the healing, only that he becomes as still as a corpse, after which Jesus lifts him to his feet.

Again, though, notice how Jesus heals the epileptic boy: he casts out demons. Yet today, we know that epilepsy is a seizure disorder that affects the nervous system and can be related to a brain injury or to family history. It is an intense burst of electrical activity in the brain like an 'electrical storm' that completely overwhelms the finely balanced neurological electrical system. The text suggests the boy is having what doctors today call a tonic-clonic seizure (what used to be called a grand-mal seizure), which has both rigid (tonic) and jerky (clonic) movements. Doctors today would typically use a class of drugs called anti-convulsants, using other treatments only where this first line of therapy is ineffective. They do not try to cast out any demons.

So we are back to epistemology again. Do we take the Bible to be the inerrant Word of God, dictated by God to the various authors, meaning exactly what it says and saying exactly what it means, for all time, world without end? In order to use the Bible's words as a 'lamp to my feet and a light to my path' (Ps 119:105), is it necessary to believe unalterably that every word – at least in the various translations – must be taken at face value and forever? Or do we need room for a more sophisticated approach? Do we need room for metaphor? Do we need room to acknowledge that the Bible is written from the point of view of the ancient world? Is it possible to have a more sophisticated Christianity that values and encourages human intellectual endeavour while, to use Marcus Borg's phrase, 'taking the Bible seriously, but not literally?'

So how is all this relevant to the gay issue? It is relevant because if there needs to be room made for modern conceptions of mental illness and disorders like epilepsy, then maybe we need to do the same for our greater understanding of human sexuality. And the Bible does have a few things to say about human sexual relations. And you probably know that it also says, in just a few places, some pretty momentous things about same-sex sexual behaviour which, if taken literally and out of context and as God's purpose for humanity for all time, would mean that the approximately 350,909,790 gay people in the world today are in big trouble, even risking eternal damnation.[3]

There are many examples of how the older biblical view has had to defer to a modern conception of the world and countless books and scholarly papers have been written about this topic. Like other disciplines, both theology and biblical studies have had to look deeply into their own respective souls in order to avoid epistemological oblivion, as happened to alchemy. For some, this comes as an enormous challenge. To be confronted with the idea that perhaps the Bible is *not* the last word on everything is a huge shock. Some turn away in disbelief; others dig in and resist ever more stridently. A group of creationists in the United States, led by an Australian, have spent multiple millions of dollars building a museum to the Genesis account of creation, weaving the dinosaurs, not referred to in the Bible at all, into their story with amazing casuistry, and agitating for 'creation science', now called 'intelligent design', to be taught in schools.

Does God feel aggrieved that I don't believe in a firmament over-hanging the earth from which the rain comes, as is described in Genesis? I don't think so. Is God put out that, if I get sick, I will go to the doctor for treatment rather than to the priest for exorcism? I don't think so. Is God put out that I am gay? I don't think so.

I was brought into this world as a human being, a being with consciousness. And I know that along with consciousness, the greatest of our gifts, humanity is also formed with sexuality, which is as much a part of us as is our intelligence and personality. We are sexual creatures, and there should be no shame in this. We therefore need to understand human sexuality based on a modern worldview that values science and reason.

Over the course of human history sexuality has taken two principal forms: heterosexuality and homosexuality. They have been there across time, so the historians tell us, and across all cultures, so the anthropologists tell us. Gay people should be free to and encouraged to enter into the fullness of their sexuality in the same way that everyone else is. They deserve, in Jesus' wonderful words, 'to have life and to have it more abundantly.'

Being Gay or
Lesbian Today

We cannot launch into a discussion about gay and lesbian people without first clarifying exactly who we're talking about. We must ask what it means to be gay or lesbian, at least in the way that we understand the terms in today's world. For, as you will see in a later chapter on biblical issues, it is absolutely critical to define the phenomenon we are discussing. The Bible is quite specific in the terms it uses and you must understand that there is a marked difference, a chasm in fact, between what the Bible refers to in the ancient world and what we mean when we talk about gay and lesbian people today.

In the West in this new century and millennium, we are very conscious that gay and lesbian people are around us. In February every year, Sydney celebrates the Gay and Lesbian Mardi Gras, a very public, internationally renowned festival in which gay people show the world that they are gay and not ashamed of it. Individuals and groups dress for the occasion in all manner of costumes, most often to declare and celebrate their sexuality in a world that would tell them to be quiet about it, but sometimes also to satirise society's and occasionally the church's non-acceptance. After the fun and excitement and parties most will take off their costumes and go back to their routine lives, working at the hospital, the school, the bank, the library, the university or the building site.

Gay and lesbian people are on our televisions. We laugh along with *Will and Grace* and follow the lives and loves of the characters in *Queer as Folk*. There have been gay characters in *Six Feet Under*, *Dawson's Creek*, *This Life*, *Buffy the Vampire Slayer*, *Brothers and Sisters*, *Brideshead Revisited* and *Friends*. Gay people are also on the silver screen. The best-known movie example of recent years is *Brokeback Mountain* from 2005, which won three Oscars. Its depiction of the lives and struggles of two cowboys who fall in love gained plaudits from around the world and won its two principal actors Oscar nominations. The late Heath Ledger, in particular, was lauded for his moving performance as Ennis Delmar, a man who found and lost love. *The Wedding Banquet*, made in 1993 and nominated for an Oscar for Best Foreign Language Film, had two main gay characters. *Y Tu Mama Tambien*, *The Object of My Affection*, *The Sum of Us*, *The Opposite of Sex*, *Philadelphia*, *Four Weddings and a Funeral*, *In and Out*, *Mambo Italiano*, *My Best Friend's Wedding*, *My Own Private Idaho*, *Priest*, *Summer Storm*, *Torchsong Trilogy*, *Wilde* and the *Donald Strachey Private Investigator* series are all movies that are either specifically about gay people or have gay characters in them.

Many of us know someone who is gay: a brother, a sister, a cousin, a friend, a team-mate. We may work with a gay person or be educated by a gay or lesbian person in a school or college or university. At the very least, we might know of someone famous who is gay. In Australia, there is former High Court Justice Michael Kirby, Greens leader Senator Bob Brown, singer Anthony Callea, former international rugby league player Ian Roberts, world-famous concert pianist Stephen Hough, 2008 Olympic diving gold medallist Matthew Mitcham or the former federal president of the Australian Medical Association, Dr Kerryn Phelps. Internationally we think of comedian Ellen DeGeneres, screen actor Sir Ian McKellen, singers k.d. lang and Ricky Martin or US Olympic diving gold medallist, Greg Louganis, to name but a few.

What we're not talking about

So what does it mean to be a gay person? Right-wing Christian fundamentalists tend to go straight to the bedroom when answering this question. For them, being gay is all about sex: how a gay person has sex. Have you noticed the rather unhealthy obsession with sex that anti-gay religious advocates seem to have? This is often the very transgression of which they accuse us – they say that *we* are obsessed with sex. With so much injustice, poverty and horror in the world, sex is often all they seem to want to talk about. Adult behaviour in the bedroom is also often the focus of their theological discourse, rather than the life, example and teachings of Jesus.

For them, being gay is about having sex with another person of the same gender. 'Gay people put this here and touch that there and hey presto, you've got yourself a gay.' Yet they would be totally horrified if we were to describe what it means to be straight, merely by how straight people have sex. 'You put this here and touch that there and hey presto, you've got yourself a straight.' There is more to being straight or gay than just whether you have sex with a man or a woman. It is more than just the sex act that constitutes a person's sexual orientation. Being gay or being straight is not just about what we do. It is much more about whom we love and who we are. To reduce being gay, or for that matter being straight, merely to the sex act is to treat someone as less than a person, as a behaviour.

Depersonalisation is the term that psychologists use to describe the act of treating someone as less than a person. The ultimate example of this kind of depersonalisation in our present context is gay hate crimes. These are perpetrated by individuals who have subscribed to the basest parts of human nature and are the products of families or societies where hatred and prejudice are permitted as part of everyday life. Such attitudes are usually hidden in some way, or coloured or glossed, as often as not with some kind of religious overtone. The most infamous of these hate crimes of recent years was the 1998 torture and murder of American Matthew Shepard, an act of barbarism so heinous that it made news reports the world over and inspired movies and plays.

Aged only 21, Matthew, a gay, gregarious, intelligent, optimistic man who spoke several languages and was studying politics at the University of Wyoming, accepted a lift home from a bar after midnight on 7 October from two men posing as gay. They took him to a remote rural area east of Laramie, where they bashed him around the head repeatedly with a gun, tied him to a split rail fence and tortured him, then left him to die in the cold of the night, unconscious and still bound to the fence. Eighteen hours later, in a coma, he was found by a cyclist, who mistook him for a scarecrow. Matthew never regained consciousness and died in hospital on 12 October.

Gay people and scholars have long given the name homophobia to the specific prejudice against gay and lesbian people. The prejudice with which Matthew Shepard's murderers grew up existed as part of the socio-political and religious world of their time and place – not that the authorities would have espoused such views openly. Prejudice was just the accepted norm. But when authority figures and institutions ignore hatred, bigotry and ignorance, they can develop into monstrous and anarchic influences. In this case, they became murderous and stole from Matthew his life and his future, and from his parents, a wonderful and loving son.

Who we are talking about

If being gay is not about the bedroom and not about a behaviour, then who *are* we talking about? Gay and lesbian people are physically and emotionally attracted to people of their own sex with whom they can form loving and sexual relationships. Just like their straight counterparts, gay and lesbian individuals come in all shapes and sizes.

We are Caucasian and Asian, black, white, tall, short, rich, poor, educated, uneducated, intelligent and not so intelligent. Some of us are people of faith and others are not. We are people with mothers, fathers, brothers, sisters, partners and children. We are introverted, extroverted, sensitive, insensitive, confident, unsure, garrulous and shy. We work as professionals, in blue collar jobs and as tradespeople. Some of us are studying. We have strengths and weaknesses, dreams and regrets, likes and dislikes and successes and failures in life. We have mortgages and personal loans, invest in the stock market and property and pay our taxes. We go to the beach, the movies, the ski fields, the pub, the café, the shopping centre and the sporting fixture. We have relationships and histories. We look after our loved ones, feed our pets, mow our lawns and weed our gardens. We talk to our neighbours and put the bin out one night each week. We go on holidays, celebrate Christmas and go back to work in the New Year. We have lives to be led, partners we love and cherish and have the same physical and psychological needs as the rest of the community. In short, gay and lesbian individuals are people, with all the variety, richness and dignity that human beings possess. Gay and lesbian people are *not* a behaviour.

As much as being gay is not a behaviour, neither is it some trendy thing that you decide to become. Being gay is not about parties or sex any more than being straight is. Neither should it be about denying who you are, being secretive about your desire or allowing others, even authority figures, to disrespect you or to proclaim that your natural orientation is wrong, disordered or contrary to God and the church. Being gay is about accepting the fact that you are attracted to your own sex and that you are not ashamed of it. It is about liking, even loving, who you are and living your life in that mindset – not someone else's idea of your life, but *your* idea of your life. And living your life is one of the most powerful and freeing things anyone can ever do.

Important
Background Research

We are in a position today to better explain, discuss and theorise intelligently about homosexuality. We do not know it all but we are on a lot surer ground than we were in earlier times, even just 50 years ago. To say that everything we need to know about human sexuality, of all kinds, is found in a book written over a 1000-year period between c.960 BCE and 100 CE is totally laughable. Conventionally minded religious people may not agree with this statement, since they would see sexuality as essentially an unchanging moral issue, but such a view does not stand up to scrutiny: even morality is not necessarily static.

Take the potent example of slavery, which has been practised from the ancient time of the Bible right through to the modern period: the Bible has even been used to justify it. Yet people the world over have rejected slavery and the ownership of human beings as barbaric. Our ideas of morality change as knowledge, culture and people change. So why should our notions of human sexuality stay rooted in knowledge that is over 2000 years old?

Language is very important. It makes our innermost thoughts external and real and gives shape to what we believe. As I said in the preface, in writing about having a homosexual orientation, therefore,

I prefer to use self-descriptive inclusive language to describe same-sex attracted people, rather than language coined by opposite-sex attracted people. And the terms 'homosexual' and 'homosexuality' are examples of the kind of terminology I prefer to avoid.

The history of the word 'homosexual' is a little murky but most believe it to have originated as a legal term, coined by lawyers in the mid nineteenth century to decry appalling treatment of same-sex attracted men under the Prussian Penal Code. Because it is not a word coined by gay people about gay people, but by, we assume, straight people, it can be described as being *heteronormative*. This is how sociologists and social psychologists describe the point of view of some that opposite-sex attraction is seen as normal while same-sex attraction is seen as deviating from that norm and thus aberrant or abnormal. So, in this book, as often as possible, without being clumsy, I will use the terms gay and lesbian sexual orientation or more briefly, gay and lesbian orientation, rather than the terms 'homosexual' or 'homosexuality.'

How many gay people are there?

This most interesting question has been the subject of considerable debate for quite some time. Over the course of my adult life, it has been accepted gay lore that most people – about 90 per cent – are heterosexual, and that a minority of people – about 10 per cent – are gay. That is, about one in ten people will be gay. Go down into the main street of the city or town where you live and count off every tenth person. According to this figure, statistically, but not actually, every tenth person will be homosexual. Is there any research to back up this figure?

In his 1948 study on males, American entomologist Alfred Kinsey found that approximately 75 per cent of the men were straight and about 8 per cent exclusively gay. The remaining men fell somewhere between these two poles. But how does this compare with newer research? Recent reputable studies have been published in which the proportion of men endorsing exclusive homosexuality ranges from 0.9 to 2 per cent and women between 0.2 and 1 per cent.[1] So there is no consensus about the numbers of gay and lesbian people in the general population. I have seen figures ranging from the above, which refers only to exclusive homosexuality, to figures between 3 and 16 per cent, all using differing methodologies. However, one thing is clear. When we talk about a person having a gay or lesbian orientation, we are not talking about sexual orientation labels we apply to ourselves, or sexual behaviours, both of which are open to wilful distortion or diversity, such as sexual experimentation. Rather, we are referring to an individual's basic sexual attraction, that place to which fantasies, thoughts, 'perving' behaviour and even dreams go – the place I call 'home base'.

So using home base as a focus, there does appear to be a figure that differs quite significantly from the popular 10 per cent. It suggests that approximately 2 to 3.5 per cent of men are exclusively same-sex attracted or gay, and that 0.5 to 1.5 per cent of women are exclusively same-sex attracted or lesbian[2] – in other words, about one in 30 men are gay, perhaps one in 25, and about one in 70 women are lesbian. To put this the other way around, about 96 per cent of the population is straight and about 4 per cent gay.

Although it is essential to give serious consideration to this research, it is also important to note another quite different point that could make the figure a little higher. Based on research done in the 1990s, we know that many people identifying as gay or straight have found their actual sexuality to be more fluid than this rigid labelling might suggest.

I am a good example of this. Although I now characterise myself fully as a gay man, I have had girlfriends in the past, have fallen in love with women and do not find the thought of straight sex repugnant, as do some gay men. I can easily recognise a beautiful woman and even be attracted to her. Although I accepted the label of being gay almost 20 years ago, I still recognise that I am perfectly capable of having straight sex. Still, straight relationships and straight sex are not home base for me. This is why, quite early after my acceptance of my own sexuality, I discarded the bisexual label, as it simply did not describe my life or my behaviour, emotional state or desire. I am capable of having and even enjoying straight sex, but I am not a straight man. I am gay. It is quite likely that, in the research cited above, there were some individuals like me who, because of the rigorous narrative of the research methodology, did not include themselves in the 'exclusive same-sex attracted' category, yet who, for all intents and purposes, lead a gay lifestyle because it is home base.

Moreover, some people accept their gay or lesbian orientation labels in a number of steps, sometimes called transitions. It is also entirely likely that some individuals did not place themselves in the exclusive category when they might have done so had the research been conducted, say, 12 months later. With that also in mind, and although some may dispute it, I feel comfortable in accepting a round figure of about 5 per cent, or one in 20, for the number of gay people in the population.

Debates

One of the great debates in the latter part of the 20th century and the beginning of the 21st has been that over the gay gene. Is homosexuality genetic? Is there a biological basis for being gay or lesbian? This is an extremely complicated question with no simple answer.

The debate has raged between those who adhere to the theory that genetic influences determine our sexuality, the theory of *biological essentialism* or *biological determinism*, and those who adhere to the theory that culture and society have the greater role to play in human sexuality, the theory of *social constructionism*. If we are to look at what the science is saying here, we need to examine both of these propositions before we examine the specific evidence on genes. Let's begin with essentialism.

Biological essentialism or determinism holds that our biology – our genes, hormones and brain tissue, the very essence of how we are physically fashioned – pre-determines the pathway of our sexual orientation. In other words, biology is destiny. Further to this proposition is the idea that such biological factors precede any cultural and social influences and actually limit the effects that such influences are able to impose. What happens to you in your mother's womb determines your sexual orientation when you are going through adolescence and cannot be altered by socio-cultural circumstances and experiences.

Sociologists have postulated a different theory to explain the formation of gay and lesbian orientation. Although some would disagree, the theory of social constructionism seems to be more a refutation of biological essentialism than a stand-alone theoretical position. This view suggests that biology is malleable: not only does the biology affect the individual, but the individual affects the biology, though only in a limited way. Because human development occurs through the medium of history, culture and society, human sexuality, too, is enveloped in cultural attitudes, mores, beliefs, societal experiences and historical connections. It can therefore come into being only within these frameworks. Ultimately, sexuality is constructed by personal experience as expressed within a culture and society, not imposed by blind biology.

The cake

Both these theories are plausible, but both have flaws. Since they are mutually exclusive, they both cannot be right, so the solution has been to amalgamate the two views. There is no science to support the idea that biology alone pre-determines orientation; likewise, it is not possible to say that history, society and culture alone frame the possibilities of orientation. Most scientists studying these issues now adhere to what has been called the interpenetrative approach.

In their 1984 book, *Not In Our Genes*, Richard Lewontin, an evolutionary geneticist, Steven Rose, a neurobiologist, and Leon J. Kamin, a psychologist, state that the biological and social strands are not separable but complementary.[3] According to these researchers, and others, individual sexual proclivities exist only as part of a society and emerge with social interaction. As individual humans, we are composed of a multitude of differing characteristics, each of which can be described on its own. But when these characteristics combine and interpenetrate with the social environment, the result is 'a complex personality and character that is qualitatively different than its parts'.[4]

To explain this they use the analogy of a cake, in which the ingredients are combined in certain amounts and then baked at a particular temperature. The taste of the cake cannot be reduced to percentages of butter, flour, and so on, although each ingredient makes its contribution to the final product. Applying this analogy to sexual preference or taste, we can assert that genes, hormones and brain tissue all contribute to heterosexual or homosexual preference but we cannot reduce such a preference to any single ingredient or to various quantities of these ingredients which, in themselves, have undergone transformations in the process of human experience. The cake is not just butter nor, after baking, is the butter present in its original form.[5]

Sexual orientation comes about by these processes: the biological and genetic, the psychological, and the sociocultural environment, including the historical and political, in which it all takes place. So to make our gay cake, we mix in the following ingredients: genes, hormones, brain tissue, cognition, needs, emotion, motivations, society, culture, history and politics. Combine them in an individual with intentionality and personal agency and bake in the oven of human experience. Allow each ingredient to combine with the others so that it no longer exists in isolation, but only in relation to the other ingredients, which have all changed too.

The Biology of Being Gay

Because there is so much information available about the biology and genetics of homosexuality I have decided to place the most important theories before you. Although I hope you will accompany me on this interesting journey, not all the material is always easy to understand so if you find the going a bit too heavy, feel free to skip ahead to the next section. Glen Wilson and Qazi Rahman's 2005 book, *Born Gay*,[1] neatly brings together much of this research in one convenient place. They suggest that the family is the first area to consider in looking at whether there is a genetic component to gay sexual orientation.

Familiarity

If a trait is thought to be genetically influenced, geneticists would reasonably expect it to bunch together or aggregate in families. In our context of gay and lesbian sexuality, they would expect there to be a greater aggregation of homosexuality in families where there are gay men and lesbians than you would find in the general population, which I have argued to be about 5 per cent. Geneticists would also expect gay men to have more gay brothers than would straight men, and lesbians to have more lesbian sisters than would straight women. This is in fact what the evidence points to.

The following research reports studies that assume the participants in each were telling the truth about their sexual orientations. A study of 101 men, 50 straight and 51 gay, found that 4 per cent of the straight men had gay brothers, while for the gay men the rate was around 22 per cent.[2] By *any* estimation, that is a massive difference. A study reviewed in 1998 found that gay men have between two and five times as many gay brothers as straight men.[3] The median rate for the gay group was 9 per cent, while for the straight men, the rate was no greater than that for the general population. A further study, published in 1999, found a rate whose highest limit was 10 per cent of gay brothers of gay men.[4]

The findings for women vary more than they do for men. In two studies, rates between 6 per cent and 25 per cent of lesbian women had lesbian sisters, compared with rates of between 2 and 10 per cent for straight women.[5]

So it appears that a gay 'trait familiarity' does indeed exist. Wilson and Rahman make the point that were we not to find clustering of homosexuality among families, we should give up the search for the so-called gay gene immediately, since trait aggregation in families is an important prerequisite for a trait to be considered to be genetically caused. However, we also know that many traits can also be caused by the environment, especially the non-shared environment, that is, the parts we don't share with our siblings. For example, psychologists have produced evidence that personality is influenced by about 40 per cent genes, 35 per cent non-shared environment and 5 per cent shared environment (with a 20 per cent error margin).

So how does this apply to sexual orientation? It is both the genetic and the non-shared environment that is the key to the constituency of sexual orientation. Just look at the concordance rates of gay siblings among the identical twins (monozygotic or MZ) in the table on the next page, twins who share 100 per cent of their genetic material.

Concordance rates of homosexual siblings in MZ and DZ twins

Sex	% in MZ twins (100% shared genetic material)	% in DZ twins (50% shared genetic material)	% in adoptive siblings (no shared genetic material)	Study year
M	52	22	11	1991[6]
M & F	65	30		1993[7]
F	48	16	6	1993[8]

Interestingly, the first 1993 study, by E. L. Whitam, M. Diamond and J. Martin, also reported on a group of three sets of triplets:

1. identical brothers, both homosexual, and one sister, heterosexual
2. identical sisters, both lesbian, and one fraternal sister, heterosexual
3. three identical brothers, all homosexual.

With such strong data to support a genetic role in the causation of gay and lesbian sexual orientation, we can actually quantify the size of the role. In the 1991 study in the table above, Mike Bailey and R. C. Pillard calculated the size of the genetic component, or heritability, in males as lying between 31 and 74 per cent. At either end of this range, such a figure stands as a huge component of a man's genetic makeup. In their 1993 female study, the third cited in the table, Bailey and A. P. Bell calculated the heritability as being greater than 50 per cent. Another study published in 2000 calculated the heritability of homosexuality for men to be around 30 per cent and for women, around 50 to 60 per cent.[9]

The fundamentalist churchmen and women who insist that gay or lesbian sexual orientation is of the devil or is caused by demonic oppression should read this evidence, which cannot be dismissed out of hand just because it differs from traditional Christian notions of what human sexuality 'should' be. There can be no doubt that there is a significant genetic component in the causation of sexual orientation. This research puts the lie to the notion that gay people just wake up one day and decide to become gay. It puts the lie to the notion that sexual 'preference' is an option.

You cannot choose whether you will be same-sex attracted. Sexual orientation is part of our biological makeup, whether we are gay or straight. Since, added to the geneticists' findings, we know, from anthropology and history, that same-sex attraction has existed throughout the ages and across all cultures, we can safely assume that homosexuality is a deeply ingrained biologic and genetic pattern that is both persistent and consistent as a usual variant of human sexuality. This research also puts the lie to the notion that gay people are somehow being used by the devil or demonic forces, as held by some fundamentalist and Pentecostal churches. If that's true, then the devil must be in our genes as well as our jeans!

Now let's take a look at some of the most interesting biological lines of inquiry being investigated at present.

X chromosome linkage

The first is the possibility that the genetic component of homosexuality may come from the mother's side. In a first of its kind study, Dean Hamer and his colleagues looked at the molecular level of human sexual orientation.[10] They recruited a sample of 76 out gay men and examined in great detail their family pedigrees. First, they found that 13.5 per cent of the men's brothers were also uncloseted gay. This result was consistent with the existing research, so no real surprises there.

However, in looking back through their families, the researchers noticed that the men also had more gay uncles and cousins than the base rate, both about 7 per cent, and that this phenomenon was found on the mother's side of the family. This was intriguing: it suggested that the genetic component of homosexuality *might* be passed on to a boy through the X chromosome that came only from his mother. Two further studies replicated this finding but others have not identified this effect, so we remain uncertain.

Xq28

Another tantalising line of inquiry, though, has emerged from the same Hamer study. When the researchers conducted a DNA analysis on a selected group of 40 pairs of gay brothers they discovered that 82 per cent of the men shared a region on the X chromosome called q28. The team therefore decided on a new study, recruiting a new sample of 32 pairs of gay brothers, 36 pairs of lesbian sisters and the straight brothers of gay pairs.[11] The results confirmed the previous study: 67 per cent of gay brothers shared the Xq28 region, but none of the lesbian sisters did. The straight brothers of the gay pairs shared a 22 per cent chance of sharing the Xq28 markers, which is less than the 50 per cent overlap predicted by mere chance. Another study found that 66 per cent of 54 pairs of gay brothers shared markers in the Xq28 region.[12]

Again, it is likely that there is some effect here but the way it manifests itself is hidden for now. We might gingerly conclude that genes in the Xq28 region affect sexual orientation in men, but not in women. The whole genes–orientation association is an extremely complex process and our present understanding falls short, but it does appear that there are probably a number of genes that affect orientation, not just one 'gay' gene.

Pre-natal androgen theory

Yet another line of inquiry has focused on the influence of hormones on the foetus in the womb. Dominant among biologists today is the pre-natal androgen (PNA) theory, which holds that male sex hormones, androgens, play an important role in determining the sex of an unborn child which, early in the pregnancy, is virtually sexually indistinct. In simple terms, the PNA theory works like this.

Although we cannot tell the sex of a child early in the pregnancy, a male child will already be genetically male, that is, he will have an X chromosome paired up with a Y chromosome. Likewise, a female child will already be genetically female, that is, she will have two paired X chromosomes. During the first two trimesters of the pregnancy, the foetus will have the undeveloped rudimentary physiology of both male and female genitalia: the male Wolffian duct and the female Mullerian duct.

But should the child be a genetic male, something powerful occurs in the final trimester of the pregnancy. The male Y chromosome sparks off a whole cascade of hormonal changes that cause testes to be made, which in turn begin to release the androgen, testosterone, that masculinises the Wolffian system, turning it into male genitals and, simultaneously, releasing another hormone that destroys the Mullerian duct. The foetus now becomes discernibly male.

For a female to be born, no such Y chromosome exists to launch the masculinising hormonal cascade in the first place, so the Mullerian duct develops into female genitalia. Glen Wilson and Qazi Rahman make the point that, because of this presence or absence of androgens, the default gender for all mammals is female. In other words, if nothing happens to change things – if there are no androgens – all mammals, including humans, are born female.

Now, biologists make the reasonable hypothesis that since genes do in fact affect sexual orientation, they probably do so in ways that are associated with the development of the male or female brain in the foetus. Androgen effects on the androgen receptors in the developing brain cause masculinising development and behaviour, while lack of androgens and the presence of female oestrogens cause feminising development and behaviour. A further plausible hypothesis is that certain centres in the brain, specifically those to do with sexual attraction, for example the hypothalamus, might be more susceptible to these hormonal effects. Interestingly, the hypothalamus does in fact have more androgen receptors in men than in women.

So, the PNA theory proposes that homosexuality might partly be caused at the time of early foetal brain development, in males by undermasculinisation of the brain, owing to lower levels of androgens, and in females by overmasculinisation of the brain, owing to higher levels of androgens. Biologists know that these so-called organisational effects are irreversible.

So why do we now hypothesise that pre-natal hormonal levels are influential in sexual orientation? Because animal studies have suggested a link. In laboratory tests, female guinea-pigs, rats and monkeys have had their hormonal levels manipulated when still foetuses and act sexually by mounting other females.

If the PNA theory is true, then what does it mean? Does it suggest that homosexuality is caused by gender malfunction? No, it does not. Given the high numbers of gay and lesbian people in the world, we can now accept the consistency of the presence of same-sex attracted people, who show no signs of pathology, illness, sickness or physical weakness as a result of their orientation. Neither have gay people been bred out of existence as weaker mutations of the human family. We may just have to learn to accept that there *may be* an undermasculinising of the foetal brain in gay men and an overmasculinising of the foetal brain in lesbian women as an effect of the presence or absence of androgens. And if that is true, then it is perfectly usual for a consistent minority of human beings.

A word, though: this does not mean that all gay men are feminine or all gay women are masculine. Far from it. We need to remember that there is great variation in the gender presentations of gay people just as there is for straight people.

Fraternal birth order

This intriguing research shows that if you are male, the more older brothers you have, the more likely you are to be gay.[13] This finding is robust and has been identified in several studies. The effect does not happen in the case of older sisters or adoptive older brothers, nor younger brothers or sisters. It is specific and unique to the number of male children your mother carried in pregnancy before you, if you are male. It has been calculated that if you are a guy, for each biological older brother you have, your chances of turning out to be gay increase by a third.[14] Just in case you're interested, I have two older brothers.

The brain

Finally, we take a brief look at the human brain. Earlier, I mentioned that the hypothalamus is directly associated with sexuality. A sex centre in mammals, it is a small region located in the base of the brain. Different areas within the hypothalamus may control different aspects of sexuality, for example, 'sexual orientation, sexual motivation, approach behaviour, and sexual performance'.[15]

Some fascinating research examining certain areas of the hypothalamus has been published. First, we know that some of these areas of the brain show sexual dimorphism, that is, they are different between males and females. If the PNA theory is correct, then perhaps undermasculinisation in gay men and overmasculinisation in lesbian women can be identified in brain physiology. If the structures in gay men differed from those in straight men and looked similar to those in women, and conversely, that the structures in lesbian women differed from straight women and looked similar to those in men, then we might have demonstrated the effect of the hypothesis.

A 1990 study found just this in a male sample.[16] The researchers found a difference between gay and straight men in a group of cells in the hypothalamus called the supra-chiasmatic nucleus or SCN, which is believed to be predominantly associated with the sleep–wake cycle and the reproductive cycle across seasonal changes. They found that this area was larger and longer in gay men than in straight men, a characteristic closer to that of women.

However, the most famous of these brain physiology studies to date is that of Simon LeVay,[17] who examined a sexually dimorphic area in the hypothalamus called the interstitial nuclei of the anterior hypothalamus (the third section) or INAH-3. LeVay examined brain tissue from autopsies on both gay and straight men and straight women. He hypothesised that the INAH-3 of gay men would be smaller than the straight men's and more like the women's, which is exactly what he found. A later study tried to replicate these findings but was unable to do so conclusively.[18]

Conclusions

So, what does all this mean? Well, for one thing, the biological research indicates that gay and lesbian people do not happen by accident: there are causative influences. For me, this means that the church cannot rely on the tradition, the teaching, or the words of the Bible and simply denounce a phenomenon that is entirely human. The church needs to understand that for gay people, being gay *is* entirely natural. It is not unnatural as was proposed in the medieval period and reiterated by the Catholic Church in modern times. Using the word 'unnatural' is problematic because it carries so much historical, psychological and sociological baggage. However, to indulge the reader of that persuasion for just a moment, then what *could* be considered unnatural would be for a straight person to try to be gay and for a gay person to try to be straight. The one is not a deviant form of the other. A gay person is not a distorted straight person. When you are same-sex attracted, being gay is the most natural thing in the world. A visiting Martian studying human sexuality would conclude that there are two major forms of sexuality in the human race, straight and gay, the former far outnumbering the latter, but the latter forming a consistent and normal minority variation.

If you are a clergyman who adheres to strict traditional Christian teaching that homosexuality is sinful, disordered or demonic, then you need to think again about what you believe and what you try to foist upon individuals under your pastoral care. If you are a family member of a loved one who is gay, you need to understand that there are elemental forces at work that none of us as human beings have any control over. Our sexuality is one of these. Your loved one needs your love and support and acceptance. It's difficult enough in a straight world without your family rejecting you on misplaced moral grounds.

If you are gay, young or older, closeted or out, and you love God and are trying to follow the Way of Jesus, know that when God created us as humans, He didn't make mistakes. You are not a mistake. Don't let anybody tell you that you are. The forces that went to make up the biological component of your sexuality have been happening to other gay people since before recorded history. God loves you and wants the best for you. He wants you to become all that you can be, just as He does for each of us, gay or straight. God hasn't lost a single night's sleep about your being gay. Rather, I suspect the only sleep God loses is over the way all humans can so easily forget about His life in and through us in the way that we disrespect each other and forget to be compassionate. As he is with straight people, God is a lot more interested in His life in you and your life in Him than in your sexual orientation.

The Psychology
of Being Gay

There are a number of important areas to discuss in looking at the psychology of being gay and lesbian, so I have placed them over three successive chapters: the theoretical component is in this chapter, followed by the 'coming out' experience in Chapter 7 and then the psychology of sexuality in Chapter 8. Psychology's bread and butter is the teasing apart of thoughts, emotions and behaviours, so we must remember that there is no one single set of descriptors that captures the way *all* gay and lesbian people think, feel and behave.

Alfred Kinsey

Let's begin by looking at some seminal research from the middle of the 20th century. In 1948, as was mentioned in Chapter 4, Alfred Kinsey and two colleagues published their findings on the sexual practices of over 5300 American males, recruited, not from prisons, hospitals or asylums, but from the general population.[1] To their surprise and shock, over one-third, some 37 per cent, of the participants between the ages of 15 and 56 reported that they had experienced a homosexual encounter leading to orgasm.

As a result of these findings, Kinsey concluded that the existence of just two types of sexuality, opposite-sex attraction and same-sex attraction, was probably not the whole story. Instead, he proposed that there might be a continuum of sexuality, where exclusive opposite-sex attraction was at one end of the continuum, exclusive same-sex attraction at the other end and some mixed sexualities in between. In other words, he thought that human sexuality might be more fluid than previously believed. He proposed the following, which later came to be called Kinsey Scale:

0   Exclusively heterosexual

1   Mainly heterosexual with a small degree of homosexuality

2   Mainly heterosexual with a significant degree of homosexuality

3   Equally heterosexual and homosexual

4   Mainly homosexual with a significant degree of heterosexuality

5   Mainly homosexual with a small degree of heterosexuality

6   Exclusively homosexual.

Notice how the higher the number, the more gay you were thought to be and the lower the number, the more straight you were thought to be.

In early research, people were asked to place themselves somewhere along this continuum. Soon researchers started talking about a Kinsey 5 or a Kinsey 2 – a K5 or a K2. However, it wasn't too long before researchers began to notice that people's self-labelling didn't always match their actual behaviour. Some males, for example, might label themselves as exclusively heterosexual, a K0, but actually be having quite regular same-sex sexual encounters.

This type of disparity eventually led researchers to alter their approach to characterising sexual orientation. Much work was undertaken that eventually showed a number of ways to determine sexual orientation. Which of these, though, was the most accurate? Which was the most reliable? Let's look at the four methods that researchers have described.

Four ways of determining sexual orientation

1. *Self-labelling*

   This is the label that an individual applies: I am gay, I am lesbian, I am straight. The trouble with this method is that it can easily be subverted. People can lie. People can be in denial. This is the type of difficulty we noticed above with the example of a 'straight' man, KO, who has clandestine sex with other men from time to time.

2. *Behaviour*

   This refers to how people actually act. You might think that this method is closest to the truth but, like self-labelling, it can distort reality. Take, for example, the married man who is really gay. To the outside world, he appears straight. He has a wife, he may have children, he may go for a drink with his mates at the pub or he may go to church. His behaviour would signify to any reasonable person that he is straight, yet inside, he knows he is gay. I see a number of these men in my consulting rooms every year. Think, too, of straight men in prison or in the military where there is no possibility of opposite-sex sexual behaviour, so same-sex sexual behaviour can occur in its stead.

3. *Fantasy, dreams, erotic thinking, 'perving' behaviour*

   This method refers to the way individuals, within the privacy of their own interior life, think, fantasise and dream about sexual activity. It also includes which gender we like to look at when we think someone is attractive, called 'perving' in the Australian vernacular. Of all the methods easily available to us, this is believed to be the closest to an individual's actual orientation. Our fantasy life, our erotic thinking, our dreams and our perving behaviour typically take us to the kind of sexual activity we truly desire.

   If while masturbating, a male generally fantasises about other males, it is a reasonable assumption that he has at least some degree of same-sex attraction within his makeup. So too, with our dreams. Erotic dreams are perfectly normal: we all have them from time to time. If you find yourself having erotic dreams with a partner consistently of the same sex, you might reasonably ask if a degree of same-sex attraction is present.

If you are sitting in a café and you can't stop looking at an attractive individual, that person's gender can be an indicator of your sexual orientation.

4. *Physiological measurements*

This method cannot really be used by the general population since it involves the placing of sensors around the penis or inside the vagina. This is highly invasive and should only ever be part of a research project that requires clearance from a university or hospital ethics committee. This kind of research technique is called plethysmography. The plethysmograph is an extremely sensitive instrument that measures, in men, *any* increase in engorgement as blood flows into the penis to create an erection and, in women, colour changes in the walls of the vagina (technically, vaginal photoplethysmography).

Plethysmography can tell a straight man from a gay man in the blink of an eye. You hook the sensors up to the volunteers, both gay and straight, and show them arousing images of naked or semi-naked men and women. All volunteers will have an increase of blood flow to the penis. Straight men will respond much more to the images of women than they will to men, while the gay men will respond much more to the images of other men. It is a very clear and robust distinction and has been replicated in several studies. You can't trick plethysmography. You can't pretend to be one orientation and actually be another. The technique is sensitive enough to detect the slightest change and will catch the would-be dissembler. The closeted sporting jock will be caught out every time.

Results from women are less clear-cut. They tend to show a more bisexual response. What does this mean? We can conclude only that either bisexuality is the norm for women, which is unlikely, given the current understanding from psychology, sociology and anthropology, or that plethysmography is not as valid or sufficiently reliable in identifying women's sexual orientation.

There is one more very interesting note in this kind of research before we leave it. Some plethysmographic studies have included strongly homophobic men in their volunteer participants. In *Born Gay*, Wilson and Rahman report that strongly homophobic men show more erectile response to images of other men than they do to women, regardless of how much they protest to the contrary or declare that they are straight, and more penile response compared with straight male volunteers who are comfortably secure in their sexuality and show more tolerance of gay people. If you think back to the gay hate crimes discussed in Chapter 3, this research proves very interesting. There is evidence to suggest that strongly homophobic men are trying to deny their own homosexuality by passing themselves off as hypermasculine straight men bathed in machismo, a defence mechanism that Sigmund Freud called *reaction formation*, where, to allay anxiety and distress, one acts and behaves the exact opposite way to what one really feels. There is some evidence to suggest that the murderers of Matthew Shephard might have been acting out of reaction formation.[2]

Clearly, only the final two of these four methods are at all reliable. Although the plethysmography studies have the last word on men, they certainly don't offer the same level of certainty with women, and they are not feasible for everyday use. So, realistically, it will have to be the third in our list: self-reported fantasy, erotic thinking, dreams and perving behaviour.

The Kinsey profile

Researchers eventually began to notice that the single-digit Kinsey number was really not complex enough to adequately describe an individual's sexual orientation. The scale intervals were not all equal and did not accurately describe *every* individual's experience of sexuality. Not all K5s for example had the same experiences.

As a result, behavioural scientists and sexologists began to embark on research aimed at clarifying how sexual orientation should be characterised. Eventually a newer model was devised, with scientists converging on the notion that human sexual orientation could be described with enough complexity by focusing on three broad areas in each individual. Different authors use slightly different terminology but they are essentially the same three factors.

Sexual feelings – this category describes the basic sexual urges that an individual feels. It incorporates (a) the kind of desire that one experiences, (b) the direction of that desire, that is, whether it is aimed at the same sex or the opposite sex, and (c) the fantasy and erotic thinking that goes with that desire.

Sexual activity – this category describes the kind of sexual behaviour in which an individual actually engages and whether it is rarely, occasionally, primarily or exclusively with someone of the same or the opposite sex. It also includes perving behaviour, although there is some overlap here with sexual feelings.

Romantic feelings – this describes the emotional connection that an individual has with a sexual partner or the decisions that an individual makes regarding the sex of partners and love.

This model provided a much broader, less simplistic view of how individuals experience their sexuality and allowed for nuance and change. Finally, researchers had a tool that would give them a closer idea of how individuals actually experienced their sexuality. Instead of using the single-digit Kinsey number, researchers began to survey individual's sexual feelings (SF), sexual activities (SA) and romantic feelings (RF). Some asked people to give themselves a Kinsey rating on *each* of the three factors. This provided them a three-digit number, sometimes called a Kinsey profile. Individuals could locate their sexual orientation themselves, as for example, sexual feelings K6, sexual activity K4 and romantic activity K6, giving a Kinsey profile of 646. The original Kinsey descriptors still hold true, but now apply to each of the three factors discretely.[3]

You can fill out your own Kinsey profile if it helps you locate your journey in sexuality. Don't forget, though, that the result will give you only a general indication of how you might be experiencing your sexual orientation. The rule of thumb among sexologists is this: that sexual orientation is set early in life and changes minimally. Sexual feelings are believed to be the most basic element in orientation and so more stable than sexual activities or romantic feelings. Hence, your sexual feelings rating is probably the key number in your profile. If you locate yourself authentically and honestly, your SF rating is a good indication of where your true orientation is ultimately likely to lie.

Your sexual activities rating can be determined by a number of different factors and it does not necessarily have to be congruent with your sexual feelings rating, as we saw above in the examples of the married gay man or inmates in prisons. Perhaps you are still attending church and feel that any kind of sexual activity outside marriage is against God's law, so you are not experiencing your sexuality at all.

Or perhaps, as a church member, you have done your best to conform to a straight lifestyle and have attempted opposite-sex emotional relationships or perhaps even sex.

Your romantic feelings rating is also very dependent on whether you characterise yourself as being gay or straight and how far you have come on your journey of self-understanding. If you have same-sex attraction and are attending church and continuing to hear that love can only ever be between a man and a woman and never between two people of the same sex, then you are probably extremely confused. Your struggle could be in its early stages or you could be further advanced and already know that you may desire to love someone of the same sex. When I was in my previous church, I already knew that I wanted to love and to be loved by another man, not just have sex with another man. I craved tenderness from someone of my own gender. Depending where you are in your sexuality journey, both the sexual activities rating and the romantic feelings rating can change as your experience and your attitudes emerge, develop and begin to become established.

Note that I describe this as a sexuality journey. It is a process. You don't wake up one morning and understand everything about your sexuality. You will have noticed, if you have same-sex attraction, that this will have begun to emerge during puberty and beyond. When we are young we have little experience of life and love or the world and how it works and we take time to mature. The same thing occurs with our journey of sexuality.

The self

I now want to change direction and begin to explore the notion of sexual identity itself. I belong to the group of psychologists who view sexual identity as a component of a larger unified self. We view the brain as one part of the mechanism through which a self functions, the body being the other part, with a unified cognitive and emotional system in place that gives us consciousness, continuity and a sense of personal identity. From a spiritual point of view, this, in my view, is what the Christian church has traditionally meant when it talked about the soul.

So let's take a look at some general points that can be made about the self. Because the self is construed as being akin to personal identity, it is suggested that:

1. a self needs embodiment, that is, being related to a particular body and therefore gender;
2. there should be subjective experience, that is, consciousness, some sense of self and of agency, and cognition, ways of organising that experience;
3. we are intrinsically related to others in a social medium of culture;
4. there may be unconscious feelings at work within us of which we are not or hardly aware; and
5. there is some sense that these strands are in complex interrelation with each other.[4]

It is difficult to argue against any of these statements. The first four are more or less self-evident in our daily lives and we would suspect the fifth to be true from our knowledge of the complexity of human behaviour. This self is often characterised as being made up of different facets, such as temperament, personality, intelligence, memory, personal biography, cultural history, belief systems, the experience of the group, social norms, the experience of time, the sense of finiteness, the sense of morality and the sense of sexuality. All of these are essential for us to function successfully as humans and each is an interacting constituent of the unified self. So how does our sexuality fit into this overarching model of the self?

Sexual identity

For most adults, there is an underlying sense of being a sexual creature, that is, a conscious realisation that we have powerful sexual urges and find certain stimuli attractive, desirable and erotic. For most of us, this sexual awareness is oriented either toward the same or the opposite sex.[5] This overarching sexual awareness is what psychology calls *sexual identity*, while its direction is referred to as *sexual orientation*. In other words, I see sexual orientation as being a component of the larger category, sexual identity, which, in turn, is a component of the larger category, self.

Traditionally, sexual identity is seen as a developmental process that occurs more or less naturally as one grows up in a particular family and culture. It is part biological, as we progress from puberty through adolescence, and part socialised, as we learn from others what is and is not acceptable. Most individuals turn into young straight people as a matter of course. Becoming straight just happens and is assumed, provided there are no cues to the contrary. It is not consciously and voluntarily undertaken as a process and teenagers don't typically experience the conscious adoption of a straight sexual orientation as a rite of passage.[6] Likewise, later in life, straight orientation is mostly taken for granted. For example, when you meet someone for the first time, you naturally assume that they are straight.[7]

It is a very different story for young gay people. From puberty they have a profound sense of being different and a growing awareness that their burgeoning sexual identity is same-sex oriented. For gay adolescents, whether out or closeted, their orientation can become a prism through which they view the whole world and their existence in it. This happens more particularly after an acceptance of the label, gay or lesbian.

Sexual orientation vs sexual preference

You may have noted that nowhere here have I used the term sexual preference. This has not been accidental. Sexual orientation is a stable facet of the self, deeply rooted within our biological makeup. So, too, with the psychology of being gay. The fundamental psychological difference between gay and straight people, that is, gender attraction, cannot be altered. By the time a person reaches young adulthood, their sexual orientation has become apparent in most ways and is unlikely to change.

The term sexual preference is problematic because it implies the existence of choice where there is none. 'Preferred sexuality' is a nonsense. You have not chosen to become straight or gay. Your sexual orientation emerged and developed on its own, without your permission. Whether we are comfortable or uncomfortable with our sexual orientation, there is no choosing, no preference.

Gay and lesbian sexual orientation

A gay or lesbian orientation does not happen overnight. From a psychological point of view, how do most gay people experience this journey?

Vivienne Cass, one of Australia's foremost researchers and theorists in this area, proposes that gay and lesbian sexual orientation, what she calls *homosexual identity*, evolves in a staged process coincidental with physical maturation. She calls this the homosexual identity formation (HIF) model. Cass holds that as the body develops secondary sex characteristics through puberty, sexual desire becomes increasingly conscious and important. At the same time, the homosexual identity begins to develop. Cass suggests that it grows out of the sorts of thoughts that come to mind when an individual thinks about the category 'homosexual' or 'gay person'. She suggests that these self-images will also develop from society's views within the culture.[8]

With empirical evidence to support her, Cass proposes that the evolution of a gay identity is a six-stage process. Real life, of course, doesn't usually turn out to be quite so neat and tidy or as linear as theoretical constructions, even the ones supported by evidence. For example, some individuals stay in a stage longer than they are 'supposed to'; some move backwards to an earlier stage; some progress through the stages in a different order; some even skip stages altogether. Still, this staged theory is thought to be the best and most fully tested psychological theory of homosexual identity formation that we have. In research, both gay men and lesbians have reported that they recognise the stages to a significant degree in their lives.

Cass suggests that, in the early stages, individuals think seriously about their self-images in comparison with what comes to mind when they think of the word 'gay'. These comparison images are often stereotypes since these are the most readily available. This means that these comparisons are not always comfortable ones, especially if, like most people, you don't happen to fit the stereotype. Cass believes that these earlier stages are more personal and interior.

In the later stages, however, a fully developed sense of self as a gay person requires more direct communication with others, both gay and non-gay, who constitute the individual's social environment. As individuals become more comfortable with their interior life, they also become more comfortable when interacting with the exterior gay world and can begin to understand its ways, its rules, its consistency and its constancy of response. Cass theorises that this consistency of interaction creates stability of identity. In other words, the more comfortable I feel within myself with thoughts about being gay, the more comfortable I will be in interacting with other people on this level and, therefore, the more stable my gay or lesbian sexual identity becomes.

The table on the next page shows the Cass model with Eliason's descriptions.[9] Take your time with it and read each stage slowly and carefully.

In terms of being in the church, you can easily see that if a person is going to get stuck at any of the stages, it will probably be in the early personal and interior stages, 1 and/or 2, of identity confusion and identity comparison. Note that in identity confusion, a person might be attracted to someone of the same sex in church, or a friend, or someone they know. If the individual experiencing these feelings is a young person, they might become infatuated or even have a crush on someone. In the 'hip and happening' Pentecostal churches, filled with well-dressed, cool-looking, sexually attractive young people, it is not uncommon for same-sex attracted individuals to form a crush on someone. If Australia's prominent Hillsong church really knew just how many same-sex attracted young people there were in its ranks, they would be horrified!

There is a great cost to be borne, and great confusion and disruption to self-identity, if a same-sex attracted individual is trying to remain straight because of traditional church sexual teachings. In some instances, the disharmony between what is felt and yearned for, and what is acted upon openly, can cause depression or anxiety disorders and, in some, even substance abuse. Some fundamentalist pastors or teachers still use this kind of mental anguish as 'proof' that homosexuality is not only a sin but also a mental illness. Let me be very plain: it is not a mental illness, as we shall see more fully in the next chapter. It is the denial of their sexuality that sets young people up for such a profound tug o' war between their internal world and church teachings, what psychologists call *cognitive dissonance*. It is this that can tip a young person over into a depression or an anxiety disorder. It has nothing to do with their being gay per se.

And you don't have to be a young person for this to happen. Forever trying to be someone that you're not would take a toll on anyone. If you're straight and find this hard to believe, then try acting gay in public constantly for just one week and see how you go.

Cass's homosexual identity formation stages theory

Stage	Name	Description
1	*Identity confusion*	An individual has experiences or feelings that might be labelled as homosexual. These feelings disrupt the self-identity as heterosexual and cause confusion. The confusion may be resolved by rejecting the possibility of homosexuality, thus foreclosing further development. Conversely, a decision to explore options might occur, and lead to the next stage.
2	*Identity comparison*	The person examines her/his own behaviour compared to the feedback given by others, or the identity of 'homosexual' in general. If the self-perceptions as homosexual are too negative, the person may decide to curtail any further exploration of that identity. Alternatively, she/he may decide to make contact with a homosexual person or community.
3	*Identity tolerance*	The person tentatively tries out the label of 'homosexual' and makes contact with other homosexuals. The quality of the initial contacts is very important. During this stage, disclosure of identity to heterosexual others is very limited, and the person may lead two separate lives.
4	*Identity acceptance*	If the initial contact with homosexual individuals or cultures/communities is positive, the person may move rather rapidly to a state of acceptance of the self-identity. Selective disclosure to friends and family begins.
5	*Identity pride*	In order to achieve congruence, the person may dichotomise the world into homosexuals and heterosexuals. If the heterosexual world is considered to be too negative about homosexuality, the person may reject them as inferior to homosexuals. A sense of loyalty and pride of homosexuality develops.
6	*Identity synthesis*	Congruence has been achieved and the identity fully accepted. Now it becomes integrated into the total self-identity. Homosexuality becomes merely one aspect of this integrated total identity, and the private and public images are merged. This generally results in a sense of peace and inner harmony.

Some, of course, resolve the confusion by denying their true identity, suppressing their desire and accepting traditional church teaching. For others, it spells the end of their faith. In the second stage, identity comparison, a young same-sex attracted Christian person might compare their church life with gay stereotypes, find the comparisons too confronting or intimidating, decide they could never be that way and perhaps conclude that they would be sinful in the eyes of God if they lived their lives in such a manner, and so shut down all further exploration. They probably cease their exploration before finding out that there is so much more to gay life than the stereotypes.

This decision, of course, will cause further cognitive dissonance. These powerful urges, for sex and for love, will not go away, even with all the praying, fasting and counselling in the world. I tried this unsuccessfully for over 20 years. They are an integral and wonderful part of the self.

Lastly I would like to draw a distinction between homosexual identity formation and first-time coming out. They are not the same thing. Whereas the former is a process that can take many years and is primarily mediated by an internal gauge, first-time coming out typically occurs in the earlier stages and the driving internal considerations are directed towards others, not the self. Gay identity formation is about integrating your sexual identity into your overall personal and social life. First-time coming out is about presenting your sexual orientation to other people. It is a little like traversing a long road that happens to have a bridge maybe about a third of the way along. The entire length of the roadway is gay identity formation; the bridge is first-time coming out.

Coming Out

There is usually no more significant moment in the lives of gay and lesbian people going through gay identity formation than the very first time they tell someone about it. Imagine it. You're a young man and you say, 'I like guys.' You're a young woman and you say, 'I like women.' There is no equivalent process in the straight world. Young straight people do not have to struggle with becoming straight in a society populated by gay people. There is no rite of passage at 18, no baptism or bar mitzvah through which young straight people are inducted into the straight world. There is no secret, interior and highly personal experience in which they must understand what it might mean to be straight and then begin to integrate themselves into the straight community. Not so for young gay men and women. All of the above applies to them, and happens slowly over a period of time, usually years.

The process of gay identity formation includes a stage where individuals may tentatively begin to disclose to others their own journey of sexuality. Typically, the earliest thoughts of doing this occur at the third stage, identity tolerance. Once this is successfully traversed, further disclosure ensues in the fourth stage, identity acceptance.

The process, known colloquially as coming out, originally referred to an expression that openly gay people used to describe their own tense pre-disclosure years. They talked about being in the closet, and the idea has captured the imagination of gay people all over the world. A closet is a place that is, by definition, closed off, a place where you keep all manner of sometimes unsightly and unsavoury paraphernalia that is meant to be out of the view of polite society. Succinct and clever, the concept of the closet became a metaphor for the kind of lives that gay and lesbian people lived: hidden, secret, shameful. The coming out process captured the idea of gay people disclosing their orientation, implicitly stating that they will no longer keep their life out of sight but will emerge into the light. This coming out into the light signifies truth: no more living a lie. The light signifies freedom: no more feeling compelled to act in a way that is contrary to your nature. The light signifies relief: no more carrying of the intense emotional burden of keeping a dark secret. The light signifies pride: the beginning of the long process of learning to live a shame-free life. When you've been in the darkness of the closet for many years, the light feels like a pretty wonderful place.

The life-lie

If a gay person doesn't come out, what is the alternative? A life in the darkness of the closet. Make no mistake, when the church or a family or friends ask their loved one to remain in the darkness, it is no small thing. While they get on with their lives, making of them what they will, the gay person is left to ponder an entire lifetime of denying their very self, their very soul. Don't make the mistake of confusing this kind of denial with the ancient Christian teaching of self-denial. That is not what we're talking about. Self-denial is about placing others' needs before your own, about loving the hard-to-love, about putting myself out to help someone else, about doing without in a rampantly acquisitive world. All of these are appropriate in certain circumstances. The denial of self expected of gay people when they are overtly or culturally pushed deeper into the closet is nothing less than the attempted eradication of part of the psyche. It is asking them to live a life-lie.

Attempting to deny your sexual identity by remaining in the closet only sets you up for a lifetime of distress and pain. The psychic energy, as psychologists call it, that it takes to live a lie for even a short time is immense and incredibly draining. Trying to do this over an entire lifetime is utterly exhausting: it is not surprising that a person's well of emotional resources inevitably runs dry. Given what we now know about the formation of sexual identity, it is cruel and unjust to ask this of anyone.

Perhaps an example might help. Think of those police officers who go undercover to join crime gangs or the underworld. They have to immerse themselves fully in the harsh realities of the criminal culture, with all its cruelty, greed, deceit and barbarism. They are forced to act and behave in every way contrary to their own nature, their own sense of morality. They must adopt the criminal culture's ways of living, talking, laughing, loving, eating, drinking, driving, playing, dressing. It is nothing short of total immersion and they must act this way 24 hours a day lest they be discovered.

The psychological cost to police officers who do this kind of work is enormous. After their undercover work is complete, it is not uncommon for them to end up in a psychologist's consulting rooms for ongoing counselling and a doctor's surgery for medication. They are often physically and psychologically spent, emotionally drained from having to live a lie. Many refuse point blank to ever do undercover work again. Many take years to heal. What causes this depth of trauma? It is the unrelenting need to be someone they are not, always teetering on the brink of emotional exhaustion from the energy this takes, while constantly under scrutiny and always filled with the terror that they will be discovered. Welcome to the world of the closet. Any pastor, priest, minister or church authority, any cardinal or cleric, any parent, sibling or friend who asks this life-lie of a gay person is not only refusing to show them the kind of love and acceptance that all humans need, but is asking them to bear a burden that cannot be borne without immeasurable damage to their soul.

By contrast, coming out, in the right way, is an overwhelmingly positive experience for most. However, the journey to the door knob of the closet takes time. For some, the process can be relatively short; for others, it can take years, even decades. I have lost count of how many closeted gay people I have seen in their 30s and 40s, usually exhausted, still living a 'straight' life, stuck in Stage 1 or 2 and paying the price of denying their true selves. I feel for them deeply. I recall only too well my own years of turmoil, loneliness and attempted eradication of self, before I finally conceded and acknowledged the glaringly obvious, the unwavering reality that had been with me all along, and allowed myself to come out.

The closet is especially strong, and may even feel as though it's padlocked, if you happen to be a Christian and a church-goer. Church culture is permeated by non-acceptance of same-sex desire. Further, there are actual sanctions against such desire. There is denunciation from the pulpit, the declaration of its sinfulness and even, in some churches, the threat of hell. Family values are espoused and encouraged at every turn. When the church talks about family values, it is code for heterosexual nuclear family normality: straight mums, dads and kids are the standard. For the church, families consist of a father, a mother and children. Even two married people without children are more or less considered families, whereas two gay people in an equally committed and lengthy relationship are not. Then there is the youth group, or the parish youth team, or the Antioch group, or the Bible study group or the music practice group. Everyone seems to be straight. Everyone seems to be pairing off. For a young same-sex attracted individual, the place fairly reeks of heterosexuality. Everything in the church seems to militate against anyone *ever* coming out.

In my last church, if someone disclosed same-sex desire, a pack of elders and pastors would surround them, lay hands on them, pray over them; the more fervent would 'take authority over the evil one who had oppressed this much-loved person'. It was pretty harrowing stuff. I do not doubt their sincerity, or perhaps even their 'good' intentions, but there can be no denying the harm this behaviour causes. I've been through a plethora of such Christian 'healing' by well-meaning but ignorant church people.

The young church person struggling through the stages of homo-sexual identity formation internalises and believes these messages of non-acceptance. 'Yes, I am dirty. Yes, I am sleazy. Yes, I am sinful. Yes, this is something I should be ashamed of.' This reaction, which also comes from society's non-acceptance, is referred to as *internalised homophobia*. In other words, gay and lesbian people growing up in a straight, non-accepting environment cannot help but internalise some of the homophobia around them, which can cause tremendous difficulties and is something that gay individuals have to be wary about for life. Those early negative messages from the days of youth are not easily forgotten. Chapter 12 deals with coming out in the church, but there are some important points about safety that I want to address here first.

Why people don't come out

I am indebted to Andrew Marshall's book, *Together Forever?* for the following headings.[1] Allow me to flesh out five reasons that impede individuals from coming out.

Society's attitudes

We live in a world where straight is considered normal. Although psychology and modern science no longer see gay and lesbian sexual orientation as deviant, much of society still does. It is never easy to be in a minority, be it colour, ethnicity, disability or orientation. Being different from everybody else is no small thing. This can definitely put people off coming out. Inevitably though when considering coming out, gay and lesbian people have to weigh up the differing costs of the closeted life-lie or being part of a minority.

Internalised homophobia

As mentioned above, when we have heard negative messages about homosexuality, cruel jokes at the expense of gay people and vicious name-calling all our lives, we tend to internalise those negative messages. Internalised homophobia keeps us hating ourselves and it keeps us quiet. It keeps us shamed and ashamed. It is not surprising that such a powerful force might hinder people coming out.

Projected homophobia

More properly called *displaced homophobia*, this is a process whereby we act out our anxiety and self-hatred on something or someone else. We kick the wall, punch the pillow, shout at the dog or take it out on parents and friends. You will recall our earlier discussion on gay hate crime. Apart from being explained significantly by reaction formation, it can also be explained by displaced homophobia. Many confused people who are stuck in this kind of cycle will struggle to 'see the light' and learn to accept themselves.

Is it really necessary?

This is the question that some Stage 1 or 2 gay people ask when they compare themselves with straight people. 'Straight people don't have to declare their sexuality, so why should we have to?' They forget that straight people don't have to go through an equivalent sexual identity formation process. Marshall also makes a very powerful point in answer to this question. He suggests applying a simple test: listen to straight people talk and count how many times they announce their sexual identity indirectly. A guy will talk of his girlfriend or his wife, or say to his mates, 'Check her out', as a good-looking woman passes by. A married woman will talk about her husband or children or what she's cooking for the family dinner that night. If you ask, 'What did you do last weekend?', in less than ten minutes, you'll hear indirect declarations of straight sexual identity. Coming out *is* necessary if you don't want to live the life-lie.

The relationship with your parents

This is a biggie. Gay and lesbian people can feel that by disclosing to their parents they will be letting them down. They fear the look of disappointment on their faces when they utter the fateful 'g' word. They tell themselves, 'They'll never handle it. They'll never get over it. It will destroy them. They'll be disappointed in me. They'll never be the same again.' I've yet to see the parent who was destroyed by a child's coming out. Yes, they *will* never be the same again. They will have to come to terms with the disclosure and integrate it into their lives, just as you, their son or daughter, had to do. This takes time, so make sure you give them the space to think, to read, to ask questions, to talk to a professional with expertise. Most of the time, coming out to parents is a positive experience, albeit a difficult one.

What lies at the heart of the reluctance to come out to parents is the fear of being rejected, the fear of being pushed away by the very ones who are supposed to be on our side, to love us come what may. But it is vital to remember that, for a parent, short of the death of a child, there is no greater burden to carry than rejecting a child. This very rarely happens. Parents may not agree with a child's lifestyle or career choice or marriage partner, but they will seldom allow this to push them to the ultimate act of rejection. Interestingly, parents frequently know or suspect that sexual orientation may be an issue for their child. Many gay people have told me that when they came out, their parents finally had the freedom to tell them that they had guessed as much all along, but didn't want to pre-empt anything or offend. They felt it was better to have their child tell them when they were ready, rather than jumping the gun.

Allow me to recount briefly three coming-out-to-parents stories. The first concerns a former client in his early 20s; the second is about a man in his late 30s known to me; the third is my own story. The 20-something man was one of those people who you knew instantaneously was gay. There was no doubt at all. All his clinical depression and substance abuse was caused by his life-lie. He was still in the closet to his parents. He acknowledged that he had to come out to them; after all, everybody else knew. He also acknowledged that they almost certainly already knew anyhow. The last time I saw him, he was still fighting the idea every inch of the way. He simply couldn't do it, couldn't tell them what they already knew, and he was seriously abusing alcohol to try to numb himself from the pain. As far as I know, he never did disclose to them. He felt ashamed (internalised homophobia) and that he would be a disappointment to them. Having met his parents once in my waiting room, I am certain that they wouldn't have rejected him. They obviously loved him dearly and were worried about his well-being.

Most people would never pick the man in his late 30s as being gay. He was the complete opposite of any gay stereotype you could possibly choose. He had a long-term partner who went everywhere with him and was part of his life in every way and well known to his parents. However, to them, the partner was his 'friend'. It was accepted that it was always his friend he brought home, rather than a girlfriend. Again, to my knowledge, he has never told his parents. His reasons? They wouldn't handle it; it would devastate them; they're too old. He has never trusted the parents who love him to be able to integrate this knowledge into their world. By predicting dire consequences, based primarily on his fear, he has underestimated his parents' maturity and ability to deal with difficult issues. As a result, heading into his

40s, he remains stuck in the darkness of the closet and deprives his parents of knowing who their son really is.

I did come out to my parents. I was 37 years of age and my parents were both almost 70. When I told them, we all had a small cry and then we talked. They said that they were disappointed that I wouldn't be able to have a family. I could understand this and conceded that it was sad for them. They had wondered about me some years before but had long since ceased any kind of speculation. Once I had explained my journey of self-understanding, they felt that it all made sense and they could see where and how the pieces fitted together. After hours of discussion, they said that I would always be their son, that this would not change anything between us, that they loved me no matter what and that they would always be there for me. At 70 years of age, that's pretty damn good, don't you think?

Right and wrong ways to come out

Coming out at an appropriate time is the best way forward for the psychological health of a gay or lesbian person, but a word of caution, lest anyone should just rush out and start declaring it to the world. There are many ways of coming out described in countless books and articles, but I offer here my own revised view of the model suggested by Andrew Marshall, who offers a five-stage or five-rung stepladder. I like this approach because it is simple, straightforward and sensible.

Coming out

to the world

to the family

to straight friends

to other gay people

to yourself

Life, however, is not so neat and tidy and many people take the steps in a different order. For that reason I prefer to use the same basic headings but to use a circle rather than a ladder to illustrate the model. Your sense of self is at the centre of the circle and you can come out to various segments when and where you choose.

I generally tell clients on the cusp of coming out to make sure that they come out first only to people they can trust. In other words, when beginning the coming out journey, only disclose to those you know will respect your life. Don't tell anyone if you're not sure how they will react. Stick to those you are confident will be supportive because they like you or love you.

Remember, too, that in some circumstances, it is clearly unsafe to come out. You must protect your personal safety at all costs. Coming out to those whom you know or suspect will try to harm you in some way, become aggressive or violent, or heap scorn upon you is just plain silly. In standing up for your rights and self, there is no need to be indiscriminate: there are some people out there who will *never* get it. You need to pick your battles, as it were, especially in the early days. Sometimes it's just not worth the risk. If you're safe and sensible, coming out can be an exciting and exhilarating time.

One final point about coming out. You may have noticed earlier that I used the phrase 'first-time coming out' several times. This is to emphasise the fact that for all gay people, coming out does not just happen once or in a few short months. Even when you've told everyone on the circle about your sexuality, there is still more coming out to do. It is a simple fact that gay people live in a predominantly straight world and must continue to come out for life. Because every gay person has at least a small degree of internalised homophobia, we are all vulnerable to allowing ourselves to be coerced back into the closet, back into being ashamed from time to time. This must be striven against persistently and consistently. The forces that would push us back into the closet are relentless and we cannot accede to them, if we value our mental health and the dignity of our own lives. Whenever I introduce my partner to someone new, I come out all over again. Whenever my partner and I go grocery shopping together as an obvious couple, we come out all over again. This is a lifelong transaction with the world. It is part of being gay.

Sound People, Sick Therapy

Historically, in the Western world, homosexuality has been viewed in a number of different negative ways down through the ages, and through three principal professions in the modern era: priests, doctors and lawyers. We'll take a look at the first two here.

Priests

We are aware that homosexuality was well known in the ancient world and continued to play a role in European life after the collapse of the Roman Empire. In his book *Christianity, Social Tolerance and Homosexuality*,[1] John Boswell suggests that during this time, and before the High Middle Ages, sexual acts between adults of the same sex appear to have been tolerated (in the strictest sense of the word) or ignored by the Christian church throughout Europe. Towards the end of the 12th century, however, antagonism toward same-sex sexual activity became common throughout European religious and secular institutions. The church and its theologians condemned this behaviour as *contra naturam*, against nature, and therefore unnatural – and a sin against God. Thus gay people were characterised as sinners.

By the 18th century, however, the human condition was recharacterised in Western philosophy. This was the Age of Enlightenment, when reason was given prominence; a time of great discovery and investigation by such men as Captain James Cook and Governor Arthur Phillip, in Australasia, and Benjamin Franklin and Thomas Jefferson in America.

In this period – early modern Europe – there was a reconceptualisation of the straightforward two-gender paradigm. The view developed that male and female each had a heterosexual and a homosexual version, thus giving four genders. The homosexual version of men was associated with femininity and the homosexual version of women with masculinity.[2] Using today's language, this meant that same-sex attracted men were seen as effete or effeminate and same-sex attracted women were seen as butch. This view survives in some quarters, where ignorant or homophobic people perpetuate the stereotype that all gay guys are limp-wristed, lisping and camp and all lesbians are butch, low-voiced dykes. Thus in the 18th century, gay people were thought to be straight people reversed.

Doctors

In the second half of the 19th century and the first four decades of the 20th, one colossus bestrode the theory and practice of psychiatry: Sigmund Freud (1856–1939). Although a lot of what Freud theorised has been dismissed in modern psychology owing to lack of evidence, the impossibility of testing it and the better understanding provided by newer research, Freud's theories were the gold standard for a long time so it is important to mention them briefly. For the doctors who came after him turned the 'reversal' of the 18th century into the 'pathology' or illness of the 19th century.

Freud created a complex model of how humans grow psychologically – his famous staged theory of psychosexual development. He also noted that sometimes development does not follow its 'normal' path and a person with same-sex attraction results. The table on the next page shows Freud's model for males.

It is a fairly obvious but important point to note that this model used what we in the 21st century view as stereotyped gay figures.

	Straight	Gay
Physical appearance	Male	Male/female
Mental characteristics	Masculine	Feminine
Object choice	Female sexual partner	Male sexual partner

Nonetheless, Freud viewed gay men as being inverted straight men, even though he did not coin the term.

Although Freud did not believe that such inverts could be turned back to a heterosexual psychology, he did not necessarily view them as being sick, as the following excerpt from a famous letter to a mother about her gay son attests: 'Homosexuality is assuredly no advantage, but it is nothing to be ashamed of, no vice, no degradation, it cannot be classified as an illness; we consider it to be a variation of the sexual function produced by a certain arrest of sexual development'.[3] The term used in his time for non-procreative sexual activity, taken originally from the church, was perversion, so Freud also used the term 'pervert'. This word has a wealth of negative connotations: it is used to describe quite deviant, mostly unsavoury sexual behaviour such as exhibitionism and voyeurism. The 19th-century view of gay people as inverts and perverts laid the foundation for the pathologisation of homosexual people by the medical profession.

The *DSM*

Freud's successors were not as enlightened as the great man himself. By the beginning of the 1950s, just a decade or so after his death, the medical profession had pathologised homosexuality so that it was viewed as a sickness. The American Psychiatric Association's (APA) psychiatric bible was the *Diagnostic and Statistical Manual of Mental Disorders*, or the *DSM*, as it is usually called. It was designed to list and describe all psychiatric illness, which it describes as mental disorders. The first edition, published in 1952, included homosexuality as a mental disorder in its chapter on perversions. The second edition, the *DSM-II*, published in 1968, continued to include homosexuality as a psychopathology.

After a marathon two-year debate brought on by researchers,

gay psychiatrists and gay activists, in 1973 the *DSM*'s Nomenclature Committee recommended to the APA that homosexuality be removed from its list of mental disorders. The majority of members accepted the motion, based on their widespread clinical experience. This was a momentous day in Western psychiatry and psychology. From that moment on, modern medicine no longer officially viewed gay and lesbian sexual identity as psychopathological. Gay people could be viewed by the medical establishment as normal, just like everyone else.

At the same time, the committee suggested a new category to replace homosexuality: *sexual orientation disturbance*. This new diagnosis was applied to gay men and women who felt disturbed or conflicted by their sexual orientation. Although these changes were approved by the general APA membership, not everyone endorsed them. There was vehement resistance from a number of renowned psychiatrists, who held strongly to the old post-Freudian idea that homosexuality was caused by fixated or arrested sexual development in childhood with the Oedipal complex not correctly resolved. However, the tide had turned and nothing could stop the research that would confirm and augment the earlier seminal work that sparked the whole APA debate.

It was in 1980 that the third edition of the *DSM* was published. The *DSM-III* really took root in the American psychiatric landscape and became the routine sourcebook for all psychiatric consultations. This edition replaced the sexual orientation disturbance category with a category called *ego-dystonic homosexuality*. The term ego-dystonic is still used in psychiatry and clinical psychology. It means that (a) you do not really understand just how psychiatrically ill you are, that is, you lack insight to your own condition, or (b) that the disorder you have does not feel appropriate to your sense of self. So when the *DSM-III* referred to ego-dystonic homosexuality, it referred to a person who is gay, but who finds this orientation a source of distress and therefore wishes to become heterosexual. Note that the *DSM-III* still did not view homosexuality as a disorder; rather, it qualified the idea of the distressed gay individual who didn't want to be gay.

In fact, you will immediately recognise the *DSM-III*'s predisposing factors for ego-dystonic homosexuality: negative societal attitudes toward homosexuality that have been internalised, while at the same time, wanting to live a socially sanctioned lifestyle of marriage, children and career. It sounds a lot like the closet, doesn't it? It also sounds a lot like being gay in church. Remember, the *DSM-III* was published in 1980 and although the United States had gone through the sexual revolution of the 1960s, its Bible belt and down-home small town culture was still not able to face homosexuality. It is no wonder that young gay men and women growing up in that culture, including in its church, were unhappy with their lives and wanted change.

However, the position of the *DSM-III* could not really be sustained. It held that homosexuality was not a psychopathology, yet said that those who had internalised their shame and distress in the ego-dystonic homosexuality category could validly move to change. In effect, it was trying to have it both ways. It seems that psychiatrists were on to this from the get-go. Mental health professionals made very little use of the ego-dystonic homosexuality diagnosis and by 1987, when the revised version, the *DSM-IIIR*, came out, the category was dropped altogether. It was replaced in the *DSM-IV*, published in 1994, by the catch-all, generic, non-orientation-specific category of *sexual disorder not otherwise specified*; still used today, and will be used in the new *DSM-V* to be published in May 2013.

In January 1975, the American Psychological Association supported the American Psychiatric Association's December 1973 decision to remove homosexuality from its official list of mental disorders. The psychologists adopted a resolution stating that homosexuality implied 'no impairment in judgment, stability, reliability, or general, social or vocational capabilities' and urged 'all mental health professionals to take the lead in removing the stigma of mental illness that has long been associated with homosexual orientations'.

The research of Evelyn Hooker

The seminal research that originally sparked the APA debate was done by Dr Evelyn Hooker, a hero in this story, although she remained uncomfortable with that epithet throughout her long life.

The illness model of homosexuality proposes that the existence of persistent homosexual feelings in an individual or group of individuals is unequivocal evidence that psychological disturbance will be a consequence of that psychosexual state. Put another way, the presence of homosexuality means that you can absolutely predict psychological disturbance. The logical outcome of this model is that if you can identify *any* homosexual individual or group that does not demonstrate psychological disturbance, then the model is refuted.[4]

Evelyn Gentry was born in 1907 on the Colorado Plains and at the age of 13 moved with her family to Sterling, Colorado. After graduation, she attended Johns Hopkins University in Baltimore, Maryland, where she gained her doctorate in psychology in 1932. While teaching at UCLA in the 1940s, she met and befriended a young gay man named Sam From, who gradually introduced her to his friends. She and her first husband, Don Caldwell, were invited to regular outings with a group of gay men.

She noticed that they seemed remarkably well adjusted, but she knew that this was not supposed to be. In those years homosexuality was considered a psychopathology, so you couldn't be gay – that is, have a mental disorder – *and* be psychologically well adjusted at the same time. The two conditions were supposed to be mutually exclusive. Sam and his companions urged their friend to research them and their lives. Although she attempted some initial exploratory work, the project was mothballed after she and Caldwell divorced in the late 1940s. She remarried in 1951, this time to a distinguished English literature professor at UCLA, Edward Hooker, and with her life happier and feeling more stable, she applied to the National Institute of Mental Health in 1953 for a grant to continue the study into homosexual men. She won the grant against almost insurmountable odds and began the study.

In the 1992 Academy Award-winning documentary, *Changing Our Minds: The Story of Dr Evelyn Hooker*, produced by David Haugland, Evelyn Hooker describes the times in which she conducted the research. After 1948 in the United States, under Section 290 of the penal code, gay men were arrested as sexual offenders in what became known as pervert arrests. It was a terrible time for gay people. Medical practitioners were performing hysterectomies on lesbian women and certain physicians were castrating gay men, while testosterone therapy was routinely used on gay men under the false premise that they were lacking in testosterone. Psychiatry was using electro-convulsive therapy. There is footage of this in the Haugland documentary. As one psychiatrist is about to switch on the ECT machine, he says to the poor wretch strapped to the table, 'This will help you to get well.'

What did Hooker's study consist of? First, she wanted to recruit participants to her study who were not psychiatrically ill. Typically, any subjects for research done on homosexuality around this time (and by opponents after her ground-breaking study) were recruited from mental hospitals, prisons or the armed forces, but Hooker wanted everyday people. Thirty gay men volunteered. After interviewing them extensively, Hooker matched each with a straight man of the same age, IQ and level of education. She now had 30 pairs of gay/straight matched men to whom she administered the three most commonly used projective tests of the day: the Rorschach, the Thematic Apperception Test (TAT) and the Make A Picture Story (MAPS). Projective tests present ambiguous stimuli so that, as they respond, the subjects will inadvertently reveal unconscious desires, drives, fantasies and conflicts. The idea was to see if the experts, without knowing which was which, could pick the gay man from the straight in each of the 30 pairs.

The Rorschach is the famous ink-blot test. Subjects examine ten ink blots and explain what they see. Experts in Rorschach were able to predict all manner of mental disorders, criminality and even, to a certain extent, future physical sickness. The TAT consists of a series of cards with scenes showing one or two people undergoing some important life experience. The test-taker is asked to make up a story about the scene, explaining what is happening, the thoughts and feelings of those depicted and what happened to make this situation occur. The scenes are ambiguous enough for them to be projective.

The MAPS consists of 22 stimulus cards each showing a differ-ent scene. These scenes range from 'structured situations (bed-room, bathroom, schoolroom, baby's room) to more ambiguous presentations (a doorway, a cave, and a totally blank card)'. Also provided are 67 cut-out figures that include 'men, women, boys, girls, policemen, mythical characters, animals, people who are disabled, nudes, and others'. The subject has to choose a stimulus card, then place selected cut-out figures on it and 'tell a story explaining those choices'.[5]

All three of these tests were then gold standard and those expert in administering them were not easily fooled. Bruno Klopfer was a Rorschach expert: as Hooker says in the Haugland documentary, 'If anyone in America could pick the gay men using the Rorschach, Klopfer could.'

Hooker took the tests of the 30 pairs of matched participants and completely removed any identification. Only she could know which was the gay or straight man in each pair. Three projective test experts, unknown to each other, were given all 30 pairs and asked to systematically go through them and to determine three things:

1. any evidence of psychopathology;
2. a rating of the level of psychological adjustment on a five-point scale ranging from 'poor' to 'well-adjusted'; and
3. the gay man in each pair.

The results proved iconoclastic. First, of the 60 men, 51 were found to be 'well adjusted' and five 'poorly adjusted', with the remainder uncertain. The two Rorschach experts rated over two-thirds of all the men, both gay and straight, in the highest three categories of adjustment. Klopfer and the other Rorschach expert were not able, in any case, to tell which in each pair was the gay man. The third expert, who used the TAT and MAPS to rate psychological adjustment, could see no difference either. In utter disbelief, and struggling to accept the result, he actually asked Hooker for a second try. When analysing the results closely, Hooker found that none of the experts could do better than random chance and that the majority of gay men were in the top three categories of psychological adjustment. Either the experts' fame was misplaced or there was no difference.

Hooker delivered the findings to the meeting of the American Psychological Association in 1956 and published them in the *Journal of Projective Techniques* a year later under the title 'The Adjustment of the Overt Male Homosexual'. In her paper she wrote, '[W]hat is difficult to accept (for most clinicians) is that some homosexuals *may* be very ordinary individuals, indistinguishable, except in sexual pattern, from ordinary individuals who are heterosexual. Or – and I do not know whether this would be more or less difficult to accept – that some *may* be quite superior individuals, not only devoid of pathology but also functioning at a superior level.'[6]

Her findings shattered over half a century of psychiatric dogma. Hooker's work throughout the 1960s in researching gay men as individuals and later in groups, as well as her constant speaking engagements, inspired others to follow in her footsteps and ensured that the truth would not be kept down. Although she was not solely responsible, Evelyn Hooker's pioneering study paved the way for the removal of homosexuality from the *DSM* in 1973. In 1992, the

American Psychological Association awarded her its highest honour, a lifetime achievement award. Evelyn Hooker died in 1996 at her home in Santa Monica, California aged 89.

I end this section with a wonderful letter written to Evelyn Hooker just after the Haugland documentary had been shown at the Berlin Film Festival in 1992. It sums up the appreciation of both the gay and psychological communities for her work.

> Dear Dr. Evelyn Hooker,
>
> My boyfriend and I just saw the documentary about you at the Berlin Film Festival. We want to say thank you for all the work you did. We're pretty sure that life would have been a lot different, and a lot worse for us, if you hadn't done your research.
>
> I asked a close, straight friend of mine, who is a medical student at Berlin, why you wanted to do this work. I mean, it just didn't make sense. Why did this straight lady care about gays? My friend replied that it was probably because you felt that it had to be done by somebody, sooner or later. He said that you must have thought that the studies you undertook would help people in some way. He called it scientific altruism.
>
> Well, whatever the real reason is, I think that your work was more than just doing a good turn for man. I think you did it because you knew what love was when you saw it and you knew that gay love was like all other love. No better, no worse.
>
> So I guess if we are thanking you, we should thank you not for the work itself, but for your desire to show to the world what you had already understood, or at least suspected, on your own.
>
> With much respect and admiration.[7]

Some important points about research

Evelyn Hooker's research was just the beginning for the whole topic of homosexuality to be viewed as a worthy domain of scholarly endeavour. Over the ensuing years, much work was undertaken that augmented Hooker's basic findings, but using different means. Before we look at those studies, though, I want to take a brief look at some important methodological issues that are common to this kind of behavioural research because understanding them is absolutely essential if one wants to comprehend the science of psychological adjustment.

There are five important issues to remember.[8] They show us how good research is undertaken so that valid robust findings can be concluded, but also how bad research is undertaken, with findings that are immediately questionable, due to faulty logic or poor methodological decisions.

1. What is considered a disturbance

Proponents of the illness model, typically psychoanalytically trained psychiatrists who had made a name for themselves 'treating' homosexuals, proposed that when certain patterns in the families of homosexuals are identified, this is evidence that homosexuality per se is a psychological disturbance. The theory is that if these patterns are not found in the families of heterosexual people, then such absence is evidence of the pathological nature of homosexuality. However, just because differences might be found between populations, this does not prove that homosexuality is pathological. This becomes not a question of pathology, but of meaning. A more valid question would be: 'If a difference were found, what would such difference mean?'

Gay and straight people actually do differ from one another in a variety of ways. We would expect them to do so. But do such differences mean that gay people are psychologically disturbed? The answer, as you will see, is a resounding no. You cannot infer pathology merely from difference. Psychological testing shows overwhelmingly that although some differences can be found between gay and straight people on a number of measures, there are not many and, where they are found, they are typically very small. Further, no signs of pathology or psychological disturbance are evidenced by these findings.

2. What is considered normal

I studiously avoid the word 'normal' when discussing a client's behaviour or emotional state. Axe murderers aside, when authority figures such as priests, politicians, doctors or therapists talk about others being normal or abnormal, you know you're on a very slippery judgemental and subjective slope. Psychologists prefer to talk about a normal *range* of phenomena. If normal behaviour is to be measured on a set of psychological tests or by day-to-day adjustment in life, or the absence of a particular trait (e.g. being highly strung), then we need to accept there will be a range of behaviour that falls into what is considered normal. People who score the very lowest or the very highest will both be considered to be in the normal range. For example, both highly extroverted and highly introverted individuals would both be considered in the normal range of social expression. The mean or average scores of individuals from each end of the continuum grouped together would both be considered normal, even though the groups are completely different.

It is not uncommon for different populations or groups of people to redefine the normal range for their particular group. For example, physical expressions of affection between straight men would be completely different in men with an Anglo-Saxon heritage from men with a European or Asian background. Both groups behave very differently, yet both groups are considered perfectly normal within their own group, i.e. they both fall within the normal range for their particular population.

3. Statistical significance and normal range

Statistical significance means that differences found between groups in research experiments will have to be large enough for the researchers to be able to confidently announce that they have not made a mathematical error. There are very strict rules governing this. The word 'significant' here has a vastly different meaning from its every-day or clinical use.

Interestingly, although differences between groups can be statistically significant, they can still be considered to be in the normal range. Just because a difference is statistically significant does not necessarily mean that the behaviour or trait is outside the normal range. This then becomes a question of interpretation. What does such a difference mean? Is there any ramification for an individual's everyday life or for clinical consideration? Finally, interpretations about such differences should be made with regard to other independent empirical data, not just a particular theory.

4. Base rates

If we accept, and I think we should, given the scientific findings, that homosexuality per se is not evidence of the presence of psychological disturbance, does this mean that there are no gay people who are disturbed? The answer is clearly no, of course not. The proportion or base rate of gay people who have psychological disturbances is roughly the same as it is for straight people who have psychological disturbances. J. C. Gonsiorek provides a helpful hypothetical situation to illustrate the point. If, for example, 5 per cent of the general population is seriously psychologically disturbed, 10 per cent moderately disturbed, 15 per cent slightly disturbed and 70 per cent are within the normal range of psychological adjustment, then we might expect that roughly the same proportions will be found in the gay population, without giving one inch to the illness model proponents who say that homosexuality *is* a sign of psychopathology. Gay people are no more immune to mental illness than are straight people, so we would expect to find some disturbed gay people along similar base rates for the rest of the population.

5. What about any perceived increased rates of disturbance?

Since homosexuality is a minority status within the rest of the population, is the target of prejudice and discrimination and same-sex attracted individuals are taught to be ashamed, it is not unreasonable to think that such a group might contain individuals or sub-groupings who show increased levels of disturbance on some measures of external stress above those of the heterosexual community at large. However, even here, it does not follow that such levels of disturbance, while present, are universal in the gay community, nor that homosexuality per se is evidence of psychological pathology. It does mean that, for such individuals or groupings, a more valid comparison group would be heterosexual individuals or groups with similar levels of external stress. Using invalid comparison groups is inherently flawed because groups end up being compared with other groups that have fundamentally different base rates.

Research after Evelyn Hooker

Let's now take a look at some of the studies that occurred after Evelyn Hooker's ground-breaking effort. By the advent of the 1980s, the scientific question as to the putative link between psychopathology and homosexuality had been thoroughly investigated and answered clearly in the negative, so researchers left the field and confidently moved on to further areas of inquiry.

In 1964 two researchers, Robert B. Dean and Harold Richardson,[9] published an article proposing that non-patient samples of openly gay men recruited among college students should show no sign of psychopathology due to their sexual orientation. Using the Minnesota Multiphasic Personality Inventory (MMPI), which is not a projective test, the researchers found that the mean scores of the gay men were only slightly higher than the straight men's and any differences were only moderate: all but three were not statistically significant. The authors concluded that the results supported their hypothesis and that their data could in no way support the proposition that gay men have 'any general or severe personality disturbance' since none of the scores were in the pathological range.

Since opponents were using patient samples, four researchers decided to take on the question of whether patient and non-patient samples were equivalent. They published their paper in 1974.[10] They gave their two samples the Eysenck Personality Inventory (EPI) and the Sixteen Personality Factor Questionnaire (16PF). The patient groups scored significantly higher on the sub-scale of neuroticism (what lay people generally call being 'highly strung') and were more aggressive, tense, conservative and group-dependent than the non-patient group. This was definitive evidence to show that inpatient groups of gay people are not the equivalent of non-patient groups of gay people. It further indicates that taking gay patient samples and extrapolating from their results is simply not a valid way to describe non-patient individuals and groups. It would be tantamount to describing straight people based on data taken from straight psychiatric inpatients.

Two other MMPI studies were conducted,[11] this time with lesbian women. Both found no evidence of greater psychopathology in either the gay women or the straight women. Other valid scales were also used. Researcher Marvin Siegelman,[12] using a sub-section of the 16PF, examined the psychological adjustment of 444 gay and straight American men. Six years later, adding the Neuroticism Scale Questionnaire and the Gough Femininity Scale, he did the same study on British men.[13] Although he found some normal range differences, he correctly concluded that, based on his data, there was no difference in psychological adjustment between the groups.

Marvin Siegelman was a very systematic researcher: he followed exactly the same protocol as above when he examined lesbian and straight women in two studies, the first in 1972 and the second in 1979,[14,15] using the same instruments in both studies. The gay women in both studies scored lower on the neuroticism measure than the straight women, and higher than them on the directedness and self-acceptance measures, while the data showed no significant differences between the groups on measures of depression, anxiety, alienation, trust, sense of self, dependency and nurturance. The only conclusion to be drawn from these data was that no evidence was found to support the notion that homosexuality is psychopathological or causes maladjustment.

Numerous other studies used other objective tests (as distinct from the projective tests) and drew the same conclusions. The California Personality Inventory, the Edwards Personal Preference Schedules, the Adjective Check List, the Jouard and Laskow Self-Disclosure Questionnaire and the Tennessee Self-Concept Scale all failed to find gay/straight differences of adjustment or the presence of psychopathology in the gay samples. Areas of possible maladjustment that have been scientifically investigated in comparison studies and where no differences have been identified between gay and straight groups have been: self-acceptance, self-conduct, depression, self-esteem, relationship discord, sexual discord, gender roles and aging. I have mentioned only a handful of studies here. There are many, many more.

Sick therapy

We have traced the story of how homosexuality has been depathologised. We have seen the seminal work of Evelyn Hooker, the 1973 APA decision to remove homosexuality from the *DSM* and the flood of research that followed, augmenting the evidence and corroborating the decision. Behavioural and medical science had finally understood what homosexual people had known all along: that gay and lesbian people were normal.

Yet not everyone was happy. There was a group of powerful psychiatrists who had a vested interest in perpetuating the myth that homosexuality was an illness and who endorsed the diagnosis of ego-dystonic homosexuality before it, too, faded away. These men provided gay men and lesbians with a therapy designed to re-orient their sexual identity back to heterosexuality, that is, to turn gays into straights. In the early days, such therapy was called conversion therapy. These days, it is more often called reparative therapy. There are two principal contexts in which reparative therapy is conducted: the therapist's couch (no longer quite so commonplace) and the clergyman's pastoral office or church-sanctioned 'ex-gay ministry' group.

As Douglas Haldeman suggests,[16] there are two fundamental problems with this so-called therapy. The first is that that there are major ethical concerns about purporting to re-orient a gay person's sexuality now that homosexuality is considered by science as a perfectly normal variant of human sexuality. The second is that empirical studies demonstrate clearly that such therapy does not in fact change people's sexual orientation; in other words, it doesn't work. Let's take a look at both these objections.

Ethical objections

Once homosexuality was no longer seen as evidence of psycho-pathology, various professional bodies made very distinct and vigorous statements about how the mental health professions and the courts should respond, by calling for an end to discriminatory practices in law and therapeutic treatments. In 1992 the American Psychiatric Association issued a powerful statement regarding stigmatisation of gay and lesbian people. The American Psychological Association adopted a forceful resolution concerning gay and lesbian civil and legal rights and the American Psychiatric Association declared loud and clear its opposition to reparative therapy and was joined by the American Academy of Pediatrics, the American Medical Association, the American Psychological Association, the American Counseling Association and the National Association of Social Workers.

In such a therapeutic culture, clinicians cannot claim ignorance when they propose that the days of the illness model are not over. First of all, clinicians who do this are ignoring the manifest evidence that since homosexuality is not a disorder, there is no *need* for anyone to try to change. This is an important point. But when you hold out a 'cure' for something, you in effect create a need in the minds of the vulnerable.[17]

In a 1991 paper, Gerald Davison heads one section 'No Cure Without a Disease'.[18] He points out that, by holding out a cure, such therapists are perpetuating the discredited illness model of homosexuality and encouraging vulnerable gay individuals to believe that such a change is worthwhile, desirable and possible. In Haldeman's words, 'Many of these individuals are vulnerable to the idea of repairing in themselves what is actually society's problem: a history of rejection and discrimination based upon socially instituted homophobia.'[19]

Davison goes on to debunk the myth of neutrality among those who offer reparative therapy. These therapists say, 'Well, we're not *forcing* anyone to come to us. They come of their own free will. We're just here to offer them a service that *they* desire and because they're so unhappy with their lives, we have a duty to look after them and care for them clinically. We stay neutral in all this.' It sounds so believable, so altruistic and even so compassionate, but it's not. It's actually quite pernicious.

Therapists are authority figures. Vulnerable and desperate people are particularly suggestible to their voices. Reparative therapy can cause harm, impedes the process of self-acceptance, traps people in a lifetime of struggle and offers only false hope. To act in such a manner against all credible scientific and clinical understanding is unethical.[20]

Why do some elements of psychiatry continue to do this? Because of their continued discomfort with homosexuality and their refusal to accept that the weight of evidence is against the illness model. Their discomfort, some would argue, stems directly from the Judaeo-Christian roots of Western psychiatry. Further, they fund and undertake research that is scientifically unsound. As the Australian Psychological Society (APS) website notes, the flaws in their methodology include 'unclear definition of terms, inaccurate classification of participants, inappropriate comparison of groups, discrepant sampling procedures, an ignorance of confounding social factors, and questionable outcome measures'.

Although these studies 'have no valid empirical support', they 'serve as the basis for inaccurate representations of lesbian, gay, and bisexual people'.[21] In most Western countries, professional organisations have explicit ethical guidelines for the respectful and non-prejudiced treatment of gay and lesbian individuals and condemn reparative therapy.

Reparative therapy does not work

Let us now look at the second objection Douglas Haldeman raises: that reparative therapy fails to alter sexual orientation. It is important to remember that sexual behaviour is not the same thing as sexual orientation. Individuals can too easily hide behind behaviour when they are actually feeling something else altogether. As you will recall, the best indicators of sexual orientation are fantasy, erotic thinking, dreams and perving behaviour. The principal index reparative therapists use to 'prove' that their treatments work is the fact that some of their patients (I give the example of males here) increase heterosexual behaviours – they go through the treatment or ministry and then have heterosexual sex, decide to stay with their wives, go out with women, participate in sport or generally exhibit more stereotypical masculine behaviour.

There are two problems with this. First, behaviour is not the same thing as orientation: their underlying sexual orientation remains the same. It is gay and does not change. Christian psychiatrist Ruth Barnhouse, who does not advocate reparative therapy, says that far from changing their sexual orientation, these men are merely demonstrating that their sexual organs are in good working order. Second, rugged 'masculine' pursuits do not constitute maleness. These pursuits, like all markers of masculinity, are predicated on culture, education, socio-economic status and family history. In other words, they change when these factors are different. There are millions of straight men who don't watch football or listen to rock music or play sport or ogle at passing girls. There are millions of straight men who love classical music, even opera, like to go to art galleries, who prefer the company of women to men when socialising, are not big drinkers and who like to talk about their feelings. God forbid, there are even some straight guys into arts and crafts and some of them actually like ballet.

The two arenas where reparative therapy occurs are the therapist's couch or the ex-gay ministry of the church. In August 2009, the American Psychological Association's annual conference reported extensively on reparative therapy and 'sexual orientation change efforts' or SOCE. Their survey of the literature shows that almost all such therapy is being targeted at people with conservative religious or political beliefs.[22] I want to take a brief look at both the couch and the pulpit since they shed light on what modern psychology considers a deceitful, harmful and unnecessary practice.

Reparative therapy on the couch

After three decades of contrary research and clinical experience, some clinicians persist in regarding homosexuality from a Freudian perspective: as a failure to resolve the Oedipal issue. They speak of an over-close, over-protective mother and a cold, distant or absent father. Most people who hear this for the first time say that it sounds like gobbledygook and most gay people laugh and point out that it does not describe them or their family at all. Needless to say, like almost all of Freud's postulations, this premise has not been, and cannot be, empirically tested. So it hangs in the air like a bad smell that won't go away.

However, certain of these therapists have written of their success rates, which are minimal to say the least, and almost all talk about success in terms of increased heterosexual repertoire. At least therapist Lee Birk, who tries to change homosexual orientation using psychotherapy and psychoeducation, is honest when he says of the 38 per cent of his patients who had 'solid heterosexual shift':

> it is my belief that these represent shifts in a person's salient adaption to life, *not a metamorphosis* [my italics]. Most, if not all, people who have been homosexual continue to have some homosexual feelings, fantasies and interests. More often than not, they also have occasional or more than occasional, homosexual outlets, even while being 'happily married'.[23]

Haldeman asks the obvious question. If this passage is meant to describe 'solid heterosexual shift', then what on earth does a soft heterosexual shift look like?[24]

What we are seeing here is simple. It is not a shift away from gay or lesbian sexual orientation at all, but a treatment that teaches or 'compassionately' coerces heterosexual behaviours, sexual and otherwise, to vulnerable or desperate people. It ignores the manifest evidence that sexual orientation is best indicated by the emotional response to sexual stimuli rather than by what we say or what we do.

However, early behaviourally oriented therapists ignored all this and attempted to change orientation by use of aversion techniques. These were usually electroshock or emetogenic drugs – drugs that make you vomit. Here's how it worked. If you were a man unhappy with having same-sex desires in a very straight, conservative world that perhaps even included a church life, you might go along to a psychiatrist specialising in reorienting homosexual people, who would enrol you in a special programme. The nice people at the clinic would hook you up to electrodes and show you pictures of naked males or males together in the sex act and at the same time give you an electric shock. This was painful, very uncomfortable and extremely distressing.

To lessen this distress, the therapists would turn off the electric shocks while simultaneously presenting you with pictures of naked women or heterosexual couples having sex. Of course this felt much better, so it was a great relief *not* to have homo-erotic images shown to you. In fact, after being subjected to this kind of treatment for a while, you might even begin to dread the very thought of homo-erotic images. Ah, success! They've reoriented you. You're cured of homosexuality. Therapists began to claim 30 per cent success rates; those who didn't change were described as treatment 'failures'.

Such 'treatment' was, of course, highly unethical, even if patients consented to it. They typically did get reductions of homosexual desire, but such reductions did not last and the men simply could not sustain them by willpower. And it was not only homosexual desire that showed a decrease, but desire in general. While hooked up to a couple of electrodes that routinely shock you, you're probably not going to get very aroused at anything much at all. So typically, treatments such as these reduced general sexual arousal more than anything else.

When the men inevitably began to return to their naturally felt same-sex desire, they deemed themselves failures and felt guilty, ashamed and even more conflicted and fearful about their sexuality. Such vulnerable people are rife for self-hatred, self-loathing and self-disgust and can end up stuck in Stage 1 identity confusion for life. Thankfully this kind of thing is uncommon these days.

Reparative therapy from the pulpit

We now move on to the ex-gay ministry within the Christian church. This topic could easily fill a whole book on its own. I will limit myself to discussing the attitudes, the protocols and the results of such ministries.

First, let us be clear about who the proponents of these ministries are. Typically they are theologically evangelical or Pentecostal and are usually associated with either a local church or a church movement as an outreach to homosexual people, in much the same way that such churches have outreaches to the homeless, drug addicts, the poor and the infirm. Sometimes they are led by designated pastors of the church who oversee the work, sometimes by lay people who feel they are called by God to this work, or, commonly, they are gay or lesbian graduates of the programme who identify with the camaraderie, the rituals and the sense of belonging they felt while participating in the programme. They are often proud of their non-professional status and feel, as reformed people, that they can speak out because they have 'been there and overcome'; they 'once were lost but now are found'.

Let's also be very clear about what these ministries are doing. They purport to reorient gay and lesbian people to heterosexuality – typically gay and lesbian Christian people who have an active faith, but who are intensely conflicted about and shamed by their sexuality and how they believe it places them in God's eyes. The ex-gay movement totally ignores the scientific evidence that homosexuality is not an illness. Instead it relies on outdated Freudian concepts and misinterpretations of Biblical texts to make up plausible-sounding models to persuade vulnerable and desperate people of the veracity of their claims.

I recall only too well a young man standing up in my own previous church many years ago to give a testimonial about how God had changed him from being gay to straight, and including the statement that 'most homosexuals have a love deficit in their lives, usually their father'. When I was ashamed of myself and pilloried by conventional church dogma regarding sexuality, I readily believed this sort of thing because I needed to. It purported to explain the inexplicable. The fact that the explanation was a generalisation, was not tested empirically, relied on discarded concepts and 19th-century psycho-analytic paradigms, and was put forward by someone who was my friend and who had apparently 'beaten' homosexuality, only served to heighten my resolve to overcome my pernicious feelings and become clean again in God's eyes. Further, it did violence to both my parents: my mother, who was certainly neither overbearing nor overprotective, and my father, who has always been there for me in every way imaginable. To suggest there was a love deficit in my family is wrong and offensive.

This sort of testimonial is a common method used by the ex-gay movement. Participants, all with the same set of feelings, gather in a private place to openly acknowledge their wayward desires, rely on each other for support, listen to someone speak about overcoming homosexuality, or support the speaker in his or her ongoing struggle. They sing, pray, do Bible study, ask God to release them from a life of selfishness and, most importantly, pray the sinner's prayer by giving their lives to God and asking Jesus to be their personal Lord and Saviour, as they commit themselves to living the way He intended mankind should live, according to His statutes as laid down in His Word, the Bible. It is heady stuff and can be intensely emotionally affirming. Typically, the givers of such testimonials are referring not to a change in sexual orientation but to a change in their religious life, where they feel closer to God, closer to each other and more a part of the ministry of the church than ever before.

Those who are born again claim that when Jesus comes into their hearts to change them spiritually, he also redesigns them sexually. Christ does the work for them, based on his redemptive work on the cross, and through the Holy Spirit they must appropriate this change for themselves in their daily lives.

Because religious conversion, with all its notions of transformation from sinner to saved is central and essential to these ministries, sexuality is characterised as being fluid and not fixed. When God changes the malleable heart of a gay person in an act of personal salvation, He also changes their sexuality. Sexual identity is therefore seen as soft and flexible, not as biologically, psychologically and culturally determined and subsequently unchangeable. In the ex-gay ministry, if science doesn't match the theology, then science is wrong. It must give way.

I have no problem with anyone following the Way of Jesus and trying to live a life connected to God through God's Spirit, or even praying the sinner's prayer if that is the way they conceptualise what God desires of them, but I have yet to see an adult have his or her sexual orientation miraculously transmogrified by God from being gay into being straight. I have yet to see God intervene in someone's life in quite that way. God's Spirit certainly did not do that for me after decades of importunate prayer and sacrifice.

In such outreach groups sexual conversion is placed at the core of religious conversion and spiritual life. All of a sudden, it's not so much a gay person's heart that is the core of spirituality, but their body and what they do with it. As Tanya Erzen, ethnographer of ex-gay ministries and Professor of Comparative Studies, says:

> By becoming a born-again Christian and maintaining a personal relationship with Jesus, ex-gay men and women are born again religiously, and as part of that process they consider themselves reconstituted sexually... Their literal belief that the Bible condemns homosexual practices and identity leads them to measure their success in negotiating their new identities through submission and surrender to Jesus in all things. Even if desires and attractions remain after they have attended an ex-gay ministry, like New Hope, their relationship with God and Jesus continues intact. That relationship supersedes any sexual changes, minimizing their frustration and disillusionment when the longed for sexual changes do not occur.[25]

I find it difficult to accept the emphasis that certain churches, individuals and ministries place upon the sexual identities of their members. The culture in these places seems to be deeply preoccupied with sex – and especially same-sex identity. It often seems that you can be derelict in your faith, you can be a Christian fraud, like some of the exposed televangelists, you can go to church rarely and even swear and drink alcohol to excess, you can gamble away your family's food and home and fornicate with strangers every night of the week, but if you're straight, you're okay. You can still be part of the church and welcomed as one of God's much-loved children. Just say sorry to God and the church won't come down on you too hard. But if you're openly gay and happen to lead an exemplary life following the Way of

Jesus, you can't be part of the church or God's family. You're a sinner, you need to repent and you're turning your back on God unless you change. The Catholic Archbishop of Sydney, Cardinal George Pell, while not running an ex-gay ministry per se, still refuses to give the Eucharist to any gay Catholic who is open about his or her sexual identity. The hypocrisy and lack of charity undergirding this culture are breathtaking.

Many men who go through such 'conversion' programmes talk about their enhanced sense of masculinity. Some ex-gay ministries endorse this embracing of conventionally masculine behaviours, encouraging keeping fit and sports in general. Some also encourage their male graduands to date women and become more comfortable in their presence. This is an interesting strategy, as many gay men find the company of women very easy anyway, and the feeling is often mutual. Some ministries offer workshops that teach gay women how to put on makeup and adopt a conventionally feminine posture, manner and behaviour.

Such behavioural changes do not indicate any change in underlying sexual orientation. Individuals who do manage to increase these so-called straight behaviours end up leading an emotionally exhausting life of struggle and sorrow – the life-lie. They will often even describe themselves as 'ex-gays', thereby assigning themselves to some kind of limbo, an in-between place. They certainly will not call themselves 'gay' and cannot in honesty call themselves 'straight'. Many tend to remain within the ministry's ranks for a long time because its culture helps them to live their 'heterosexual' lives between meetings. But they have embarked on a never-ending journey with a forever unattainable destination – be straight or be celibate.

Erzen's fieldwork shows that, in the ex-gay movement, it is far more reprehensible to abandon a commitment to Jesus than it is to stray from the fold sexually. In other words, it is accepted that group participants will continue to experience same-sex desire and from time to time may even seek out a gay sexual encounter. However, such individuals are encouraged to acknowledge their weakness, repent of their sin and return to the embrace and support of the ministry. This cycle of lapse, repentance, relapse, return and recovery becomes their life.

I leave the last word here to Douglas Haldeman and his paper on 'the scientific evidence on the effectiveness of conversion therapies'. Reparative therapy in the context of ex-gay ministries is serious business and does serious harm to people's lives.

> Recently, founders of yet another prominent 'ex-gay' ministry, Exodus International, denounced their conversion therapy procedures as ineffective. Michael Busse and Gary Cooper, co-founders of Exodus, and lovers for 13 years, were involved with the organization from 1976 to 1979. The program was described by these men as 'ineffective… not one person was healed'. They stated that the program often exacerbated already prominent feelings of guilt and personal failure among the counselees; many were driven to suicidal thoughts as a result of the failed 'reparative therapy' (Newswatch Briefs, 1990).[26]

A word to pastors, priests and youth group leaders

If you are a priest, pastor or church leader who is considering the merits of the ex-gay ministry wing of the church for any under your pastoral care, I urge you to think again. Gay and lesbian sexuality, like heterosexuality, is neither wilfully chosen nor wilfully changed. I have yet to see God perform a transformative miracle in any gay individual's life to make him or her straight. You are asking a person to be in denial for the rest of their lives and to be tormented, either by desire or by the loneliness of coerced celibacy. Either way, it is a life of torment. You have no right to ask that of anyone: it is tantamount to psychological torture.

There is simply no need to burden your flock with outdated and unscientific models based on medieval thought and highly controversial sacred text verses written in the ancient world and presented to them as God's dictated word. There is another way. I invite you to read the second section of this book to investigate the fact that not all Christians think this way. Countless millions of Christian people understand God in a very different way and I invite you to stay with me and my gay readers to explore this with an open mind.

The Bible
and Christianity

In the early days of coming to terms with my own sexuality I was mystified by the response I received from the one or two old friends at my previous church. They said, 'Well, I don't agree with it, but you have to do what you think is best,' or words to that effect. 'I don't agree with it.' Since when does one's response to human sexuality become one of agreement or disagreement? You can't disagree with the phenomenon of homosexuality or, for that matter, heterosexuality, any more than it makes sense to disagree with eagles, knives and forks, left-handedness, freckles, the music of Schubert or athleticism. 'I'm sorry, mate, but I don't *agree* with heterosexuality.' Just as absurd a statement and what on earth would it mean anyway?

Now, why would sane, educated, Christian people say such a thing? I think it comes down to them from the pulpits and the teaching of their pastors and priests and has as its basic premise the misunderstanding that sexuality is about what one does rather than about who one is. Most often, the pastors and priests rely on the Bible to augment their statements, giving them, as it were, God's seal of approval.

The Bible does say a number of things about homosexuality, which we will examine in detail in the next chapter, but just for now, let it be said that the few verses involved are not usually read and interpreted today in a favourable light by traditionalists. However, such interpretations do not even remotely take into account what we now know about homosexuality. The peddlers of this type of preaching believe they and their teachings are exempt from modern scholarship, that truth, and even God's reputation, are at stake. Why do they feel so strongly about what this book says regarding human sexuality while ignoring every other book on the subject that presents homosexuality in an accepting and favourable way? I believe that it's all to do with how you approach the Bible.

The Bible

Perhaps no current religious debate, especially in the non-Catholic church, is as contentious and divisive as that over the place of the Bible. Denominations the world over are tearing themselves apart over such controversial doctrinal matters as homosexuality, women, abortion and priestly orders while relying on vastly different interpretations of passages of scripture to bolster or prove their positions.[1] Biblical scholar and author Marcus Borg, in his wonderful book *Reading the Bible Again For the First Time: Taking the Bible Seriously But Not Literally*,[2] suggests that this debate is primarily found in three distinct issues:

1. creation vs evolution – a debate not found throughout the church, but certainly vehemently argued by its various proponents in certain quarters;
2. personal morality – particularly sexual practice, with homosexuality at the forefront; and
3. historical biblical criticism – research by scholars, not necessarily part of the church structures, into the historical Jesus and the early church.

It is easy to see that the way one views the Bible is strongly associated with how one views Christianity as a whole. For example, when someone sees the Bible as the dictated, inerrant Word of God for all time, then faith, ethics, sacrament and even God are all cemented in, with little room for movement or fresh understanding. However, one of the greatest reform movements to sweep the world church is the Progressive Christianity or Emergent Church movement, which is not fearful of human intellect or the spirit of inquiry and seeks to have modern scholarship elucidate faith in the context of a modern world. Naturally, such views are vociferously condemned by those who see the Bible as a fixed, unexaminable text. For them, those of us who feel it necessary to be believers in a different way are heretics, apostates and backsliders. Let's take a brief look at the competing views so as to better understand how I will be discussing gay and lesbian orientation a little later. I am particularly relying here on the first part of Borg's book.

The three great questions

Borg says, quite rightly, that our lenses affect the way we read. These lenses are filters or ideologies, or, to use the terminology of social psychology, schemas, through which we view the Bible and therefore Christianity. For countless hundreds of millions of people, both within the church and especially for those who have already left it, the traditional lens for reading scripture has become a stumbling block to faith and makes the Bible irrelevant and unbelievable. In today's world, it is just too great an ask to believe that Moses smote a rock and water gushed forth, or that bread fell from the sky every day for the children of Israel as they crossed the desert after the exodus from Egypt, or that women should keep silent in church and, if they have any questions, ask their menfolk when they get home. Many now either create new lenses to look at the Way of Jesus and the Bible or abandon Christianity altogether. Sadly, many have already made the latter choice.

The controversies over the place of the Bible revolve around three areas. What you believe about these, and how you answer the essential questions implied within each, will frame and mould your entire view of the Bible and Christianity. The three areas are the origin of the Bible, the authority of the Bible and the interpretation of the Bible. Different groupings within the church have distinctively different beliefs about these three areas. Ian Barbour offers a loose continuum of theological belief that becomes more theologically and ecclesiastically controlled as it progresses: 'naturalism (including materialism), pantheism, liberalism, neo-orthodoxy, traditionalism, conservatism, biblical literalism – fundamentalism'.[3] The first two would be considered outside the church.

On one side of the great divide are conservatives, biblical literalists and fundamentalists, with a surprising number of different denominations in bed together: certain Baptists, Pentecostals, revival centres, charismatic churches and even some Anglicans. This is not to say that all people within these groups are fundamentalist or conservative in their approach to the Bible, but most are. These people believe in the inerrant word of God, infallible and in every event 'a light unto our path'. Borg quotes a bumper sticker that I heard a 'Spirit-filled' Methodist minister include in a Bible-thumping sermon way back in the late 1970s: 'God said it, I believe it, that settles it.' This is literalist fundamentalism: if it's in the Bible, then God said it, and this is what we should believe forever and that's the end of the matter, no need for questions or discussion.

The literalist-fundamentalist answers the three great questions like this:

1. *The origin of the Bible*
   The Bible is from God. It is *God's* word. It is therefore of divine origin and not human. Some people in this group believe God virtually dictated the Bible to each author. It is therefore sacred scripture and is not like any other book;

2. *The authority of the Bible*
   The Bible is therefore accurate, without error and authoritative. It is applicable to the lives of its readers for all time and without revision. As the only authority that exists to teach humanity the way of salvation and the truths of the things of God, it is essential reading;

3. *The interpretation of the Bible*
   The Bible is therefore to be interpreted literally, meaning what it says and saying what it means, unless the passage is obviously meant to be metaphorical, such as 'the trees of the field clapped their hands'. The Bible is factually true so its descriptions of events are descriptions of events that really happened.

This group takes the Bible very seriously and often stridently criticises other groups for 'watering' it down and thereby avoiding its moral authority to state how we should live and what happens to us after we die. They see themselves as guardians of the truth and of the one true church. It's very much an 'us and them' mentality.

On the other side are moderate to liberal Christians, mostly found in such mainstream denominations as Anglicans, Lutherans, Uniting Church, Quakers and Presbyterians. The Catholics have much more in common with this grouping than they do with biblical literalists or fundamentalists. Most of them agree that vast swathes of the Bible cannot be taken as either factually or historically true or as expressing the will of God. They accept the existence of metaphor, culture and anthropogenic (manmade) laws, statutes, attitudes and customs as part of the Bible's structure.

The origins and beliefs of fundamentalism

After the invention of the printing press in the mid-1400s, the separate sacred books of scripture began to be published with a single binding and came to be known as the Bible, from the Greek *biblios* and Latin *biblia* for book. When this happened, it became easier to think of the Bible as a single volume with a single author, namely, God. Until very recently, most Christians saw the Bible through the filter of what scholars call *natural literalism*. This means that such individuals read and interpret the Bible literally, but without effort. Reading the Bible this way poses no problem at all, as it would never enter into their thinking to interpret it any other way. It is a naïve, in the true sense of the word, way to interact with the Bible. Given the state of the understanding of the world and science in the Middle Ages, we can excuse such an approach then; it is less easy to excuse in the modern world.

By contrast, there is *conscious literalism*, which does recognise that there are tremendous difficulties in reading and interpreting the Bible literally, but insists that we should do so regardless. Unlike natural literalism, conscious literalism is anything but easy and effortless. Borg puts it this way: 'It requires "faith", understood as believing things hard to believe'.[4] Among my own acquaintances, I have heard many times the remonstration that, at certain churches, you have to check your intelligence in at the door.

We tend to think that evangelical fundamentalism has been there from the beginning, but the fundamentalism we know today as a mainstream Protestant movement is probably only about 100 years old. As theologian and author Philip Kennedy suggests, its teaching 'inoculate[d] religious doubt with massive doses of certainty'.[5] And this is precisely what fundamentalism still offers today: certainty in an ever changing world, a fixed and precise moral compass that anchors us to the true faith and to what God would have us do in all matters of life. But both evangelical and modern Catholic fundamentalism are appeals to authority, not to demonstrated phenomena. They are declarations of what is, arguing from the authority of the Roman church and/or from the authority of the Bible. However, as Kennedy puts it in a rather arcane manner, 'proclamation is not apodictic elucidation'.[6] Just because you say it does not necessarily make it so.

Fundamentalism, whether Christian, Islamic or Jewish, is, in Borg's words, 'a reaction to modern culture'.[7] Modernity is the enemy, with all its enquiry, discussion, nuance, relativism and empiricism. Fundamentalism feels much more at home with what it has known from times past. It is best friends with dogma, authority, hierarchy and immutability.

As Kennedy says, fundamentalism mistakenly assumes 'that an orthodox version of Christian faith emerged among the followers of Jesus, and needs to be defended today against modern biblical critics'. He further points out that for its first 400 years, Christianity was

> a maelstrom of controversy in which rival factions vied for the appellation 'orthodox'. ... For fundamentalist Catholics and Protestants, 'orthodoxy' refers to an original unified body of doctrines, dating from the time of Jesus' apostles, and shared by most Christians everywhere. In reality, as the scripture scholar Bart Ehrman elucidates, 'orthodoxy' in the sense of a unified group advocating an apostolic doctrine accepted by the majority of Christians everywhere, did not exist in the second and third centuries. For the first three or four centuries of its existence, Christianity was a motley collection of rival groups advocating a rich mixture of diverse theologies.[8]

Marcus Borg suggests that modern fundamentalism is characterised by six ideas: it is literalistic (in its interpretations of the Bible), doctrinal (believing its teachings have the truth), moralistic (there are right and wrong behaviours), patriarchal (using male language for God, people, the church and institutions), exclusivist (their version of knowing Jesus Christ is the only way to be in relationship with God) and focused on the afterlife ((about eternity and going to heaven).

Why the shift away from fundamentalism?

This, I think, is one of the most interesting questions in modern Christian thinking today. Borg says there are four reasons why the fundamentalist way of viewing the Christian faith has become so unconvincing.

1. *Religious pluralism*
   In today's internet-connected world, we are more aware of non-Western cultures and their religious traditions in ways that could never have been dreamed of a century ago. We see these cultures portrayed on our television screens in documentaries, movies and entertainment shows. Most modern Western countries are multicultural societies and we have grown accustomed to interacting with people from other backgrounds As Borg asks, 'Does it make sense that the creator of the whole universe would be known in only one religious tradition, which (fortunately) just happens to be our own?'[9]

2. *Historical and cultural relativity*
   Similarly, we are now much more aware that our place in time, history and culture, and our socio-economic status, all affect how we understand the world. For example, when the first contraceptive pills were being prescribed to women in the 1960s, some people reacted with great shock and discomposure, and some young women on the pill were thought to be fast and forward and even morally loose. Yet today, nobody gives this ubiquitous kind of contraception a second thought. We find it difficult today to accept that one collection of truths, even the Bible, can be absolute for all time.

3. *Modernity*

As we have seen, the age of modernity began in the 18th century with the period known as the Enlightenment, when reason and scientific explanation began to be more valued than older explanations. Scientific method gradually developed into a sophisticated explanatory device, based on careful observation, measurement, replication and the notion of falsifiability. Modernity also brought its own way of conceptualising the world, the universe and man's relationship to it all – a worldview that always demonstrates what is real and knowable through science.

As a result, we have become sceptical of anything that cannot be scientifically validated. If you can't measure it, then it's not real. Because God doesn't exactly fit into a nice neat scientific box, in some philosophical circles He was killed off over a century ago. For the same reason, spirituality itself foundered on the rocks of scientific absolutism: 'you don't need faith any more, you've got science'. Modernity has also led us to blur the distinction between factuality and truth. We have become preoccupied with factuality and this has had its own influence on biblical study and on Christianity in general. It is interesting to note that the two polarities, conscious biblical literalism and scientific reductionism, have both made factuality pre-eminent. The first sought to demonstrate the factual and historical accuracy of biblical texts; the second sought to make faith work with the worldview of modernity: space, time, energy, matter.

4. *Postmodernity*

The world is now in such a rapid state of flux that we do not know what to call it. For the time being, scholars have used the term 'postmodern' – the period after modernity. Perhaps, in time, a new epithet will emerge to describe this new age, which has been so profoundly altered by the advent of the internet and the information revolution.

These four issues – religious pluralism, historical and cultural relativity, modernity and postmodernity – have proved massively influential in persuading many in the educated West that traditional religious explanations of life are inadequate. Sadly, the church has not been able to refashion its message and countless millions have walked away, no longer considering themselves people of faith in the traditional way. The old stories and the old explanations simply will not do in this new world, at least as they have usually been told. Many just do not make sense to us. So if faith is to remain alive at all, there must be new ways of doing and talking about it. It is not by accident that John Shelby Spong provocatively called his 1998 book, *Why Christianity Must Change Or Die*. He says that the new way 'reveals the willingness to explore the truth of God without seeking to protect God from the disturbance of new insights' and 'also reveals that any god who is threatened by new truth from any source is clearly dead already'.[10]

Fundamentalists would have us believe that theirs is the only way to live the Christian life. For Barbour, their voices are the loudest and most sensational in the Christian church today, especially in the Western world. Apart from occasional news stories about the pope or the clerical abuse scandal, their views are most often heard in Christian news stories. Yet not all Christians experience their faith this way. In fact, as of 2001, according to the World Christian Encyclopedia,[11] the standard source for Christian membership statistics, 33 per cent of the world's population, 2.1 billion people, was Christian, but only a third of that number could legitimately be regarded as strictly fundamentalist in their theology or their interpretation of the Bible. Expressed differently, more Christians do not live their faith the biblical fundamentalist way than do. When I finally understood this, it was a great source of liberation and comfort. I knew I was not alone.

An alternative view

With millions of others, ministers and biblical scholars included, I now see the Bible as a human construct, a set of separate writings penned over a period of about 1100 years, from approximately the 900s BCE to approximately 150 CE, and finally agreed upon and combined together by a group of *men* at the Council of Nicaea in 325 CE. It is a collection of writings, now bound in a single book, about two ancient faith communities, the Jewish community, in the Old Testament, and the early Christian faith community, in the New Testament. The Bible records the words and thoughts of these two groups as they wrestled with life in an ancient and barbaric world and their relationship to God. The Bible contains not the words *of* God, in the way a fundamentalist would use the phrase, but words *about* God.

The Bible is the response of the two communities to their religious and, yes, mystical experiences of the holy or the numinous or the sacred. I have no doubt at all that these authors felt inspired by God to write of their experiences and put their thoughts in words that their audiences would understand. They use the power of simple stories, family 'histories', songs, letters and prophecies to shed light upon the life of faith. However, with other scholars, I don't believe that God dictated the words to the writers who then wrote them down verbatim. This would reduce the authors to the level of the hypnotised secretary or the God-channelling mystic. If you read the Bible with an open and intellectually honest heart, you cannot believe that God wrote every bit of it. A close reading will not allow you to believe that the God whom Jesus talked about could be so capricious, so self-centred, so demanding of blood sacrifice, so needy, so desirous of propitiation, so full of wrath, so vengeful and even so genocidal as the God who is often portrayed in the pages of the Bible. No, there is abundant scope now for viewing these writings as possessing plenty of human tribal agendas. Can the God of the cosmos seriously be so interested in the minutiae of an ancient religious purity code that, among other things, demanded the detestation of shellfish or marine creatures with an exoskeleton? These are surely the words of ancient man.

It is important to remember, too, that God is not bound by human language. In fact, I believe we can never fully understand or come remotely close to describing the living, ineffable God. But we must use language in order to talk about God: we have nothing else. We need, however, to acknowledge its limitations – our syntax, our semantics, our word constructions, the etymology of translated words, the nuances of meaning of a single word in different locales, the change in meaning over time. With a nod and a wink, I suggest you take, for example, the word 'gay'. In times past, a man described as gay was a womaniser, relentlessly chasing after the 'fairer sex'. Today, if you describe a man as gay, well, he's not exactly a womaniser, is he? Our language is not set in stone, ossified for all time: it changes as humanity itself changes.

Nevertheless, the Bible for me retains its uniqueness. It is still like no other book, for it also records the life and teachings of Jesus of Nazareth, the greatest exemplar of goodness and the life of faith in Christianity and, I suggest, the world. Its authors were inspired by God to write, but they did so with their own limited understandings and even their own agendas, perhaps not understanding that their words would carry overlaying meanings for generations to come. It is primarily a religious book, written in the ancient world by numerous ancient authors. It is not a science text. Neither is it a sex manual for the modern day, and nor does it even address many modern concerns. In Borg's words, the Bible speaks 'about how *they* saw things, not about how *God* sees things'.[12]

How do we interpret the Bible?

Modern biblical studies are not an attempt to undermine or sabotage Christianity. Rather, they represent scholars' fearless endeavours to bring intellectual rigour and fresh insight to our understanding of God and faith, even though their discoveries may challenge or even occasionally overturn the understanding of previous generations.

Today, there are at least 16 scholarly and interrelated approaches to the interpretation of the Bible. The table below from Philip Kennedy lists them according to three groupings.[13]

Meaning is with the author	Meaning is with the text	Meaning is with the reader
Source criticism	New criticism	Reader-response criticism
Form criticism	Literary criticism	Narrative criticism *(meaning also with author)*
Redaction criticism	Textual criticism	
Historical criticism	Form criticism	Advocacy criticism
Canonical criticism	Structuralism	Deconstructive criticism *(meaning also with text)*
Rhetorical criticism	Social criticism	

Most scholars agree that a combination of these approaches offers the best way to examine the Bible and to yield interpretations of text that accord with modern knowledge. Further, taking a leaf from the approaches in the first column above, it is essential to acknowledge the complexity of interpreting ancient text. Unlike the fundamentalist view, it is no simple matter. And it is not just us who believe this. Take, for example, Simon Peter's little declaration about Paul's writings (II Peter 3:16): 'His letters contain some things that are hard to understand'. If Peter struggles to understand some of Paul's theology after such a short span of time and in such close proximity to him, then we in the 21st-century West should be under no illusions that biblical interpretation is all just plain sailing: 'God said it, I believe it, that settles it.'

There is no doubt that the Bible is the foundation document of the Christian faith but we need to read it carefully since there is much in its pages that is violent, sexist, misogynistic, patriarchal, tribal, nationalistic and homophobic, just as you would expect in texts from the ancient world. The best method for interpretation of the Bible, therefore, is a combination of the modern scholarly approaches listed in the table above. The approach I take is one that millions of others in the Emerging Church movement have taken: the critical-historical approach and its more devotional cousin, the historical-metaphorical approach.

The historical approach

The word 'historical' here refers to the meanings of the texts as authored by specific individuals in specific times for a specific audience. As Borg says, 'What *did* this text mean *in the ancient historical setting in which it was written?*'[14] It's easier to make a more reasonable interpretation of a text today if we know what it meant to the people for whom it was written. Borg puts it well:

> Historical study takes seriously the vast historical and cultural distance between us and the Biblical past.... The historical study of the Bible is one of the glories of modern scholarship. It has been immensely illuminating. Without it, much of the Bible would remain simply opaque. Setting Biblical passages in their ancient context makes them come alive. It enables us to see meanings in these ancient texts that would otherwise be hidden from our sight. It unearths meanings that otherwise would remain buried in the

past. Moreover, it allows us to hear the strangeness of these texts that come to us from worlds strange to us. Thus it helps us to avoid reading the Bible simply with our current agendas in mind and frees the Bible to speak with its own voices.[15]

The metaphorical approach

A metaphorical or non-literal reading of the Bible does not deal with the historical, factual or literal meanings of a text; rather, it goes beyond to the question, 'What does this story mean as a *story*, independent of its historical factuality?'[16] Metaphor tells us at once what something is and what it is not. It states confidently that 'the sound of the car back-firing was a gunshot to her ears'. Contrast this with the 'softer' literary device of simile, which states that something is *like* something else: 'the sound of the car back-firing was *like* a gunshot to her ears'. The metaphor states that it is a gunshot, but at the same time, we know it is not. Moreover, metaphors carry extra layers. For example, it may be a gunshot in its volume, its ferocity, its intensity or the pain it gives the observer; or in the shock and incredulity of something bad happening without warning; or in its ability to break in upon a wider world absorbed in going about its own business. Metaphor opens up for the reader new worlds of possible meaning and understanding.

The rationalisation for using the metaphorical approach in tandem with the historical approach is sound. First, the historical approach needs something more to bring it alive for the modern reader interested in things spiritual; otherwise it can get stuck in the past and even feel a bit dry. Second, there are obvious passages in the Bible that can be interpreted only as metaphor.

> Where were you when I laid the earth's foundations? Tell me if you understand. Who marked off its dimensions? Surely you know. Who stretched a measuring line across it? On what were its footings set or who laid its cornerstone while the morning stars sang together and all the angels shouted for joy? (Job 38: 4–7)

Sensational writing to be sure, but pure metaphor.

Further, where passages do not appear to be metaphorical, there is still good reason to investigate multiple layers or personal nuances. As a literary text, the Bible is a religious classic. All classics of whatever genre – for example, the plays of Shakespeare and the novels of Dickens or Austen – deserve to be read afresh in every generation and enjoyed not only for what they are as texts, but also for what they can bring to our understanding of the human condition. As a religious text, the Bible can do this while also bringing to us a world of spiritual contemplation and intimacy with God. I don't mind watching Baz Luhrmann's film version of *Romeo + Juliet* with loud, revved-up cars and grunge guitars because it reminds me of the power that exists in unquenchable, ineradicable love. I don't mind reading the Job quote above and marvelling at the awesomeness of God in the universe and how He can be interested in me in my smallness.

The historical approach keeps the metaphorical grounded. You can't just imagine any old thing that has nothing to do with the text as text itself. The two approaches complement each other and use many of the scholarly critical approaches shown in the table above. Examine the scriptures in this way with a fresh eye and a mind open to the grander themes posited in the Bible and don't be afraid of metaphor or allegory. After all, Jesus himself favoured this type of teaching. His parables and aphorisms are as much alive today as they were in his own time.

What the Bible says about sex

To begin with, it is instructive to realise that the Bible is not full of sex; nor does it concentrate on sex in any way. There are only about 50 references to sex in the entire 66 books of the Bible, and these are 'inadvertent remarks',[17] incidental to the recording of the life of the two faith communities. In fact, the Bible says more about sex by what it omits than by discussing issues specifically. It implies, rather than explicates, that the consenting adults among its dramatis personae are living a robust sexual life. As Ellens says, 'It is surprising that the wide range of normal and healthy sexual play between consenting adults, within and outside of marriage, hardly comes up for comment anywhere in the Bible.'[18]

Now, of course, those who know their Bible well will immediately think of the book of Leviticus in the Old Testament. Surely this book speaks about sex. Well yes, it does, but as part of a larger, overall ancient purity code that included food, clothing, worship, legal matters, warfare, marriage and divorce, ownership of possessions, the status of women, land and countless other minutiae of the rules that governed the lives of the ancient Israelites. There is no focus on sex and references to it are not substantial. There are only eight sexual acts that the Bible spells out as being forbidden: promiscuous sex, incest, paedophilia, necrophilia (sex with the dead), bestiality (sex with animals), adultery (sex with someone not your spouse if you are married), homosexual behaviour by heterosexual persons, and rape (forced, coerced or violent sex with someone not consenting).

Rather than harping on about sex or speaking about it in a condemnatory tone as though it is dirty, sinful or evil, the Bible just accepts that sex is widespread, common and normal. It implies, as Ellens suggests, that sex is 'a delightful and natural desire and experience. The Bible is for it … [and] enjoins us to enter into such communion with the care and tenderness that holds the personhood of "the other" as a sacred trust.'[19]

Maybe I need to qualify my remarks here: there actually is one book in the Bible that does focus on sex, and that is the Song of Songs, sometimes known as the Song of Solomon. This book is an ancient Jewish poem that celebrates the joy of sex between two apparently unmarried people, possibly even Solomon and the Queen of Sheba, as some scholars have suggested. The Song of Songs is enthusiastically erotic and the lover and his beloved are described in achingly close detail as they kiss, caress and explore each other's bodies. The book portrays an act of lovemaking, complete with metaphors for each other's genitalia, how much they love each other's bodies and what they want from each other. The description is powerful, earthy, devoid of overt spirituality and overflowing with sexual desire.

The lovers' act is portrayed as being joyous and normal and very human. And it is what it is. Although various metaphorical layers can be superimposed on it, such as a description of Christ's love for the church or of God's love for humanity, it is still worth reading it for how it portrays itself. Perhaps the Song of Songs is the Bible's answer to the 'sex is dirty, sex is sinful, sex is degraded' brigade. Rather, the 'literal celebration of rich robust sex and sensuality is not unbiblical'.[20] And by extension, neither is it ungodly, profane, inferior or second best.

The overmoralisation of sex

In fact, the Bible does not go out of its way to moralise sex per se. In its pages, sex is characterised as 'a central human reality, like eating, sleeping, hunting, gathering, building, and worshipping',[21] but all that had changed by the Middle Ages. As church teachers began to overemphasise spirituality at the expense of sensuality, sexuality was repressed and denied and it was not uncommon for it to be sublimated in a putative clerical vocation, God's 'calling' to monastic life. Unfortunately, this can still happen in the modern age.

Ellens makes the excellent point that whenever the equilibrium between sexuality and spirituality overbalances to either side, humanity has been the poorer. Today, when we almost define our lives by sexual attractiveness and desirability, we can often overlook the need for a spiritual life. In the Middle Ages, the opposite happened: sex became second best to the life of the spirit. It was considered inferior to the nobler godly way – impure, even degraded and filthy, something that had to be denied.

Two saints

The church was done an enormous disservice by two of its greatest early saints and their attitudes to sex: St Augustine and St Jerome. As a young man, St Augustine (354–430 CE) lived the life of what was then considered to be a libertine. He had a son by a concubine, with whom he had a 15-year relationship, and his so-called hedonism and scholarship outside the church drew him into heretical belief and secular studies in rhetoric. As an adult, Augustine converted to Christianity, apparently after hearing an unseen child's voice in his Milan garden telling him to 'take up and read'. Augustine opened the scriptures at random and read verses 13 and 14 of Chapter 13 of Paul's Epistle to the Romans: 'Let us walk honestly, as in the day; not in rioting and drunkenness, not in chambering and wantonness, not in strife and envying; but put on the Lord Jesus Christ, and make no provision for the flesh, to gratify its desires.'

Augustine spent the rest of his life confessing his sinfulness and dedicating his life to sexual abstinence and denial of desire. This overreaction to his former life and to the text he had read was more than likely some kind of *sublimation* of his own desire and sexuality, a defence mechanism by which anxiety is reduced through engaging in behaviours that are deemed worthy and of noble value, such as art, music, religion and study.

In his *Confessions,* Augustine writes that when he was 16 he moved to Carthage.

> There seethed all around me a cauldron of lawless loves. I loved not yet, yet I loved to love, and out of a deep-seated want, I hated myself for wanting not. I sought what I might love, in love with loving, and I hated safety... To love then, and to be beloved, was sweet to me; but more, when I obtained to enjoy the person I loved. I defiled, therefore, the spring of friendship with the filth of concupiscence, and I beclouded its brightness with the hell of lustfulness.[22]

There you have it. For Augustine, desire is filth and of hell.

Following the Way of Jesus is a wonderful and positive endeavour, but Augustine's sense of personal sinfulness and his rigorous repudiation of human sexuality turned into something else. He was a truly wondrous teacher and thinker, yet a greatly flawed man. The same heart and mind that wrote, 'Thou hast created us for Thyself, and our heart is not quiet until it rests in Thee', 'Since love grows within you, so beauty grows, for love is the beauty of the soul' and 'God loves each of us as if there were only one of us', also wrote, 'Women should not be enlightened or educated in any way. They should, in fact, be segregated as they are the cause of hideous and involuntary erections in holy men.' Eventually Augustine was ordained a priest and became a bishop and famous preacher. More than anyone else, he helped to mould the character of the early church.

St Jerome (c.347–420 CE) was also enormously significant in fashioning the early church. He translated the Bible from its Hebrew and Greek into Latin, known as the Vulgate, the church's eventual official Latin translation. He was a profound scholar, writing, apart from the translations, theology, letters, historical writings and commentaries. As a young student in Rome before his conversion, Jerome had followed his natural homosexual inclinations, living a life of pleasure and study. Same-sex sexual encounters were not uncommon in Rome, nor believed to be necessarily abnormal. However, after his conversion to Christianity, Jerome interpreted some of St Paul's texts as being anti-homosexual and forbidding the practice of homosexual sex. He became so wracked with guilt and shame that he entered into a life of fierce asceticism and total self-denial. He lived in the desert for a time with other desert hermits, but after being exposed in compromising situations a few times, he ultimately moved to Bethlehem, built a monastery and lived out the rest of his life as an ascetic priest surrounded by widows.

Jerome believed that human sexual reproduction was a consequence of the Fall in the Garden of Eden.[23] By the year 400, Christians were already supremely anxious and hung up about sex. Jerome was even hostile towards marriage itself, again relying on St Paul, who believed that celibacy was better than marriage. Jerome's thoughts filtered through the church, augmenting 'a mainstream Christianity that became infected with a pronounced streak of distrust towards bodily existence and sexuality'.[24] He could not countenance any of the apostles having sex and was confident that even the married apostles abstained from intercourse with their wives since sex would surely diminish their purity and drive towards God. Like his contemporary, Augustine, St Jerome was one of the greatest Christian scholars of antiquity, but also a flawed man. As a result of his highly defensive attitude to sexuality,[25] Jerome became one of the strongest proponents of clerical continence, that is, abstention from marriage and sexual activity for the clergy. It was Jerome's vociferous teachings, among others, that influenced the Western church later to mandate and, later again, to enforce celibacy for its priesthood, which has been an unnecessary and cruel impost on the lives of Catholic clergy for centuries.

I end with the words of Ellens speaking generally about sex and the Bible. 'Aside from those few sexual behaviors which are proscribed, that is, forbidden, there is no form of "conformity" that is idealized, or of nonconformity that is marked out as "tragic" or "sinful".[26]

The Evangelical View of Homosexuality

This is the chapter that I really did not want to write. I did not want to write it because it is here that I discuss each of the main verses in the Bible that mention homosexuality. It's not that these verses frighten me or intimidate me in any way; rather, it is because fundamentalists use these verses like sledgehammers to undermine the character, faith and personhood of gay people. To do so by adopting the voice of God is, in my mind, among the great sins of the Christian church. Lives are hurt and good people are wounded and even destroyed.

I have seen this for myself when a person of faith comes in for sexual orientation counselling. Occasionally, the attitudes of churchmen arise and the Bible is quoted. Always it's one of the sledgehammers, usually the old favourite from Leviticus that apparently describes homosexuality as an abomination. Can you imagine what it feels like to be told that your natural self is an abomination to the God whom you love and with whom you try to walk a life of spiritual reflection? Of course people are going to be ashamed, offended, horrified and confused when they hear this sort of thing.

Homosexuality in the Bible

The Bible does not offer any one particular way in which people should behave sexually or prescribe any one relationship status. But neither does it forbid any sexual activity outside the eight types of sexual acts enumerated in the last chapter, all of which do dishonour and disrespect to either the partner or the self. The same applies to homosexuality. The Bible has nothing at all to say about homosexuality as we know the phenomenon today as a lifelong orientation. Where it does mention same-sex sexual activity, it speaks of it in a very specific cultural context.

In the whole Bible there are only six references we might believe have anything to do with homosexuality that are worth looking at: three in the Old Testament and three in the New Testament.

Old Testament	*New Testament*
Genesis 19: 1–29	Romans 1: 18–32
Leviticus 18: 22–24	I Corinthians 6: 9–10
Leviticus 20: 13	I Timothy 1: 10

Ellens believes that, in the Old Testament passages, neither homosexual orientation nor homosexual behaviour is the main matter at issue and that homosexual orientation per se is not addressed in *any* of the passages, although homogenital behaviour seems certain to be.[1] I endorse this position and take it further: a thorough reading of the texts offers not even a glimpse into what we know today psychologically as sexual identity. These passages cannot and do not address human sexuality from the point of view of a modern, enlightened understanding of the complex genetic, biological, psychological and social factors involved in the constitution of either sexual orientation or gay identity formation. I am not saying that the Bible should, only that it does not, and this is a glaring chasm in the way traditional Christian teaching treats the gay issue.

Since the Middle East of the ancient world had no concept of gay sexual orientation as we understand it today, it made no distinction between orientation and behaviour. Just like the Canaanite, Babylonian, Greek and Roman cultures surrounding them, the Jewish people, both before and after the time of Jesus, did not make this differentiation. As we have seen, a gay sexual orientation goes right to the heart of a person, to the very core of who they are and how they are in the world, to their deepest sense of self. You will see as we take a look at these scriptures that when the Bible talks about homogenital contact, it is not referring to our description at all.

So how should we examine these verses? Obviously not with a literalist approach that refuses to consider what the authors were intending to say to their own audience and which cherry-picks quotes out of context, culture and history. After all, isn't that what some people did in the 18th and 19th centuries with verses that referred to slavery in the ancient world? Well, we don't use the Bible to endorse slavery today, and we won't make that mistake regarding sexuality. Rather, we will look at the ancient languages in which the texts were written and how their audience would have understood them.

One evening in Sodom

Of all the verses in the Bible that supposedly talk about homosexuality, the verses in Genesis 19: 1–11 about Sodom are those most frequently quoted. Before we go on, I invite you to open your Bible and read this passage for yourself.

On the face of it, it looks pretty damning of homosexuality, doesn't it? The traditional interpretation of this passage, which began about the 12th century, reads it this way. The men of Sodom were all wicked and the rumours of their wickedness had reached God who, as a result, was thinking of destroying them all. Their wickedness was that all the men were homosexuals and when the two strangers, the angels, visited the city, all the men tried to rush the door of Lot's home, where the visitors were staying the night, in order to have sex with them. The focus of this interpretation was on homogenital contact. Homosexuality, then, is obviously wicked. As a consequence of this interpretation, the word sodomy came into use in the English language as a description of anal intercourse, and homosexuals were called sodomites. It's pretty powerful stuff, I'm sure you will agree. The thing is, though: it's incorrect.

Let's take a closer historical-critical look at the passage. The story really begins in the previous chapter, Genesis 18: 1–33. Abraham, the great Hebrew patriarch and Lot's uncle, is sitting near the trees at Mamre at the entrance to his tent trying to keep cool in the heat of the day. Three men, one of whom is said to be the Lord, and the other two angels, come by. When Abraham sees them he hurries over, showing great deference and inviting them to spend the day under his protection. He feeds and shelters them from the desert and any ne'er-do-wells. Later, as they are about to leave, Abraham finds out the real reason for their passing by. They are on their way to the nearby city of Sodom to find out whether the rumours of its wickedness are true, and should they be so, to destroy the city completely. The two angels head off to Sodom and the Lord remains with Abraham to converse.

Abraham, knowing that his nephew Lot and Lot's wife and daughters live in Sodom, begins to bargain with the Lord, suggesting that it wouldn't be just if He were to destroy the righteous with the wicked. And so he bargains for Sodom on the basis that perhaps there are 50 righteous men there. For 50, the Lord agrees not to destroy the city. And Abraham presses on for fewer and fewer righteous men each time. And each time the Lord relents, only to have Abraham press Him further, on and on. 'What if only ten can be found there?' he asks and God answers, 'For the sake of ten, I will not destroy it.' The Lord then leaves and Genesis 19 begins, with the two angels arriving at the gateway of Sodom in the evening.

Let us make a closer inspection of what is happening here. Unfortunately for the literalists, the first thing to notice here is that the presentation of God in these two chapters does not furnish us with a characterisation of an omniscient deity. God is portrayed as not knowing whether Sodom is wicked or not. He's heard rumours (Genesis 18: 20–21) and needs to check them out. Further, the two angels don't know if Sodom is wicked either. When they arrive in the city, they are at first inclined to spend the night in the square (Genesis 19: 2), presumably in order to see what might occur and to have their hypothesis confirmed or refuted. If we are to take the Bible literally, then we are faced with a God who is not all-knowing.

The second thing to note is that we are given not one but two portrayals of what the subject here really is – the law of hospitality. In the ancient Middle East, the law of hospitality was not just a convention about being nice to others. It ensured the safety of travellers and sojourners as they went through the desert from town to town. Strangers were at the mercy of the inhabitants of the towns or cities, who would typically demonstrate their ownership of the local territory and their governance of the region. To our modern sensibilities, this could be done in a harsh, brutish and even violent manner. If the townsfolk were so inclined, one or other of them might even debase the stranger by sexually abusing him in order to reinforce their superiority. Like women of the time, he would be treated as nothing more than a piece of property.

The same thing still occurs in prisons and during war. Like all rape, it is a power act, not a sexual act. The only way that travellers could avoid such abuse or aggression or violence was if one of the town's inhabitants publicly declared that he would take the person under his protection, that is, offer him hospitality. From that moment on, the traveller could relax, revictual and prepare for the remainder of his journey without fear that he would be set upon by the locals.

Here, Abraham is the first to offer hospitality. In Genesis 18: 3–5 we read: 'He [Abraham] said, "If I have found favour in your eyes my lord, do not pass your servant by. Let a little water be brought, and then you may all wash your feet and rest under this tree. Let me get you something to eat, so you can be refreshed and then go on your way – now that you have come to your servant."' In the New International Version (NIV) Study Bible, the notes make the following points about the law of hospitality:

1. Abraham gives prompt attention to the needs of his guests;

2. He bows low to the ground;

3. He politely addresses one of his guests as 'my lord' and calls himself 'your servant', a common way of speaking when addressing a superior;

4. He acts as if it will be a favour to him if they allow him to serve them;

5. He asks that water be brought to wash their feet, an act of courtesy to refresh travellers in a hot, dusty climate;

6. He prepares a lavish meal for them;

7. He stands nearby, assuming the posture of a servant, to meet their every wish.[2]

This is a significant point. If hospitality, not homosexuality, is the point of the story of Sodom, then we are given the clearest possible descriptions of how hospitality is to be dispensed. Abraham really shows us how it is done. You can easily see how protective and even deferential it is, and the cultural importance of the gesture to both the host and the traveller.

The second portrayal of hospitality is that shown by Lot to the two angels. With Abraham's behaviour fresh in our minds, let us take a close inspection. We read again the first three verses of Chapter 19.

1. The two angels arrived at Sodom in the evening and Lot was sitting in the gateway of the city. When he saw them, he got up to meet them and bowed down with his face to the ground.

2. 'My Lords,' he said, 'please turn aside to your servant's house. You can wash your feet and spend the night and then go on your way early in the morning.' 'No,' they answered, 'we will spend the night in the square.'

3. But he insisted so strongly that they did go with him and entered his house. He prepared a meal for them, baking bread without yeast, and they ate.

Now it's pretty clear from this that Lot, like his famous uncle, knows about the law of hospitality. Furthermore, we cannot fault his attempts to offer protection to the travellers. Without doubt Lot realises that the Sodom village square crowd could get territorial and be quite brutal with travellers, which is why he insists they come to his home where they can publicly receive his protection.

Let us now move on to the darker parts of this narrative. The first thing to notice is that Lot is not the least bit surprised that some of the men want to force sex on the travellers. He shows zero shock at the mention of same-sex sexual behaviour. This component of the interaction doesn't faze him at all. In his riposte to them, he doesn't even mention it by name. What does upset him, and upsets him greatly, is the fact that he has already taken these men under his roof and understands them to be thus protected. The *only* thing he says is, 'But don't do anything to these men *for they have come under the protection of my roof.*' Notice the focus of his concern: the potential breach of their cultural law. Any assault on the men will be a gross violation of the law of hospitality and what is left of Sodom's reputation as a civilised city will be destroyed. Not good for trade, not good for Sodom all round. In fact, since we know that God has heard a rumour about Sodom's wickedness, perhaps we can take it that the reputation of the city is progressively getting worse and that it's already known far and wide as a dangerous place.

The second thing we need to examine is in verse 8, where we read Lot's unbelievable suggestion that he bring out his two daughters so the mob can appease their sexual appetites with them. What sort of a father is this? He offers his daughters to be raped instead of handing over two travellers he has just met. I have read many commentaries on this verse and most of them I find unconvincing.

Ellens has the only interpretation I have read so far that might explain Lot's apparently abhorrent behaviour. It is certainly persuasive enough to be given consideration. Even so, the misogyny of the ancient world is plain and it is not to be emulated, regardless of its place in the Bible. The treatment of women in these tribal times was horrendous and the Bible is no exception to other ancient texts in showing us just how lowly women really were. Ellens makes an argument that Lot is not being serious. He is trying to calm a bad situation by attempting a bit of levity, hoping that the mob will get the joke and perhaps laugh it off and leave Lot and his protected guests be.

Lot knows the townsfolk. He knows of the reputation of Sodom. He has probably seen violence of one sort or another visited upon other unfortunates in the past. This is why he has begged the travellers to accept his hospitality. Taken in this light, Lot's doorstep suggestion could be seen as ironic. Ellens wonders if the girls, their mother and even the angels might have been laughing inside the house when they heard Lot's suggestion, knowing full well that the last thing these men want is the girls. It is a nasty situation and Lot thinks it's worth a try. This explanation is not watertight by any means, but I do find it at least plausible and sufficient to make sense of the text, given what we know about fathers and their children. Lot's offer doesn't work. It only incites the mob to fury. They try to rape him and break down his door and, true to their threats, they show absolutely no interest in the girls.

Sex is not the point of the story: there is no judgement, positive or negative, regarding either homosexual or heterosexual behaviour. As Ellens says, 'What is at stake is the inviolable prescription for hospitality to strangers in the social code and legal code of the ancient Near East.'[3] The Sodom story is mirrored in the Gibeah story in Judges 19 where the intended victims of the twin sexual assaults are same sex and opposite sex respectively. Both violations are abhorrent to their culture because of the importance attached to a breach of the hospitality code. 'Both the stories of Sodom and Gibeah deal with sexual violations. But the fact that the sex victim is interchangeable without lessening the repulsion of the biblical authors, shows clearly that it is not homosexuality or heterosexuality that is the primary consideration here, but violence.'[4]

If the conventional interpretation of the story of Sodom is correct, then we might reasonably expect the other references to Sodom in the Bible to at least mention it. But that is precisely what we do not find. The Bible mentions Sodom 54 times, mostly just in passing, but nowhere does it place the sin of Sodom as homosexuality. Sodom is wicked, certainly, but that wickedness is never once designated as being homosexuality.

Ezekiel 16: 48–50 describes Sodom's sin as being arrogant, overfed and unconcerned and not helping the poor and needy. Isaiah 1: 10–17 lists Sodom's sins as sacrifices, burnt offerings, rams, fattened animals, libations of bull's, lamb's and goat's blood, meaningless offerings, incense, various festivals, feasts and congregations. God enjoins them, in verses 16 and 17, to 'Stop doing wrong, learn to do right. Seek justice, encourage the oppressed. Defend the cause of the fatherless, plead the case of the widow.' In Jeremiah 23: 14 Sodom is associated with strengthening the hand of evildoers so that innocent people are hurt, and also with adultery, a property violation in the ancient world and thus a crime against justice. In Zephaniah 2: 8–11, Sodom is associated with pride again.

Jesus himself makes reference to Sodom, which can be read in the Gospel of Matthew, Chapter 10: 5–16. Here is a summary of the main points. Jesus is commissioning the 12 disciples to go out and tell other Jewish people how to relate to God according to his way. He tells them not to take anything for the journey but to rely on the worthy people of each town to put them up and look after them. Does this remind you of anything? Further, he tells them to bless any household that supports and protects them as being worthy: 'Let your peace rest on it; if it is not, let your peace return to you' (13). Finally he says, 'If anyone will not welcome you or listen to your words, shake the dust off your feet when you leave that home or town. I tell you the truth, it will be more bearable for Sodom and Gomorrah on the day of judgement than for that town' (14–15).

Jesus associates Sodom not with homosexuality at all, but with treating badly the traveller who is telling townsfolk of God's kingdom being near. He understands that some will repudiate the disciples and he likens these people to the people of Sodom. In fact, in verse 16, he gives his men some practical advice: 'I am sending you out like sheep among wolves. Therefore be as shrewd as snakes and as innocent as doves.' Even by Jesus, Sodom is associated with violence and abuse perpetrated upon innocent travellers.

It is essential that we put paid to the conventional interpretation of the Sodom story once and for all. It has been used against gay people so ferociously and for so long that it must be vehemently repudiated. The Sodom narrative in Genesis is not required reading if you want to follow the Way of Jesus. Even when elucidated by modern scholarship, it is not particularly enriching or uplifting.

It is ironic that the real sin of Sodom, violence done to innocents, is exactly what gay and lesbian people suffer at the hands of 'God-fearing, good Christian' people and homophobic communities. They are still stigmatised, ostracised, disowned by their families, made the butt of jokes by media, denounced from the pulpit and even physically assaulted – and much of this is done within the ethic of Judaeo-Christian Western culture. As Daniel Helminiak, respected theologian and Catholic priest, points out,

> Such wickedness is the very sin of which the people of Sodom were guilty. Such cruelty is what the Bible truly condemns over and over again. So those who oppress homosexuals because of the supposed 'sin of Sodom' may themselves be the real 'sodomites' as the Bible understands it.[5]

It's an abominable thing

'Heath Ledger is now in Hell, and has begun serving his eternal sentence there,' the Westboro Baptist media announcement said. This 'church' was announcing its intention to picket the late actor's funeral service. Why? Because Heath Ledger, a straight man, had the temerity to *play the role* of a gay man in the movie, *Brokeback Mountain*. 'He got on that big screen with a big, fat message: God is a liar and it's OK to be gay.' The media release then went on to quote our next scripture,

Leviticus 18: 22: 'Do not lie with a man as one lies with a woman; that is detestable', except that, like all fundamentalists, they used the King James Version: 'it is an abomination'.

'God hates fags,' the announcement said. 'The wrath of God has been revealed before the eyes of this nation with the death of Heath Ledger.'[6] It also quoted the next scripture we will discuss, also found in Leviticus, two chapters on, 20: 13: 'If a man lies with a man as one lies with a woman, both of them have done what is detestable [abominable]. They must be put to death; their blood will be on their own heads.' This verse is virtually the same as the first, except that it adds the death penalty. Let's treat both of them together.

I'm not putting all fundamentalists into the Westboro Baptist basket: this group of hatemongers is unique even among gay critics. Rather, I am using their media release on the Ledger death as a means to introduce the concepts in these verses and the way that fundamentalists of all persuasions use these scriptures to attack and punish gay people.

First, let us place these verses in context. They are found in the book of Leviticus or 'relating to the Levites', which takes its name from the Greek translation of the Hebrew scriptures called the Septuagint. The Hebrew tribe of Levi was called by God to provide men for the Jewish priesthood, so the book of Leviticus concerns itself with the service of worship of God at the tabernacle. It is a book about religious rites, or 'cultic practices', as religious scholars call them, or 'liturgy' as we would call it today. This includes absolutely everything connected with the worship of Yahweh: the priests, their clothes, rites, sacrifice and food.

One strong main theme runs throughout the book of Leviticus: that God is holy and that His chosen people must be the same. The word holy means separate, set apart, distinct and different – as God is from any of the so-called gods worshipped by the surrounding empires. God's people, the children of Israel, also had to be separate and different from all the other races in the Middle East. They must not behave in the same way and they most certainly must *not* worship in the same way.

The book of Leviticus was written in the latter years of the sixth century BCE when the Israelites were the captives of the Babylonian empire and living in exile. Because the people had been away from their beloved Judah and its capital, Jerusalem, for so long, Leviticus was intended as a survival document, to remind and show the exiles that the Jewish people were chosen by God. For example, they had to keep the Sabbath as a day of mandatory rest and rite, follow the rules of kosher food preparation and consumption, and perform ritual circumcision on all males.

Central to Leviticus is the section known by scholars as the holiness code, which describes in detail the cultic rites and rituals that the Jews should continue to enact to keep themselves different from all others, especially the Babylonians among whom they lived. It is called the holiness code because it is *the* great call to the Jewish nation to be like God, that is, holy, or separate, set apart, distinct and different. The book of Leviticus also speaks of the 'promised land' of the children of Israel, which they took from the Canaanites. This is their spiritual home. If they become like those heathen nations by turning to idols, false gods or even trying to worship Yahweh in the manner of the heathen, their land will be cursed.

The authors of the book of Leviticus, known by scholars as the priestly writers, were thoroughly aware of the cultic rites and rituals practised by their Babylonian captors and the original Canaanite occupants of the promised land. The holiness code lists some of these heathen practices, such as fertility rites, which included sexual rituals believed to make the cycle of the seasons flow properly and behave according to the order of nature. Fertility rituals invoked new life and birth in the seasons, the crops, the animals and the inhabitants. These rituals, Leviticus suggests, included whole families, adults, children, uncles, aunts, everyone having sex with each other. It is in this context of religious or cultic sex that Leviticus mentions male-male sexual activity as being an abomination.

The first three verses of Leviticus 18 state the premise and reason for the holiness code: 'The Lord said to Moses, "Speak to the Israelites and say to them: 'I am the Lord your God. You must not do as they do in Egypt, where you used to live, and you must not do as they do in the land of Canaan, where I am bringing you. Do not follow their practices.'"' This is followed by a list of practices not to be copied, including male-male religious sex.

This is the point missed by biased fundamentalists: the holiness code in Leviticus does not ban male-male sex for sexual reasons. It bans male-male sex for religious reasons or, to use the modern phrase, liturgical reasons. The prohibition is made specifically to stop the people of Israel from engaging in the kind of sexual activity used by the Canaanites in their worship so that they would remain holy and set apart. Heterosexual male-male cultic sex was closely identified with Gentile, or non-Jewish, identity. Thus, to break the ritual laws of the holiness code is to become unclean, to appear like the surrounding heathen Gentiles who practise male-male sex in their religious rites.

A word study

The original Bible was not, of course, written in English, let alone the early 1600s Jacobean English of the King James Bible, but in an ancient language, Hebrew. We have seen how fundamentalists typically quote the King James Version so that they can use the extraordinarily powerful word 'abomination' when describing so-called gay sex. However, the original Hebrew word for abomination in this Leviticus text about male-male sex is the word, transliterated into our alphabet, *toevah*. This word has a strict meaning, is used very selectively in the Hebrew Bible and, according to Ellens, derives its meaning from the cultic rituals of the cultures of the Near East. It is not an everyday term, but a technical term, meaning 'to abhor' something for religious reasons, and when used in the Old Testament refers chiefly to idolatry.

As Ellens notes, verses such as Deuteronomy 7: 25 and 27: 15, 2 Kings 23: 13, Jeremiah 16: 18 and Ezekiel 14: 6 all refer to idols as being 'an abomination to the Lord your God'. Leviticus 18 (which is our focus), Deuteronomy 12: 29–31, 13: 14, 17: 4, 18: 9, 2 Kings 16: 3, 21: 2, 2 Chronicles 33: 2, Ezekiel 5: 9 and 11, and Malachi 2: 11 all refer to idolatrous behaviour as being an abomination. The word *toevah* is used in all these texts, associated with heathen religious rituals and idols. Ellens points out that not only was the explicit practice of heathen religious ritual an abomination, but so was anything remotely connected with it, such as the eating of unclean animals and other unclean food.

The assessment of Leviticus 18 for implications regarding homosexual orientation or behaviour, therefore, hinges upon the precise intent of that word for abomination, in verses 22 and 29. That is, this statement forbidding homosexuality as an abomination intends to convey the meaning that such behaviour, when practised as the Canaanites practised it, namely by *heterosexual persons in worship liturgies*, was, like idolatry, a bad mode of worship, that is, an abomination. It was bad worship liturgy. Not Yahweh's kind of worship service or communal behaviour [my italics].[7]

Ellens also reminds us, importantly, about other biblical passages that offer similar prohibitions. In Deuteronomy 23: 17-18, for example, we read: 'None of the daughters of Israel shall be a *cult prostitute*, nor shall any of the sons of Israel be a *cult prostitute*. You shall not bring the hire of a harlot or the wages of a dog into the house of the Lord your God for any votive offering, for both of these are an *abomination* to the Lord your God' (New American Standard Version – my italics). In I Kings: 14: 24, we read of King Asa's liturgical reforms: 'There were also *male cult prostitutes* in the land. They did according to all the *abominations* of the nations which the Lord dispossessed before the sons of Israel' (New American Standard Version – my italics). Chapter 15: 12 repeats this, again using similar language. Male-male sexual activity in religious worship is an abomination because it is associated with the Gentile nations. The focus and clear emphasis throughout the holiness code in Leviticus is not moral, not sexual, but religious or liturgical. Break these laws and you are breaking liturgical laws. As we shall see, this idea is echoed in the New Testament in Romans and Corinthians.

Helminiak notes that *toevah* can also be translated as 'uncleanness' or 'impurity' or 'dirtiness'. He suggests that the English word 'taboo', that which is culturally or ritually forbidden, would also be a legitimate translation. The Hebrews had another word, *zimah*, for something that is considered wrong in itself, an injustice or a sin. Biblical authors used this word when describing acts that are intrinsically wrong. It is telling that the priestly writers of the Leviticus holiness code do not use *zimah* to describe male-male sex in verse 22, suggesting that such sex is not sinful in and of itself. Instead they use *toevah*, indicating that such ritual sex is liturgically impure. There is a world of difference here. *Zimah* means that certain behaviours are of their very nature, sinful; *toevah* holds that some behaviours, if employed in the worship of Yahweh, are considered taboo.

In the centuries before Christ, sometime between 300 and 150 BCE, the Hebrew Bible was translated into Greek for the Jewish people living outside Palestine who could no longer speak and read Hebrew. This translation was the Septuagint. It is very instructive to note what the Greek translators did with the word *toevah*. In Leviticus 18: 22, they correctly translated this word into the Greek word *bdelygma*, which meant a ritual offence. The Septuagint recognises the difference between male-male sexual activity and male-male ritual sexual activity. And, just like the original Hebrew authors, the translators could have chosen a number of different well-known Greek words that had specific meanings for acts that are intrinsically wrong.

To end this section, I want to share with you one or two ideas that I have found helpful in trying to understand the great gulf that exists between our modern understanding of these things and that of the ancient world. The first is this idea of uncleanness or dirtiness. The Jews of that period, including in the time of Jesus, had strong rules and regulations about what constituted a state of uncleanness – being liturgically or religiously impure. All manner of things and events could make one unclean. But most people today would struggle to understand this concept. Those of us who are not Jewish or Moslem can eat what we like when we like and, within the law, do what we like, without any negative religious consequences. Yet we do understand this idea of dirtiness in other ways.

Helminiak gives the example of a child picking his nose and eating the dried snot. We think of this as being dirty and disgusting, but we don't view it as being morally wrong. We take mucus down the back of our throats every day of our lives, where it transits to the stomach and is ultimately eliminated via the alimentary canal – all quite normal and healthy. However, we find the child's action dirty, even disgusting, though it is not ethically wrong. The concept of dirtiness is mostly bound up in culture, and this was true for the ancient Israelites too, except they used the word 'unclean'.

Their worldview was delineated rigorously for them by the priests and anything that did not fit was considered unclean. Certainty, order, typicality and clarity all equalled cleanness. Confusion, hybridity, atypicality and blurring all equalled uncleanness. Thus, animals with cloven hooves, mixing two kinds of seeds in a field, wearing clothes made of two kinds of fabric or even trimming a man's beard, all found in the holiness code and strictly forbidden, were considered unclean and therefore morally objectionable. They saw male-male sex in worship acts in the same way.

Many today struggle with that same sense of dirtiness regarding sex. As children, we may encounter prudish adults who are uncomfortable with sex, sexuality, the human body and human desire, and show this discomfort and embarrassment in their behaviour. They will quickly leave a room or change a television channel rather than have to face something of a sexual nature. They also tend to avoid the topic in conversation, and when they do occasionally speak about sex, it is often in hushed tones using the language of acute discomfort, harsh judgement, defensive humour or euphemism. Children can grow up feeling that sex is somehow dirty and sleazy and not to be talked about or even acknowledged in polite company. Uncomfortable feelings can become elaborated into moral wrong.

Ritual uncleanness is particularly hard for us to grasp, yet when I was a very young Catholic boy in the 1960s, the church had a teaching that might help us to understand something of the concept.[8] Catholics were supposed to refrain from eating meat on Fridays. Some Catholic families would extend this no-meat business to every Friday of the year, while others would participate only during Lent. We were all supposed to eat fish instead of meat, on pain of mortal sin. (If you died in a state of mortal sin, you could be punished in hell.) It is interesting to note the similarity between this 20th-century Catholic teaching and the holiness code of Leviticus 18. It's very simple: it's not that eating meat was a serious sin in itself – we happily ate it on every other day of the week – but that eating meat on Fridays was a breach of Catholic teaching.

Before we leave the Old Testament and move to the New, we should take a brief look at Leviticus 20: 13, which adds the death penalty to the injunction against male-male ritual sex. In ancient Israel, death was prescribed for acts that would defile the people and so, possibly, the promised land, which would result in its destruction by the removal of God's blessing and favour. Leviticus lists a number of different crimes that would result in the death penalty in ancient Israelite society. Some were sexual behaviours – such as adultery, incest, ritual male-male sex and bestiality – while others, such as cursing one's parents, had nothing to do with sex. Each of these incurred the death penalty for different reasons, but all followed the same basic precept of Leviticus: 'Don't act like the heathen nations, which will defile you. Be different if you want to call yourselves the children of God.' However, as Helminiak says, just knowing that something was a capital offence does not tell us very much: 'Cursing one's parents and committing adultery meant very different things in ancient Israel than they do in our culture'.[9] Thus, engaging in male-male sex was seen as making things unclean and possibly defiling the land itself.

> Losing the land because of uncleanness among the people was too much to risk. The penalty for such risky behaviour had to be severe. Like a broken seal on a sterile medicine, one unclean act could defile the whole people. The flaw must be corrected. The betrayer must be eliminated. The land must be preserved. Hence, the death penalty. But such thinking has nothing to do with male-male sex today. [10]

The New Testament

This is the section where things really begin to heat up. Some fundamentalists or literalists defend their position against the kind of scholarship we have looked at by saying, 'Well, that's just the Old Testament – Christians live by the New Testament, which is what really counts.' This means that we must examine the principal scriptures from the New Testament that purport to refer to homosexuality.

Once again, nowhere in the New Testament does the Bible discuss or even refer to sexual identity. When we are looking at these passages, it is important to remember that we are looking only at what the New Testament says about certain types of homogenital acts. It is also essential to remember that these words were not written in English but in ancient Greek, so we need to understand what they meant in their own time and how they were understood by their audience. Merely relying on English versions allows too much important information to be 'lost in translation'. The Bible does not even have a word for the modern term 'homosexuality'. Wherever you find this word in English translations, you can be sure that it is a mistranslation, imposed upon the ancient word by prejudiced or naive translators, and that the Bible is actually referring to something else altogether, usually homogenital acts within specific and well-defined boundaries.

Romans 1

Peccatus contra naturam – the sin against nature. The passage from Romans that we will be addressing here is used by the literalists as the basis of their accusation that same sex attraction is unnatural. Of this I will have much to say. Some literalists also like to use this passage to suggest that HIV-Aids is God's punishment on gay and lesbian people for committing this sin against nature.

This letter was written by St Paul probably around 57 CE. He wanted to prepare the way for his coming visit to the Roman church so wrote to explain the basic message of salvation. He also wanted to explain the relationship between Jews and Gentiles in the overall plan of human redemption. As part of this, he needed to spell out to the Jewish Christians in Rome, a sizeable minority, that the Jewish purity code as seen in their dietary laws and observance of sacred days was not to be imposed on the new Gentile Christians. Paul wanted to show that Christ had set everyone free from these religious duties and that there was now a new order, the old one was gone.

Let us, then, take a close look at Romans 1: 18–32. Once again, I will quote it for you in full from the NIV.

18 The wrath of God is being revealed from heaven against all the godlessness and wickedness of men who suppress the truth by their wickedness, 19 since what may be known about God is plain to them, because God has made it plain to them. 20 For since the creation of the world God's invisible qualities – his eternal power and divine nature – have been clearly seen, being understood from what has been made, so that men are without excuse.

21 For although they knew God, they neither glorified him as God nor gave thanks to him, but their thinking became futile and their foolish hearts were darkened. 22 Although they claimed to be wise, they became fools 23 and exchanged the glory of the immortal God for images made to look like mortal man and birds and animals and reptiles.

24 Therefore God gave them over in the sinful desires of their hearts to sexual impurity for the degrading of their bodies with one another. 25 They exchanged the truth of God for a lie, and worshipped and served created things rather than the Creator – who is forever praised. Amen.

26 Because of this, God gave them over to shameful lusts. Even their women exchanged natural relations for unnatural ones. 27 In the same way the men also abandoned natural relations with women and were inflamed with lust for one another. Men committed indecent acts with other men, and received in themselves the due penalty for their perversion.

28 Furthermore, since they did not think it worthwhile to retain the knowledge of God, he gave them over to a depraved mind, to do what ought not to be done. 29 They have become filled with every kind of wickedness, evil, greed and depravity. They are full of envy, murder, strife, deceit and malice. They are gossips, 30 slanderers, God-haters, insolent, arrogant and boastful; they invent ways of doing evil; they disobey their parents; 31 they are senseless, faithless, heartless, ruthless. 32 Although they know God's righteous decree that those who do such things deserve death, they not only continue to do these very things but also approve of those who practise them.

From the very outset of reading this passage I am sure that, like me, you will have heard Leviticus bells ringing very loudly. The holiness code here is inescapable. These verses are suffused with ideas of religious impurity or uncleanness through the worship of idols and the abandonment of the worship of the true God by worshipping images of men and animals (23 and 25). The homogenital acts described are directly associated with idolatry: see verse 26, 'because of this' referring back to the idolatrous practices in verse 25. Once again, homosexual behaviour is directly linked to heathen worship practices and described negatively on that count.

The primary problem, as Paul sees it, is godlessness and wickedness (verse 18), as a result of denial of God's revelation of himself in nature (19–20), human arrogance (21–22) and heathen forms of worship (23). Because homogenital acts are part of pagan worship rites, Paul denounces such behaviour as unJewish and a departure from the Jewish call to be holy, separate and distinct. So, Paul says, it is unacceptable for heterosexual males, those who 'abandon natural relations with women', to engage in homogenital contact in their worship. He is not talking about gay people.

Some word studies

I want to take this further, because the Romans passage is the big gun in the anti-gay arsenal used by fundamentalists. I rely heavily here on the work of Helminiak, who himself stands on the shoulders of such giants as John Boswell and L. William Countryman. In our passage, in the New Revised Standard Version, there are three words used to describe homogenital acts, found in verses 26 and 27: unnatural, degrading and shameless (indecent).

Let's look at the first of these, unnatural. Paul says that 'the men also abandoned natural relations with women and were inflamed with lust for one another'. He also says that 'women exchanged natural relations for unnatural ones'. The Greek word used here, and translated as unnatural, is *para physin*. It is not used in the sense that we would talk of the beauty of nature. No, Paul uses *para physin* to denote a thing's character or kind, as in 'He is *by nature* quite extroverted'.

Helminiak quotes a few other verses by Paul to demonstrate this usage. In Galatians 2: 15, Paul speaks of 'those who are Jews by nature' and in Romans 2: 27, he speaks of Gentiles via the mechanism of metaphor as 'uncircumcision by nature'. In both places the Greek word *physeos,* or its derivations, is used. In Romans 2: 14, Paul writes of the Gentiles 'who do instinctively *(physei)* what the law requires' and in I Corinthians 11: 14, he says, 'does not nature *(physis)* itself teach you that if a man wears long hair, it is degrading to him?' As Helminiak says,

> For Paul, something is *natural* when it responds according to its own kind, when it is as it is expected to be... *natural* refers to what is characteristic, consistent, ordinary, standard, expected and regular. When people acted as was expected and showed a certain consistency, they were acting naturally. When people did something surprising, something unusual, something beyond the routine, something out of character, they were acting unnaturally.[11]

Then what about the word *para* in *para physin*? This word is usually translated as 'beside', 'more than', 'over and above', or 'beyond', all still used in the English language today, as in paramilitary, paralegal or paraprofessional. It can sometimes also be translated 'contrary to'. So when Paul describes the sexual practices of certain women who 'exchange natural relations for unnatural and are consumed with passion for one another', he is making not an ethical but a social comment. This behaviour is contrary to what is usual, different from what is normally expected. In fact, the simple word 'unexpectedly' is not a bad translation. There is no suggestion that what these women are doing is something wrong, against God, or sinful.

A further and very powerful refutation of the 'God says that gay is unnatural' theme is the fact that Paul uses the very same word, *para physin,* to speak about God's own behaviour no less. In Romans 11: 24, he is using the metaphor of grafting to describe how God is joining the Gentiles' wild olive tree onto the Jewish cultivated root olive tree. The usual way of doing this would be to graft a branch of the root tree onto the wild tree so that the latter would benefit from the former's vitality, but Paul says that God does it the other way round – He acts contrary to nature, *para physin.* Paul is not, of course, suggesting that God is acting unnaturally or immorally.

Further to this, even though, as Bernadette Brooten has discovered,[12] *para physin* had a technical meaning in Stoic philosophy, she reminds us that Paul was not a philosopher, Stoic or any other kind, but a Jewish convert to Christianity who would have used the phrase in its everyday way to mean what was culturally prevalent and socially acceptable. In this use of the term, nature and custom were virtually interchangeable, as they are for us today. When we act according to the behaviours and values of our own culture, we feel we are acting naturally and that everyone who doesn't do this is a bit peculiar. In Paul's Roman world, it was natural or customary to think of men in the sexual act as penetrators and women as being penetrated. This was 'natural' or customary thinking.

For the Jews of the ancient world, such thinking had everything to do with their purity code. Same-sex activity between women, where no penetration occurs, was hardly even worth thinking about or mentioning, which is why it is not even listed in the Leviticus holiness code. However, where men rejected or ignored this, they were deemed to be ritually unclean. For the Romans, by contrast, this was all about social status. Adult male citizens could have penetrative sex with any non-citizen they chose, male or female, free or slave, provided that they did not allow themselves to be penetrated, and that no sex occurred with another fellow adult citizen of Rome. If this were to occur, it would be deemed unnatural – in other words, contrary to the Roman way. As a Roman citizen himself, Paul was acutely aware of all these considerations. When, in Romans 1, he spoke of acts that were *para physin*, he realised that there was a diversity of sexual behaviours and that some of them were atypical. There is no ethical or moral judgement implied.

The next word on our list is degrading, which is found in verse 26. The NIV translates it as 'shameful'. The Greek word used here is *atimia*, which means 'something not highly valued', 'not much respected', even 'ill reputed' or 'socially unacceptable'.

Paul uses *atimia* in two other passages when he speaks about himself. He says in 2 Corinthians 6: 8 and 11: 21 that he is sometimes deemed to be held in disrepute or shame (*atimia*) because of his commitment to Christ. Thus, being in *atimia* is not necessarily a dreadful thing. Earlier we saw in 1 Corinthians 11: 14 that it is 'degrading (*atimia*) for a man to wear long hair'. This means that it is not highly valued, regarded as disreputable, just as long hair in the 1960s was seen by the older generation. In another passage, Romans 9: 21, Paul speaks of 'clay pots fashioned for dishonour (*atimia*)', which is a polite way of referring to chamber pots. In all of these examples, no sense of moral rightness or wrongness is implied.

The final word in our list, shameless, is the translation of the Greek word *aschemosyne* found in verse 27. The NIV translates it as 'indecent'. The word's literal meaning is, 'not according to form'. Paul uses it in the sense of 'not very nice', 'unseemly', 'uncomely', or 'inappropriate' – much as he uses *atimia* in the preceding section. Now Paul does occasionally come across as a bit of a prude and in 1 Corinthians 12: 23, where he is referring to the genitals, he describes them as 'unseemly' or 'unpresentable' (*aschemosyne*). This doesn't really work for us in the modern world. We like to think of ourselves as being much more comfortable in talking about such matters, although, as we have seen, many still find the topic of sex difficult. When I lecture to my medical students on the topic of human sexuality I emphasise how important it is to speak unashamedly and without embarrassment about genitalia and sexual acts in order to help patients feel more comfortable in addressing the topic with their doctors. A Pauline approach to genitals is the last thing a patient needs.

In I Corinthians 13, the great love chapter, Paul describes love as not being 'rude' (*aschemosyne*). The King James Version says love 'doth not behave itself unseemly'. In Chapter 7 of the same letter, Paul uses the word *aschemosyne*, translated in the New Revised Standard Version as 'improperly' to describe the man who is betrothed to a virgin and who is wondering whether or not to marry her. The man wants to know if he is behaving according to social etiquette.

It seems, then, that there is a direct parallel in the Romans passage to the Leviticus holiness code of the Old Testament. Just like the authors of Leviticus, Paul uses different words to distinguish between religious wrong (ritual uncleanness) and ethical wrong, or sin. Verse 18 contains two words that generally denote ethical wrong, *asebeia* and *adikia*. Paul uses them to speak of 'ungodliness' and 'wickedness' of people who suppress the truth. *Adikia* is also found in verse 29 among a long list of truly immoral behaviours that makes no mention of anything sexual. Paul uses neither of these words to describe homogenital acts, which he regards as socially disreputable but not intrinsically wrong.

Paul was trying to make a point to these Roman Christians, a point about purity. He no doubt knew of Jesus' own teaching about purity and uncleanness, that both were to be judged by the heart, as it says in Matthew 15: 11 and 17–20, not by the fulfilment of some religious behaviour. Paul was trying to teach that transgressions of social expectations and Jewish purity rules were not the same thing as sin. They were qualitatively different.

There is a strong argument in biblical studies circles that this section of Romans is actually divided into two segments. First, in verses 26 and 27, Paul lists the socially disreputable behaviour of homogenital acts, and then, signalled by the word 'furthermore' in verse 28, he lists the real wrongs, the sins, in verses 29 and following, where there is no mention of any kind of same-sex sexual activity. Paul is distinguishing between socially disreputable acts and ethically immoral wrongs.

Even so, I concede that Paul, based on the Romans passage, does not appear to be approving much less enamoured of homogenital behaviour. But he does not condemn such behaviour as sinful, only as socially disreputable. I can live with that. It was a different time and Paul did not understand about sexual orientation. I often wonder whether, if Paul, an erudite man, had lived in our own time, he would have grasped the modern understanding of sexual orientation. I suspect that he would have. Paul was no fool.

It is enough for me that in Galatians 3: 26–28, in my opinion the greatest Pauline statement in scripture, he states unequivocally that, in Christ, traditional barriers and boundaries are no longer tenable and do nt exist. 'You are *all* sons of God though faith in Christ Jesus, for *all of you* who were baptised into Christ have clothed yourselves with Christ. There is neither Jew nor Greek, slave nor free, male nor female, for you are *all one* in Christ Jesus [my italics].' I think, and you can believe this or reject it as you see fit, that if Paul had lived today, he would probably have added one extra phrase to the list that was entirely consistent with the rest of his theology: 'There is neither Jew nor Greek, slave nor free, male nor female, straight nor gay, for you are all one in Christ Jesus.'[13]

Finally, to suggest that HIV-Aids is God punishing gay people is to turn God into something monstrous. According to this appalling thinking, God, who hates everything about gay and lesbian orientation, smites all the world's gay and lesbian individuals, but only those from the 1980s on, with an incurable disease that just happens to wipe out millions of straight people as well: babies, children, women, men, drug addicts, the hungry and the ill of those years who needed blood transfusions. This God of the fundamentalists is pretty indiscriminate, and all the doctors, nurses and researchers working in this field are actively working against Him.

The peddlers of such warped and judgemental thinking take for their proof the last phrase of verse 27: 'men committed indecent acts with other men, *and received in themselves the due penalty for their perversion*'. Let's take a brief look at the Greek of this small passage. 'In themselves', or 'in their own persons' as some other translations have it, is better translated as '*among* themselves'. This suggests that it is not individuals to whom Paul is referring, but the whole group, that is, the Gentiles and their ways. The Greek word for 'penalty' is better translated as 'recompense,' as does the King James Version, the American King James Version, the American Standard Version and the old Douay-Rheims Version, among quite a few others. It just means a 'payment', 'something due': it is neither positive nor negative.

Helminiak argues strongly that the 'error' of verse 27 – rather than perversion, as the King James Bible has it – is not homosexuality, but in fact idolatry, that is, Gentile customs, liturgical or otherwise. Paul is using the Jews' own prejudice here to make them receptive to his argument that there is ritual uncleanness and there is real wrong. He is using their kind of talk. When the passage is read this way, you can see that the idolatry comes first and only then the homogenital acts, which we have already discussed. To be sure, Paul sees such behaviour as an error, but he does so because he believes all such behaviour makes Gentiles socially disreputable and even unclean in Jewish eyes.

One final comment needs to be made before we look at the last two scriptures. Those, such as myself, who have a gay sexual orientation constituting their sexual identity, are not acting unnaturally or being unnatural in any way. For us, to be gay is natural. We are by nature, gay. In fact, the only way for any gay individual to act unnaturally would be to attempt to live a straight life (the life-lie) and to bond with the opposite sex (unfair to the partner and damaging to both). You don't have to drum up same-sex attraction when you're gay. It is just part of you. When I hug my partner lovingly after a long day's work and we're glad to see each other, I do so, naturally. It is not an act and it is not unnatural. In this respect, I am no different from my straight brothers who hug their wives lovingly at the end of the day. After all these centuries, the gay sexual identity is still here; it has not gone away or been bred out of existence. It is a constant. It is a part of the human condition. It is not unnatural.

I Corinthians and I Timothy

Let us now turn to the final two scriptures that say something about same-sex sexual activity: I Corinthians 6: 9–10 and I Timothy 1: 10. These two verses employ two Greek words that have been extremely resistant to translation and definition: *malakoi* and *arsenokoitai*. I will treat the verses together as they both use the second of these crucial words. However, scholars have still not been able to clearly define the meaning of these two texts owing to the obscurity of these two Greek words, so the ambiguity remains.

Here are the verses in full from the NIV Study Bible:

9 Do you not know that the wicked will not inherit the kingdom of God? Do not be deceived: Neither the sexually immoral nor

idolaters nor adulterers nor male prostitutes (*malakoi*) nor homo-sexual offenders (*arsenokoitai*) 10 nor thieves nor the greedy nor drunkards nor slanderers nor swindlers will inherit the kingdom of God. (I Corinthians 6: 9–10)

9 We also know that law is made not for the righteous but for the law-breakers and rebels, the ungodly and sinful, the unholy and irreligious: for those who kill their fathers or mothers, for murderers, for 10 adulterers and perverts (*arsenokoitai*), for slave traders and liars and perjurers – and whatever else is contrary to sound doctrine... (I Timothy 1: 9–10)

Allow me to give you just a glimpse of the difficulties that translators through the ages have had with these two words.[14]

Bible Translation	*malakoi* in I Cor 6: 9	*arsenokoitai* in I Cor 6: 9	*arsenokoitai* in I Tim 1: 10
New International Version	male prostitutes	homosexual offenders	perverts
New American Standard	effeminate	homosexuals	homosexuals
King James Version	effeminate	abusers of themselves with mankind	them that defile themselves with mankind
Basic English Bible	is less than a man	makes a wrong use of men	those with unnatural desires
Darby Bible	those who make women of themselves	who abuse themselves with men	sodomites
Jerusalem Bible	catamites	sodomites	for those who are immoral... with boys or with men
New Jerusalem Bible	self-indulgent	sodomites	homosexuals
Contemporary English Version	pervert	behaves like a homosexual	who live as homosexuals

Note that Bible translators are not immune from throwing in a bit of 'interpretive' translation from time to time according to their own beliefs and cultural attitudes. For example, until the 20th century in Roman Catholicism, the word *malakoi* was believed to mean 'masturbators', a translation now rejected by most editors. Another example is the translation of the word *arsenokoitai* in the Catholic Church's New American Bible as 'practising homosexuals', which is consistent with Catholic teaching that it's not sinful to be sexually oriented as gay or lesbian just as long as you don't do anything about it. Of course the Greek has no such nuance. If you glance back at the table above, you'll see the Contemporary English Version making exactly the same mistake with *arsenokoitai* being translated as he who '*behaves* like a homosexual' and 'who *live* as homosexuals' (my italics). The modern word homosexuals, practising or otherwise, includes women, and this word *arsenokoitai* refers specifically to men, so it's all very sloppy scholarship. In the later editions of the New American Bible, the editors agreed to change 'practising homosexuals', which was positive, but unfortunately, they changed it to 'sodomite'. As we have seen, a Sodomite in the Bible is in fact simply an inhabitant of Sodom, just as a New Yorker is a person of the city of New York.

Without any definitive conclusion about the meaning of these two words, the following argument is the most credible, given Paul's much more extensive treatment of homogenital activity in the book of Romans. If Romans, the major exposition of this topic, does not give a blanket condemnation, then we cannot conclude too much to the contrary based on two very obscure Greek words merely used in a stock list of vices.

The singular form of *malakoi* is *malakos* and it is used quite commonly. It literally means 'soft'. It is used in Matthew 11: 8 in adjectival form where Jesus is talking about John the Baptist: 'But what did you go out to see? A man dressed in *soft* clothing? Those who wear *soft* clothing are in kings' palaces!' Helminiak says that, in the ancient world, *malakos* was also used critically for the not obviously virile and masculine man who might be thought to be a bit soft. In this sense it could be accepted as meaning effeminate or effete. However, such usage implies no association with homogenital activity. Effeminacy in the ancient world, as during the Enlightenment, was not so much associated with male-male sex as with men who preened, primped, plucked, polished and pampered themselves with a view to improving their looks and visual presentation. And nothing much has changed today. Many young straight men today who take pride in their appearance and clothing are thought of as a bit soft – often described by the slightly pejorative term, metrosexual.

Applied to sexual ethics, *malakoi* could mean 'loose', 'wanton', 'unrestrained' or 'undisciplined'. This is probably the nearest in meaning that we can get to this ancient word and the closest translation is that in the New Jerusalem Bible: 'self-indulgent'. In some texts, *malakos* could just as legitimately be translated as 'weak' or 'undisciplined'. Thus, *malakoi* was generally seen as being associated with moral excess. The early church fathers thought that such self-indulgence was commonly characterised by masturbation, which accounts for that translation. So the best conclusion we can make is that *malakoi* has been used in I Corinthians 6 to denote moral looseness and undisciplined, excessive behaviour or self-indulgence.

Our second word, *arsenokoitai*, is much harder to pin down. It occurs only twice in the Bible, in the two passages we are presently examining. It appears just a few times in non-biblical literature of the time, and then mostly as an element in vice lists, which are very limited in what they can tell us. Also, *arsenokoitai* is not a single but a compound word: two words joined together to make a new word. The two single word parts are easy enough to translate. *Arseno* refers to men or male, that is, adult human males, and *koitai* comes from the word meaning bedroom or bed and refers to someone who lies with – in other words, has sex with. Even more precisely, it refers to someone who penetrates sexually. So if we just take the two words, put them together and say that the compound word means a 'manlier' or 'man-sleeper' or 'man-penetrator', might we not be onto a sure thing?

I don't think so. We don't actually know exactly what the compound word means when its two parts are joined. Does it refer to the gender of the agent, that is, a male lying in bed, or does it refer to the sexual act? If it's the latter, does it refer to a man who has sex with others, or to a man who has sex with other men? Helminiak compares this semantic phenomenon with the compound word 'lady-killer'. 'In English, the word "lady-killer" means neither a lady who kills nor a person who kills ladies but a man who knows how to charm women.'[15] The original meaning of the two single words offers no clues as to the ultimate meaning of the compound word.

Boswell believes that *arsenokoitai* refers to male prostitutes, gigolos to either men or women. Countryman refines this one step further.

He believes that the male prostitutes to whom the word refers were those who cultivated amorous relationships with older wealthy people to increase their chances of gaining an inheritance after the 'loved one's' demise. In other words, *arsenokoitai* is somehow associated with 'sexual foul play around money'.[16]

Although we are unsure of the exact meaning of *arsenokoitai*, it has to be conceded that it could refer to some kind of male, although not female, homogenital activity. One clue here is to notice that the word may be a translation of a Hebrew phrase. You will remember the Septuagint, the Greek translation of the Hebrew scriptures. Here is the closest English translation of the clumsy Jewish usage of Leviticus 18: 22: 'the man who lies with a man the lyings of a woman'. The translators of the Septuagint rendered this passage into ancient Greek thus: *hos an koimethe meta arsenos koiten gunaikos.* Hebrew-speaking rabbis are believed to have abbreviated this phrase when referring to male sexual activity, using the terms *mishkav zakur* (lying of a male) or *mishkav bzakur* (lying with a male). Transliterated into Greek by the translators of the Septuagint, the result could validly be *arseno-koitai* – 'man-liers' or 'those who lie with a male'. If this argument is correct, then it seems that both the Corinthians passage and the Timothy passage are referring back to the Hebrew Bible holiness code and the prohibition of male cultic homogenitality.

We are left with a quandary. Paul offers no blanket objection to male same-sex activity in the book of Romans, but could possibly object to ritual male-male sexual activity in Corinthians. For me, the Timothy passage is not as persuasive, even using *arsenokoitai* as it does, since most reputable scholars agree now that Paul was not the author of Timothy, but that it was written by some zealous disciple who 'out-bishoped the bishop' in his attitudes to same-sex sexual activity and also to women.

Nevertheless, let's take a brief and closer look at the Timothy passage as it may shed some light.[17] When reading it, one cannot help but notice that the words seem to be clustered together in some kind of order, either in twos or threes. Using the NIV translation as quoted above, let's look at these distinct clusters.

A: law-breakers   and   rebels

B: ungodly   and   sinful

C: unholy and irreligious

D: killers of fathers and killers of mothers and murderers

E: adulterers and perverts (*arsenokoitai*) and slave traders

F: liars and perjurers and whatever.

Notice how each cluster in each line makes perfect sense with the other words in that grouping. There is a clear relationship within each of the groups A, B, C, D and F. However, Group E is anomalous: there is no clear relationship between adulterers, perverts and slave traders.

To find whether there is a relationship between the words in Group E, we need, as usual, to go back to the original Greek. The three Greek words are, respectively, *pornoi*, *arsenokoitai* and *andrapodistai*. Again, there is no clear-cut agreement on exactly what these three terms mean and they have been translated in many ways.

According to an online Bible study resource,[18] *pornoi* has as its stem *pornos*, which comes from the verb form *pernemi*, meaning to sell. Three possibilities are offered: a male who prostitutes his body to another's lust for hire, a male prostitute or a male who indulges in unlawful sexual intercourse – a fornicator. The word *andrapodistai* means a slave dealer, kidnapper or man stealer. There are two possibilities: one who unjustly reduces free males to slavery, or one who steals the slaves of others and sells them.

We already know that the two words that make up the compound word *arsenokoitai* are *arseno* (male or man) and *koitai* (bed). These three words used together in Timothy may shed some light as to how to treat its use of *arsenokoitai*. In context, we now have the enslaved or sold male prostitute (*pornoi*), the male-bedder (*arsenokoitai*) and the slave trader (*andrapodistai*). Thus, *arsenokoitai* could validly be translated as 'the one who sleeps with the male prostitute', literally, the one who lies on the bed with him. The author, using Paul's name, condemns not only the prostitute, but the man who sleeps with him, as well as the slave trader who procured him.

From this we can accept that *arsenokoitai* was probably referring to exploitation, inequality and abusive sexual practices involved in the buying and selling of sex and human beings. This was certainly happening in Corinth and was widespread in the ancient world and it still unfortunately happens in our own day. This is what Greek-speaking Jews condemned in Roman society.

It seems that the word *arsenokoitai* is encapsulated within its own time and culture and deals with the abusive sexual slavery practices that were an accepted part of ancient Roman society. If the word does refer to male-male sexual activity, it is clearly not referring to what we know as sexual orientation. Even if sex between men is referred to, the authors more than likely had specific abusive sexual practices in mind, and not all male-male sex includes these abuses. Further, it completely ignores lesbian sexual activity in the ancient world.

It is very easy for fundamentalists to trot out Corinthians and Timothy and just baldly state that they refer to homosexuals, without even realising that there was no such word as homosexual when these two letters were written. In doing so, they ignore the principal treatment of the topic in the Christian Bible, that is, the book of Romans, which offers no blanket condemnation. Thus they use the Bible itself in the course of their zeal to uphold homophobic, prejudiced and unsound beliefs with which to sledgehammer gay and lesbian people.

I end this section with one final quote from Daniel Helminiak:

> What is the positive teaching of 1 Corinthians 6: 9 and 1 Timothy 1: 10 regarding male-male sex today? Biblical opposition to prostitution, incest or adultery does not forbid male-female sex acts as such. What the Bible opposes throughout is *abuse* of heterosexuality. Likewise, if *arsenokoitai* does refer to male-male sex, these texts do not forbid male homogenitality as such. In first-century Greek-speaking, Jewish Christianity, *arsenokoitai* would have referred to exploitative, lewd, and wanton sex between men. This, and not male-male sex in general, is what the term would imply. This, then, and not male-male sex in general, is what these biblical texts oppose.[19]

Cherry-picking the Bible

The fundamentalists and literalists who make thunderous proclamations about the sinfulness or filthiness of gay and lesbian people are in fact cherry-picking the Bible. In other words, they carefully choose their pet verses, be it Saturday being the Sabbath, or believers' versus infant baptism. I heard one old Methodist preacher say, many years ago, that 'a text taken out of context is a pretext', and he was right. This selection of verses about ancient attitudes to homogenital behaviour is nothing but a pretext to run an anti-gay agenda based on bias, prejudice and ignorance.

Another side to cherry-picking is the literalists' avoidance of verses that make them feel uncomfortable. For instance, they will quote chapter and verse of the Leviticus holiness code to condemn a gay person, but ignore the rest of the code where it also condemns the barbering of a man's hair and beard or the wearing of two kinds of fabric in the one garment. This is a double standard writ large. If they really believe that being gay is an abomination before God, they should also eschew shellfish, pork and bacon, keep a few slaves (after all, St Paul didn't exactly denounce slavery in the New Testament), discard all their clothing made from more than one fibre and severely punish people who work on Saturdays, perhaps even put some of them to death, especially the kids who give cheek to their parents.

Also striking is their disregard for Jesus' command not to judge others and to love one another. Gay people are pilloried by the church and made to feel ashamed because of their sexual orientation. This is not love. It is coercion and hostility, which have nothing to do with the Spirit of God. Jesus made it very clear in his teaching that an individual's heart is the key to how that person stands before God, not whether they go to church, are married, follow religious laws or even how they pray. Jesus himself spent almost all of his three-year ministry in ritual uncleanness, much to the disapprobation of the Jewish elders who were trying to pin something on him. Jesus would have none of it. He refused to buy into that kind of religious model. Church men and women who denounce gay and lesbian people for their sexuality could well take a leaf out of Jesus' book.

So you're gay and belong to a church

What if you're gay and find yourself in an evangelical church, whether it is relatively liberal or stridently fundamentalist? What do you do? You have a number of choices, as I see it.

The first is to work out whether it's time to come out to yourself if you haven't already done so. I strongly encourage you to move out of the identity confusion stage and begin the journey of self-acceptance. Coming out to yourself is a different journey for different people: yours will be *your* journey. Should you decide to do this, I suggest that you go and talk to someone professionally. There are many psychologists and counsellors out there who can guide you through this and offer help with your personal issues and you will find them to be accepting and non-judgemental.[20] I have worked with gay or confused people, both younger and older, in this way myself countless times.

Your second choice is to work out whether your church is a safe place for you to come out to friends. You will have to gauge the culture for yourself. What do they preach and teach on the topic of gay and lesbian orientation? What kind of language is used in the youth group, in the social group, the music group or any other church-based group to which you might belong? Has anyone ever come out before? How were they treated? Just as with coming out to friends in the outside world, you need to choose carefully whom you will trust with your disclosure. If you belong to a church that can support your disclosure, then speak to those in authority, but do so from a place of confidence and of what you know to be right. Take a support person with you if you want or need to.

However, some churches are not safe places. Fundamentalist and literalist churches, often Pentecostal, will probably not hesitate to condemn such a disclosure and tell you that unless you repent and renounce any claim to living a gay lifestyle, you can't stay in the church and will have to leave. Some will even eject or 'disfellowship' you, as a number of them call it. There are a few churches that may let you remain, on the condition that you publicly renounce your orientation and, if you have been living a gay lifestyle, will ask you to seek God's forgiveness openly in a service in front of everyone. Anthony Venn-Brown, a gay former Assemblies of God pastor in Australia, who was married with two daughters, was publicly humiliated by his church when, after secretly struggling with his sexuality for years, he was forced to stand in front of his congregation and family, resign his ministry, his living and career, and announce that he was an adulterer.[21] And this was all done 'in love'.

You should not allow yourself to be put in that position by anyone or any church. It is psychologically traumatising and is nothing more than public shaming dressed in the clothes of repentance and forgiveness. It is an attempt to make you accountable to the pastor and church leadership for the conduct of your private life, something that none of the straight people in the church have to do or would put up with in their own lives.

The third choice in these churches is almost like having no choice at all. It is very difficult: it is the choice to stay or leave. Unlike some Catholic, Anglican or Uniting Churches where you might be able to go under the radar, so to speak, but still be out and uncloseted, fundamentalist, 'Bible-believing' churches will probably not allow you to do this. There is no degree of homosexuality that they will countenance, so if you stay – if they let you stay – you will more than likely be constantly told by the pastor and leadership to change your life and your 'sinful ways'. If there is no letting-up and they will not give an inch in their views, then I am afraid that the only thing to do in this situation is to leave, in order to protect your mental health.

I understand that this might be the hardest decision you've ever had to make. All your friends are in the church; there is so much history there; and there is much meaning attached to the building itself – every room has special memories. Despite all of this, though, it will be very unhealthy to remain in a place that overtly and consistently refuses to accept your orientation or partner or lifestyle. Trying to stay in such a place will only bring you distress and difficulty. Elders will call meetings to discuss you. Congregation members will ring you at home trying to persuade you to repent, or to prophesy over you that God is calling you out of this lifestyle. People will drop round to tell you that God has spoken to them or given them a scripture verse or passage for you to read so that you can give up your sinful ways. There will be words of knowledge, words of wisdom, tongues and interpretation, all telling you that you must renounce your sexual self and turn to God. Others will want to pray over you for supernatural healing; still others will want to pray over you for deliverance from demonic oppression. Trust me, all of this has happened to me, and more. It is incredibly difficult. You love these people, but they do not comprehend your situation.

Leaving your church may be a terrible wrench, but it is not the worst thing that could happen. It will take time, but you *will* be able to move on. You will grieve, as we all do when we lose something precious, but you will finish grieving and move into a new phase in your life. You will find alternative communities of friends and supportive people. And you have to remember that it is not the church or your church friends that is the primary relationship in your Christian life, but your relationship with God. Ultimately, it's more important that you live an authentic life with positive people around you – a life free of homophobia, judgement, rejection and shame. These four words all deal in emotional and spiritual death. They kill the heart, poison the mind and will keep you in a desert. Your authentic life is worth fighting for: a life of honesty and self-acceptance, a life of love, a life of walking with God's Spirit as a gay person. And you will find the place and room to thrive and flourish. It may take a little time, but you will find it. Perhaps you could go to a different church, one that is accepting of gay people. There are such churches around. There is even a gay church, if you care to try it. I say more about the gay Christian life in Chapter 12, so make sure you don't miss it.

The Catholic View
of Homosexuality

There are two parts to looking at the Catholic view of homosexuality: the official Catholic teaching on the matter; and the everyday practical ramifications of this teaching. As you might imagine, my views and the views of the Catholic church[1] regarding gay and lesbian people are vastly different. If I were still an active participant in the church, I would be considered to be in error and out of step with the church's authority. You cannot be a Catholic and dissent from official church teaching *publicly* and remain in right relationship with the church – at least from their point of view.

For those who dissent, and I'm not just talking about sexual issues here, the wheels of change in the Roman church turn too slowly. The intransigence of Rome can become too much. For a 2000-year-old institution, a century is a very short time, but for the rest of us, who must navigate our lived experience in today's modern world in the span of a single lifetime, the church seems practically moribund. The most obvious example in the 20th century is the church's teaching on birth control.

The great bifurcation

On 25 July 1968, Pope Paul VI promulgated the church's official teaching on human life, sexual conduct and marriage in the encyclical titled *Humanae Vitae* (On Human Life) and subtitled 'On the Regulation of Human Birth'. In it, he made it plain that the use of contraception was against natural law and in contravention to Catholic teaching. Millions of people around the world, not only women, but men too, both clergy and lay alike, who were awaiting a more relaxed and workable ruling, were shocked at this draconian, backward-looking attitude. Women were not even mentioned in the encyclical's title.

What did such an announcement do to the life of the church? Essays and whole books have been written on this topic; suffice it to say that the people began to decide for themselves what was going to be acceptable teaching in this matter and what was not. Those who decided that enough was enough and that they would leave Mother Church often did so with a great wound in their souls. Voting with their feet, in an institution where there is no democracy, many faithful Catholics simply could not accommodate this teaching and left, never to return. Although they maintained their integrity and conscience, it still cost them their personal history and their way of interacting with God and their faith.

Those who remained could either accept the church's teaching and continue to create unreasonably large families, a huge and unconscionable burden, especially in the developing world, or simply ignore the teaching on the grounds that it was an unworkable and impractical way to live out one's faith. Millions chose the latter, and thus the church lost some of its moral authority. It began to be seen as an out-of-touch, foreign, immovable, mediaeval, monarchical edifice that people were now ready to question, ignore or defy. The days of the primacy of personal conscience had arrived and the Catholic faithful around the world began to look to their own values forged in life's experiences as a moral compass and a guide.

This ability to bifurcate – divide into two – the church's teachings has become an established and entrenched way of being Catholic in today's world. In the 21st century, Catholics the world over have changed their views of what it means to be a good Catholic. On the whole, they feel a lot freer to judge matters of life and faith for themselves, to follow the church's teaching where they think it appropriate in their lives, and to ignore it where they deem it inappropriate, unworkable or irrelevant, and yet still remain in the church and in good conscience.

To their great credit, many of the church's clergy and religious (members of religious orders – nuns, monks, priests, brothers and friars) also follow this model. Although they usually do not speak out too loudly, these men and women of God quietly but relentlessly work for change from within and have helped to bring about a shift in the way the church talks about life and faith and the way that Catholic people interact with their 'on the ground' church.[2]

On one level I am grateful to Paul VI for *Humanae Vitae*. World reaction to it was the beginning, along with Vatican II, of the setting free of the real church, the enquiring mind and the searching soul of everyday people. Pope Paul's predecessor John XXIII understood that the church had to change, to pull itself into the modern world and to reduce the vast chasm that had opened between the church and the people. To this end he convened the Second Vatican Council, which ran from 1962 to 1965, because he understood that the church had to change and pull itself into the modern world.

In my experience, where dogma is enthroned absolute, personal individual faith struggles. In every great religious tradition, there is a place for the search, the journey and the mystery of life. To its great credit the Catholic church has always valued the mystery of life in its rhetoric, but not always in its actions. Doctrine and dogma have held sway for well over a millennium.

Yet in today's world, people are suspicious of anyone telling them what to do, what to believe and how to live their lives. It is not necessarily that they don't believe the old stories, but that they want perhaps to understand and be told them in different ways. A lifelong celibate septuagenarian or octogenarian with a red or white skull-cap telling people how to live their lives, and even how to make love, because he says so, will no longer suffice.

The authority of the Catholic church

Before we investigate the official Catholic line on our subject at hand, we must first understand the three sources of the Catholic church's authority – scripture, the Tradition, and the church's teaching authority, usually called the Magisterium: what these three terms mean according to the church, and how they work out in practice.

Whenever the Catholic church speaks, it does so very carefully. Church spokesmen have to be measured, articulate and, above all, rely, not on their own opinions or intelligence but on the authority of the church as it promulgates its attitudes and teaching about matters, both sacred and secular.

Let's first look at the Catholic view of scripture. In the church, the Bible is viewed as the Word of God, divinely inspired and inerrant in matters pertaining to salvation. As Vatican II stated, 'The Books of Scripture must be acknowledged as teaching firmly, faithfully, and without error that truth which God wanted put into the Sacred Writings for the sake of our salvation.'[3] Although the Bible's *message* pertaining to salvation is regarded as inerrant, the church accepts that the *messenger* may not always be inerrant and that occasionally personal opinions or convictions may have been wrong. Happily, the Catholic church also has a more sophisticated view of the importance of human language in biblical interpretation than the evangelical fundamentalists. It accepts 'the use of common literary devices, such as poetry, figures of speech, paradox, approximation, compressed narratives, inexact quotations, folklore, legend, song'.[4]

The church regards the Bible as being a collection of books rather than just one book. In 1546 at the Council of Trent, the church definitively listed – in technical terms, made canonical – the books it regarded as being divinely inspired. The entire Hebrew scriptures were accepted into the canon *in toto*. They are quoted by Christ and New Testament writers some 350 times in the New Testament as scripture. The New Testament writings, while making no claim themselves about their status as scripture, were included by the early church fathers along with the Hebrew scriptures from the outset. Thus the canon of scripture was never set by scripture itself, but by the church's men at the Council of Trent.

Next, we look at the Tradition, the lived and living faith of the Catholic church. It is seen as something precious that has been handed on from the beginning, century after century. The Tradition is the way that the Gospel of Christ was received as a living faith by the 12 apostles, starting from Christ's teaching of them and the other disciples, then handed on by the apostles to the early church. The

Tradition includes scripture, the essential doctrines of the church, the major writings and teachings of the early church fathers, the liturgies and rites of the church and the living and lived faith of the whole church from the beginning until now. It is seen as a continuity to be valued, lived and protected. The church often quotes Paul's words in I Corinthians 15: 3 and following, to describe the 'handing on' process of the Tradition: 'I *handed on* to you first of all what I myself received...'

R.P. McBrien makes an important distinction, between Tradition and tradition:

Tradition (upper case T) is the living and lived faith of the Church; traditions (lower case t) are customary ways of doing or expressing matters related to faith. If a tradition cannot be rejected or lost without essential distortion of the Gospel, it is part of Tradition itself. If a tradition is not essential (i.e., if it does not appear, for example, in the New Testament, or it is not clearly taught as essential to Christian faith), then it is subject to change and even to elimination. It is not part of the Tradition of the Church.[5]

McBrien suggests that the process of sorting out which bits are 'Tradition' and which bits 'tradition' involves the teaching Magisterium, the scholarship of theologians and the lived experience of the Christian community itself.

Because the apostles *handed on* Christ's teaching to the first-century church, the Catholic church believes it has a divine mandate to teach and can do so without error, because of its authority, the Tradition and the scriptures. The Magisterium, the church's teaching authority, is constituted by the reigning pope and his bishops, but also includes the scholarly competence of the church's erudite theologians.

According to Catholic Tradition, the Magisterium can issue teaching through a solemn decree, either through an ecumenical council, like Vatican II, whose head is always the pope, or by the pope alone acting as head of the universal church without a council. Alternatively, ordinary universal teaching is usually promulgated though a papal encyclical (for example, Paul VI's *Humanae Vitae*), a synodal declaration or a decree of a Vatican congregation with the approval of the pope or a full ecumenical council. It was this last, a decree from a Vatican congregation with the approval of the then reigning pope, that constituted the manner by which the church first spoke authoritatively about homosexuality.

An official belief taught by the church's Magisterium, either in solemn decree or ordinary universal teaching, is known as a doctrine. According to canon law, one can dissent from a doctrine and still remain in communion with the church. A dissenter is not excommunicated or cut off from the life of the church or its sacraments, but will more than likely be prevented from holding any kind of office within the church and fulfilling any kind of teaching role. In some circumstances, if a dissenter happens to be a priest or religious, he or she might even be prevented from undertaking a pastoral role.

In the most famous case of this type, this is precisely what happened to Sister Jeannine Gramick and Father Robert Nugent, who had committed their adult lives in ministry to gay and lesbian Catholics. They had been speaking about these issues since 1971 and co-founded New Ways Ministry, dedicated to justice for gay and lesbian Catholics and all homosexuals in the Christian church. They were forced to resign from New Ways in 1984, and in 1999 the then powerful Vatican Congregation for the Doctrine of the Faith (CDF) notified them, after ten years of deliberation on their work, that they were to permanently cease and desist all pastoral work with gay and lesbian people and that they were temporarily suspended from holding office within their respective religious Congregations. Both obeyed the notification at first but openly questioned the mechanics of the judgment. In 2000, they were summoned to Rome and ordered to stop discussing the probity of the CDF's ruling and processes. Their religious Congregations were ordered by Vatican officials to expel them should they disobey. In 2001, Gramick's order commanded her not to speak about homosexuality at all. She refused as a matter of conscience and voluntarily left the order transferring her vocation into the hands of the Sisters of Loretto, who bravely supported her in her ministry.[6]

However, if a doctrine is taught with the fullest solemnity, after exhaustive scholarship by the whole Magisterium, it is called a dogma and is regarded as being without fundamental error. The rejection of a dogma places a person outside the Catholic church: such an individual is regarded as committing heresy. However, the church does not have a list of dogmas on which all bishops, theologians and pastors agree, so agreement or dissent is not always a straightforward matter. Dogmas are considered to be irreformable – they are not subject to review by some higher authority in the church, either when they are promulgated or later in history. Once said, they cannot be unsaid. The church does concede, though, that there are limitations to human language and that dogmas may not always be articulated in the best possible way. This means there is room for theologians, always under the supervision of the Magisterium, to enrich the church by suggesting new formulations for dogmas so that they better reflect a different epoch.

Some fundamental Catholic teaching

The principal location for the church's official teaching pertaining to homosexuality is found in two decrees put forth by the CDF.[7] We will examine both of these in due course. The premises on which they are based derive from earlier teaching about human love and how it is to be legitimately experienced. They come from the same encyclical we looked at before about birth control, *Humanae Vitae*.

The arguments in *Humanae Vitae* about human love are phrased almost exclusively in the context of becoming a parent. Although it grudgingly concedes that human love may be about more than parenthood, it only *just* manages to do so and makes such love totally subordinate. Section 12 states that humans are 'called to parenthood'. Note the careful choice of language in the following quotations from the encyclical.

> It is in reality the wise and provident institution of God the Creator, whose purpose was to effect in man His loving design. As a consequence, husband and wife, through that mutual gift of themselves, which is specific and exclusive to them alone, develop that union of two persons in which they perfect one another, cooperating with God in the generation and rearing of new lives.[8]

The whole document echoes these sentiments about human sexuality being intrinsically associated with procreation.

> Finally, this love is fecund. It is not confined wholly to the loving

interchange of husband and wife; it also contrives to go beyond this to bring new life into being. 'Marriage and conjugal love are by their nature ordained toward the procreation and education of children. Children are really the supreme gift of marriage and contribute in the highest degree to their parents' welfare.'[9]

In Section 12, the doctrine states that this is natural law ordained by God and written into the biology of humanity. What is natural in the world is placed there by God.

> This particular doctrine, often expounded by the Magisterium of the Church, is based on the inseparable connection, established by God, which man on his own initiative may not break, between the unitive significance and the procreative significance which are both inherent to the marriage act.
>
> The reason is that the fundamental nature of the marriage act, while uniting husband and wife in the closest intimacy, also renders them capable of generating new life – and this as a result of laws written into the actual nature of man and of woman. And if each of these essential qualities, the unitive and the procreative, is preserved, the use of marriage fully retains its sense of true mutual love and its *ordination to the supreme responsibility of parenthood to which man is called* [my italics]. We believe that our contemporaries are particularly capable of seeing that this teaching is in harmony with human reason.

Section 11 does not mince words. Sex is for procreation and every sexual act should be associated with procreation or the possibility of procreation.

> The Church, nevertheless, in urging men to the observance of the precepts of the natural law, which it interprets by its constant doctrine, teaches that *each and every* marital act must of necessity retain its intrinsic relationship to the procreation of human life [my italics].

Finally, in Section 14, the church teaches that this relationship between sex and procreation is so essential and holy that it is forbidden to impede it in any way except in 'the use of those therapeutic means necessary to cure bodily diseases', provided that such therapies are not done with the intention of stopping conception. Vasectomies and hysterectomies also appear to be against God's will.

> Therefore We base Our words on the first principles of a human and Christian doctrine of marriage when We are obliged once more to declare that the direct interruption of the generative process already begun and, above all, all direct abortion, even for therapeutic reasons, are to be absolutely excluded as lawful means of regulating the number of children. Equally to be condemned, as the Magisterium of the Church has affirmed on many occasions, is direct sterilization, whether of the man or of the woman, whether permanent or temporary. Similarly excluded is any action which either before, at the moment of, or after sexual intercourse, is specifically intended to prevent procreation – whether as an end or as a means.[10]

I believe the church gravely misinterprets human sexuality by understanding that it is only meant for generative purposes. If there is any possibility that what you're doing might stop a pregnancy from occurring, the church says that action is morally wrong and objectionable to God. Its terms 'unitive' and 'generative' denote different aspects of human love and desire. The first means the uniting of two people in their love, allowing and fostering the growth of intimacy, mutual trust and physical pleasure. The second is about becoming fathers and mothers, which the church teaches is what we are all called to. I cannot accept this. My clinical and adult experience tells me that there are many different categories of people who do not father and mother children, yet are no less fulfilled or evolved in life than any parent may be.

Becoming a parent is not the zenith of human existence. Young people in their early teens can become parents. On 9 November 2009, the ABC in Australia reported that a 12-year-old girl in New South Wales had given birth to a boy. Her father was reported to have said, 'She is only a baby herself and now she's got a baby. She has no maternal instincts at all.' Murderers, thieves and brutal thugs can also become parents. I come across people every day in my work who have been destroyed or wounded deeply by their parents. Parenting is not a God-given skill. It is something one must learn to do well.

By its sole emphasis on generative love, the church has completely missed the boat on unitive love. It just does not understand that people have sex for lots of different reasons that are just as natural as the desire to father or mother children. Allow me to quote sexuality and relationship expert of 20 years, Dr Gabrielle Morrissey, who states the obvious: 'Sex for procreation is the minority expression of our sexuality. Couples, over a lifetime, will have far more sex for recreation.' She continues, 'Sex is your adult playtime, so have fun with it! Laugh, giggle, play games, tease and please.'[11] Judging by its rhetoric, the church does not understand human desire in this way at all. As most mature, sexually active adults understand, human beings have a remarkably wide and diverse range of sexual interests, needs and behaviours. And of course we have sex for many different reasons, only one of which is procreation. To suggest otherwise would be as absurd as suggesting that our voices were only ever meant for singing.

I believe the church's attitude in these matters is medieval. The church has always shied away from human desire, historically characterising it as base, and contrasting it unfavourably with holiness or spirituality. You will recall Sts Augustine and Jerome as exemplars of this kind of notion. I actually think the church is *erophobic*, that is, it has a fear of desire. And this erophobia is found in many of its teachings about sex, love and the body. The church does not seem to understand desire at all. And how could it? Its celibate priests, most of whom have struggled with their enforced so-called chastity, have spent centuries trying to tell us that desire is wrong, or the lesser way, or that the flesh (read, the body) is evil and sinful and must be 'crucified'. Chastity is sacred and regarded as God's way; the body and desire are profane.

Rather, I believe God to be totally for desire and sex and perfectly comfortable with our needs and the way that we are designed. But, for the Catholic church, it is beyond question that sex must only be between a man and a woman, and only ever in a manner that does not exclude the possibility of procreation. Sex is designed by God for this *final* purpose, so the teaching goes. Without this finality, that is, the possibility of conception, sex is wrong according to the church.

The Catholic church's official teaching on homosexuality

On this occasion, it is not a papal encyclical that declared the church's teaching, but two declarations put out by the CDF in co-operation with the pope. As such, they are considered to be the teaching of the Magisterium.

The 1975 Seper Declaration

The first decree, which has the authority of a doctrine not a dogma, was issued in 1975 under the hand of the CDF's prefect of the time, Cardinal Franjo Seper, under the direct order of Pope Paul VI. Its title was:

SACRED CONGREGATION FOR THE DOCTRINE OF THE FAITH

PERSONA HUMANA

DECLARATION ON CERTAIN QUESTIONS CONCERNING SEXUAL ETHICS

Persona Humana (The Human Person) consists of 13 sections followed by endnotes. I will attempt to convey the gist of each of the sections in everyday language.

Section I	People have sexuality and this sexuality helps to constitute a person. Sexuality is everywhere being corrupted. Educators are getting lax in their education about sex. The people are therefore confused.
Section II	The church cannot remain indifferent to this confusion. Everywhere, bishops try hard to clarify the situation for the faithful, but confusion persists. Therefore the Magisterium considers it necessary to declare resolutely what the church teaches regarding these matters.
Section III	People are everywhere looking to their own intelligence to work out their values. God has put his law into men's hearts and by it, will all be judged. There is a natural order in the universe and personal morality is part of this natural law that God has set in place.

Section IV   Those who suggest that these laws are appropriate only for certain times in history are in error. God's natural laws are forever and unchanging. They are not just for some but are for everyone. To go against them is to go against the Gospel.

Section V   The Gospel teaching is therefore relevant to sexual ethics. Right sexual practice is found only within the confines of a marriage between man and woman when it is open to the possibility of procreation. Sexual functioning can be moral only in this context.

Section VI   This declaration is not going to go into all the abuses of human sexuality, but will instead concentrate on repeating the church's doctrine on particular points of widespread abuse and immoral behaviour.

Section VII   Premarital sex is immoral. It is against the will of God and expressly contravenes the teaching of the church.

Section VIII   Homosexual behaviour is wrong, immoral and intrinsically disordered.

Section IX   Masturbation is a grave moral disorder.

Section X   When people commit such actions, they are committing mortal sin, which separates them from God.

Section XI   Those who cannot practise moral sex must remain virginal, celibate and practise chastity at all times.

Section XII   People should deny themselves, 'take up their cross' and attend the rites and liturgies of the church to help them live a sound Christian life of chastity, regardless of whether they are married.

Section XIII   The bishops must take great pains to teach this doctrine to the faithful and to remind parents and teachers to educate their children in the ways of chastity and sexual morality.

Section VIII, about gay and lesbian people, comes between the fornicators and the masturbators, who also seem doomed to separation from God.[12] Keep in mind, as you read the following analysis, that this encyclical was promulgated in 1975, just two years after homosexuality was removed from the American Psychiatric Association's Diagnostic and Statistical Manual of Mental Disorders. The section is only 315 words long so I include it in its entirety. (For a transcript of the whole Seper Declaration, see the website provided.[13])

At the present time there are those who, basing themselves on observations in the psychological order, have begun to judge indulgently, and even to excuse completely, homosexual relations between certain people. This they do in opposition to the constant teaching of the Magisterium and to the moral sense of the Christian people.

A distinction is drawn, and it seems with some reason, between homosexuals whose tendency comes from a false education, from a lack of normal sexual development, from habit, from bad example, or from other similar causes, and is transitory or at least not incurable; and homosexuals who are definitively such because of some kind of innate instinct or a pathological constitution judged to be incurable.

In regard to this second category of subjects, some people conclude that their tendency is so natural that it justifies in their case homosexual relations within a sincere communion of life and love analogous to marriage, in so far as such homosexuals feel incapable of enduring a solitary life.

In the pastoral field, these homosexuals must certainly be treated with understanding and sustained in the hope of overcoming their personal difficulties and their inability to fit into society. Their culpability will be judged with prudence. But no pastoral method can be employed which would give moral justification to these acts on the grounds that they would be consonant with the condition of such people. For according to the objective moral order, homosexual relations are acts which lack an essential and indispensable finality. In Sacred Scripture they are condemned as a serious depravity and even presented as the sad consequence of rejecting God. This judgment of Scripture does not of course permit us to conclude that all those who suffer from this anomaly are personally responsible for it, but it does attest to the fact that homosexual acts are intrinsically disordered and can in no case be approved of.

This section begins with an attack on my profession. Psychology is both a profession of clinicians, with many sub-branches, and a rigorous science. Like John Spong, I believe there is absolutely no area of knowledge from which the church has to protect God, and this includes the understanding that psychology brings to the discipline of human sexuality and relationships. God and the church survived Copernicus and Galileo and their new ideas about cosmology; they will also survive psychology's current and future understandings of human sexuality.

As to psychology's teaching 'in opposition to the moral sense of the Christian people', I think the church might be surprised to learn that most intelligent people in the 21st century have a more sophisticated understanding of the nature of homosexuality than their predecessors. I know many straight Catholics who don't worry too much about what the church teaches about gay and lesbian people and just get on with loving and living with them in their parishes – I don't for an instant believe that they are the only ones. In fact, the Australia Institute, an independent thinktank, in 2005 documented homophobia over various economic, geographical, educational and religious strata throughout Australia and found that of those who profess a religious affiliation, Catholics are actually the least homophobic and most tolerant, with a minority 34 per cent believing that homosexuality is immoral. This leaves a massive 66 per cent or two-thirds of Catholics in Australia who either don't believe or simply ignore the church's teachings on gay issues.

In the second paragraph, the church concedes that there are two types of gay people, who are referred to in terms of what causes homosexuality. For the church, homosexuality is a result of:

1. negative and immoral reasons:
   a. false education
   b. lack of normal sexual development
   c. habit
   d. bad example
   e. similar causes

2. natural inclinations:
   a. innate instinct
   b. pathological incurable constitution.

Let's take these systematically, starting with the first group. I will take points (a) and (d) together, owing to their similarity. False education and bad example both refer to the *contagion* theory of homosexuality. This is the totally discredited belief that if a young person is in regular social contact with a gay person, then he or she is more likely to end up being gay through 'catching' the gay lifestyle, whatever that might be. Modern psychology regards this as patent nonsense. Human sexuality simply does not work this way. You are what you are. Home base will emerge. You cannot encourage a gay male to catch 'straightness' by making him 'hang out' with straight friends, any more than you can encourage a straight male to catch 'gayness' by 'hanging out' with gay friends.

Part (b), the lack of normal sexual development, is the psycho-pathology argument: if you end up being gay, then your sexual development was somehow arrested or disordered. Considering that, statistically, 5 per cent of the world's population is gay, the church is making a pretty big call here. The problem with this theory is that, if it were true, we would expect some evidence that such a major pathology would show itself in personality or relationships or in some other observable way. Not only does this not happen but there is strong, repeated evidence to the contrary. Gay and lesbian people are as 'normal' as any 'normal' straight person, and in fact there is evidence from America's leading family and relationship institute, the Gottman Foundation, to show that, in several areas of relationship dynamics, gay people do better on some measures than straight people. Gay and lesbian people do not have disordered or arrested sexual developments.

Part (c) says that homosexuality is caused by habit. I'm not exactly sure what the declaration is getting at here. Do they mean that you have to be homosexually inclined, then practise same-sex sexual activity regularly and thereby develop a habit that causes you to be gay? But this can't be, because you're already inclined towards same-sex orientation in the first place, so the so-called habit cannot cause it. Such a reading breaks the most fundamental of philosophical and scientific laws of causation: if x *causes* y then x must occur *before* y. The alternative is the opposite reading: you're not homosexually inclined in the first place, but for some reason, you start practising same-sex sexual activity, which becomes a habit, and then this causes homosexuality. The flaws in this argument are so huge that it is not worth spending any significant time refuting it. Put simply, what straight person would habitually have sex with their own gender? It just does not make any sense. Finally, (e), 'similar causes', is so obtuse that it is not even worth concerning ourselves with.

The final statement about this so-called first type of gay person is that their homosexuality is/can be 'transitory' or 'not incurable'. Once again, the CDF does not understand human sexuality. Sexual identity or orientation is not transitory: it is there for keeps. The Seper Declaration then goes on to the 'second type' of gay person, one who is so naturally inclined this way that even the church concedes that there is probably something to this, and that such people should be 'treated with understanding'. Part (a) says that their homosexuality is innate instinct. Well, on this occasion, the CDF have got it right. 'Innate' I can accept. But the declaration goes off the rails again in part (b) by describing gay people as disordered, psychopathological and incurable. Is it any wonder that gay people get rather worked up when this stuff is trotted out by devout and pious people speaking in God's name? The declaration goes on to discuss these Group 2 gay people in terms of 'their personal difficulties and their inability to fit into society'. This is incredibly patronising and smacks of the old 'ego-dystonic homosexuality disorder' that described a gay person who was uncomfortable with his or her orientation. The disorder is not in the gay individual; the disorder is in the church.

Paragraph 3 of the Seper Declaration starts as though the CDF might be conceding that 'a sincere communion of life and love analogous to marriage' is possible between gay people. But any such hope is dashed in the final clause, which says that this idea is suggested by some people only because gays 'feel incapable of enduring a solitary life'. In my experience, most human beings desire to share their lives with a compatible partner at some point. A life of isolation, while seen by the church hierarchy as necessary for its clergy,[14] is not top of most people's wish-list. So, to suggest that we poor gay people are hopelessly inadequate because we are not inclined to lead a life of isolation and celibacy is exceedingly far-fetched.

The final paragraph comes to the crux of the church's view of what being gay means. There are two arguments:

1. same-sex sexual activity lacks finality

2. the Bible condemns homosexuality.

As a result, same-sex sexual activity is said to be intrinsically disordered.

First, the notion of finality. By this, the CDF means there is no possibility of a pregnancy. The logic goes like this. God made the world with perpetuation of the species in mind, so procreation must be moral. Gay sex lacks this finality and is therefore against the natural order and therefore against God, because it was God who set up the natural order in the first place. Thus gay sex cannot be of God.

But the logic works only if you accept the first premise, that is, that every sexual act must contain at least the possibility of a pregnancy. There are many reasons why adults have sex, and procreation is only one of them. It does not stand in splendid isolation in human sexual behaviour and the other unitive acts of sex are equally important to the enrichment of relationship. There is a second argument against this. Same-sex sexual attraction is a normal part of the human condition – a normal and consistent variation in the phenomenology of human sexuality. If we accept this, and I do, then it makes perfect sense for the spiritually minded to accept that God is the author of *all* human sexuality, including gay sexuality, which is thus as much a part of the 'objective moral order' as is straight sexuality.

Let me now briefly turn to the second reason why the Seper Declaration says that homosexuality is intrinsically disordered. First, again, it refers to 'homosexual relations', thus reducing gay people to a behaviour, and not an identity. The declaration says, 'in Sacred Scripture they [homosexual relations] are condemned as a serious depravity and even presented as the sad consequence of rejecting God'. From the analysis offered in Chapter 10, we know already that the Bible does *not* condemn homosexuality outright. The CDF is mischievous here, because the Catholic Tradition, in its attitude to biblical interpretation, is not 'conscious literalist', like the funda-mentalists, so they really should and do know better. Furthermore, millions of gay people walk in the pathway of Jesus and count themselves Christian, and I am one of them, and we most assuredly do not reject God, so our sexual orientation cannot be a punishment from God for rejecting Him. It is a non-sequitur. Anyway, what kind of a God is being presented here? 'I don't think I want to believe in you God,' says the atheist. 'All right then,' says God, 'have it your own way. I'm going to make you a homosexual as a punishment for rejecting me.' It is patent nonsense.

This same paragraph ends the declaration by being rather cavalier with the truth. It says that scripture attests 'to the fact that homosexual acts are intrinsically disordered'. I must have missed something: I know of no scripture verse, Old or New Testament, that suggests, states or shows such a thing.

I believe Section VIII of the Seper Declaration to be almost entirely flawed. I say almost, because the CDF did at least acknowledge that some gay people seem to have such a strong inclination that it might be considered innate. But that is as far as it goes. There is not one statement in the declaration that can stand up to modern scholarly scrutiny. It is weak in its science, it is weak in its biblical interpretation and it is weak in its theology. It does not provide sufficient grounds to condemn gay people and should no longer be used to do so.

The Ratzinger Letter 1986

From here we move on to the second document published by the CDF on the topic of homosexuality, 11 years after the Seper Declaration. In the interim much had been written and spoken about the topic, both within the church and in society at large. This second document, titled 'Letter to the Bishops of the Catholic Church on the Pastoral Care of Homosexual Persons', was promulgated as a letter, rather than a papal encyclical or CDF declaration. It had the same signatory format as the Seper Declaration but it was signed by the CDF's new prefect, Cardinal Joseph Ratzinger. Heading up the Vatican's powerful CDF was his last job before he became Pope Benedict XVI and in those days he answered to Pope John Paul II.

Given the same signatory format and the CDF's clear teaching found throughout the document, along with the papal order to be published, this is a letter in name only. Make no mistake, it is clear doctrinal teaching from the Magisterium and is meant to be read and accepted as such. It is as much a declaration as is *Humana Persona* and is addressed to the bishops, not to the people, so there is a sense that they are being told to get into line and start denouncing homosexuality more forcefully and more openly. Keeping their heads down and staying quiet is not an option.

At 3959 words, the Ratzinger letter is far too long to reproduce in its entirety. Instead, I will quote from it liberally, but I invite you to read the whole document for yourself if you feel so inclined.[15] It has

18 sections, but I will try to limit my scrutiny to areas where it differs from, augments or elaborates on the Seper Declaration.

Section 2 says that while the church is in a position to learn from science, it can also 'transcend the horizons of science and ... be confident that her more global vision does greater justice to the rich reality of the human person in his spiritual and physical dimensions'. I dispute this statement on a number of grounds, the most important of which is the idea that the church has enriched people's lives with its moral teachings regarding human sexuality. To reduce gay people to a behaviour and regard all sexual contact as immoral without the possibility of a pregnancy, is not to enrich humankind, but to impoverish it.

In Section 3, citing the Seper Declaration, that because there is no 'indispensable finality' in gay sexual acts, homosexuality is 'intrinsically disordered', the Ratzinger letter goes on to say that, since then, an 'overly benign interpretation' has been given 'to the homosexual condition itself'. The letter will not countenance this: it states definitively that, 'although the particular inclination of the homosexual person is not a sin, it is a more or less strong tendency ordered toward an intrinsic moral evil'. No other line of church text has caused so much debate, so much hurt and so much offence to gay people, and many straight people.

So here we have it. The Catholic church says that I am an intrinsically disordered person and worse, if that is possible, that I am intrinsically inclined toward moral evil. And this because, when my partner and I make love, there is no possibility of a pregnancy. And it says this despite the clear findings of science and sociology. This does not make sense and I do not accept it. The church's God must be incredibly small if He should judge that I am morally evil in my nature and essence to the very core, which is what the word intrinsically means, just because of my orientation.

There is room in the church's thinking for the lived experience of the people. It is actually part of the Tradition and the church needs to listen to it more. The lived experience of the church's gay people makes a lie of this doctrine, which I consider to be tantamount to blasphemy: it takes that which God says is good, and remember that God calls *all* His creation good, and declares it to be black and false and evil. Which God of love are these people serving?

And as for rejecting God, this is simply not true. Millions of gay people already follow the Way of Jesus, walk with God, pray, show compassion and offer service to others as Christians, go to church, participate in the sacramental life of the church and receive comfort, solace, empowerment and love in their spiritual life. Many stay within the mainline churches, including the Catholic church; others have begun churches that are more open, warm and accepting of gay people. There is no rejection of God here and to say otherwise blatantly misrepresents gay people. There are also many gay and straight Christians who do not attend church.

Section 7 repeats the *Humanae Vitae* line. Sex can be moral only in marriage: 'To choose someone of the same sex for one's sexual activity is to annul the rich symbolism and meaning, not to mention the goals, of the Creator's design'. In what way are gay people doing this, given that science understands *all* sexual orientation to be hormonally shunted down a particular trajectory from the womb, probably moderated by genetic make-up? Do celibate priests and bishops also annul the Creator's design, especially the ones who do not have the gift of celibacy, as St Paul calls it, which is in fact, most of them? Does their denial of their natural God-given sexual needs annul the Creator's design? Do animals in the wild which exhibit homosexual inclinations annul the Creator's design? Do straight couples who choose not to have children annul the Creator's design?

The church seems to have only one song: if it's not male and female and if there's no chance of a pregnancy, then sex is out of the question. I think the church imputes to humankind far too much power and influence over God's design and needs to take its blinkers off in order to see the enormous breadth of diversity within humankind and the marvellous superfluity with which God continues to embark on His vast creative act.

Section 7 goes on: 'Homosexual activity is not a complementary union, able to transmit life; and so it thwarts the call to a life of that form of self-giving which the Gospel says is the essence of Christian living.' I do not accept this on two grounds. First, gay relationships can be and are, as much as any straight relationship, complementary: two individuals fostering love, care, protection and mutual growth. Of course, when the CDF talks about complementarity, it's talking about sex and means that only straight people can form a complementary union because only they can have children. As an experienced marriage and relationship therapist, I can tell you that a sexual view is a pretty narrow view of what makes up relationship complementarity.

Second, theologically, is the teaching Magisterium of the church actually saying that having kids is the essence of the Christian life? I know of no full teaching or scriptural passage or even a single verse anywhere in the Bible that suggests that the essence of living as a Christian is having children. Such a notion is the stuff of cults. Jesus' teachings about the nature of God, forgiveness, love, compassion, the proximity of the Kingdom of God and the power of God to enter and heal our lives through his indwelling Spirit might be a little closer to the essence of the Way of Jesus than conceiving babies.

The end of Section 7 repeats an idea from the Seper Declaration, that 'homosexual activity prevents one's own fulfilment and happiness by acting contrary to the creative wisdom of God'. This means that gay people are not fulfilled and happy because they are attracted to the same gender – that is, they are 'contrary to the creative wisdom of God'. There are a number of problems with this proposition.

First, gay people are not unfulfilled or unhappy, at least no more so than straight people. Personally, and I know I speak on behalf of many gay people, I didn't find my true happiness and fulfilment in life *until* I accepted my self-evident sexuality. Second, as I said earlier, it's a bit far-fetched to suggest that all gay people are biological mistakes, the result of original sin in the world. That is hardly a picture of an infinitely just God – allowing us to be born gay and then damning us for something we didn't ask for. And since He would have to choose which babies would be born with a gay inclination (toward moral evil) and which babies would be born with a straight inclination (toward moral good), this would make God partial and guilty of playing favourites.

Why not, instead, allow that God made gay people too and that homosexuality is part of the natural order? After all, there is plenty of evidence of homosexuality in the animal kingdom. In 2006, the Natural History Museum of the University of Oslo staged an exhibition about this much ignored topic. The scientists reported the following:

Homosexuality has been observed in most vertebrate groups, and also among insects, spiders, crustaceans, octopi and parasitic worms. The phenomenon has been reported in more than 1500 animal species, and is well documented for 500 of them, but the real extent is probably much higher. The frequency of homosexuality varies from species to species. In some species, homosexuality has never been reported, while in others the entire species is bisexual. In zoos around 1 in 5 pairs of king penguins are of the same sex. The record is held by orange fronted parakeets, where roughly half of all pairs in captivity are of the same sex.[16]

Some homosexual pairing in the animal kingdom may be brief; others mate for life. Do such animals annul the Creator's design? Obviously not. If we believe in the vast creative act of God, then these animals are part of it. They are part of His world, part of His divine plan. Just because it's not the predominant way that animals mate doesn't mean that such behaviour does not exist and is morally wrong, objectionable or disordered. It just means that it is atypical, nothing more. Clearly, there is far more homosexuality in the animal kingdom than anyone ever believed and we are understanding this more and more as science continues to investigate this phenomenon. It is essential that anyone who argues against homosexuality based on false notions that it is against nature should be strongly challenged.[17]

Based on the incredible diversity that is biological life on planet earth, why wouldn't there be homosexuality in the human family? 'Veni Creator Spiritus', we used to sing – the hymn celebrating the creative Spirit of God in the world. Gay people are the equal recipients of God's wonderful fashioning of the clay of our lives. There are too many of us to be accidents, genetic mutations or unfortunates who missed out on God's creative power. No, gay people, too, are the children of God and much beloved, as are all the marginalised in the scriptures: the widows, the orphans, the powerless and the sick. Jesus championed the marginalised, the little people; he eschewed the religious and the pious and the powerful. God's love knows no bounds and gay people of faith believe that He has made us just the way we are. We are part of His world, part of His plan.

James Alison argues against the church's position, suggesting that this is the greatest of binding forces that the Church uses to deny the intrinsic self of gay people, 'for it is when we get this right that we'll be able to move on'.[18]

Let me reduce this to two voices: first there is the voice, proclaiming with apparent pride, but underlying fragility 'I am what I am' – already, if we consider it quizzically, an astounding biblical claim, for this is the very name of God,[19] and behind the name, the realisation that it is 'I am who I am' who makes all things to be. Then there is what I might call the ecclesiastical voice: 'You are not.' Let me be clear that it is not at all the ecclesiastical prohibition of sexual acts between people of the same sex that is really problematic, but the justification for that prohibition, the deep voice which booms beneath it, claiming to be of God: 'You are not. I didn't create you. I only create heterosexual people. You are a defective heterosexual. Agree to be a defect and I'll rescue you. But if you claim to *be*, then your very being is constructed over against me, and you are lost.[20]

Section 8 of the Ratzinger letter points its accusatory finger at those outside the Catholic church, like me, who do not accept this teaching. It accuses us of seeking 'to create confusion regarding the Church's position'. I beg to differ. The CDF's teaching could not be clearer. There is no confusion here. Our rejection of the doctrine is based not on a desire to confuse people but on the need to repudiate a set of teachings that does not bear the ethical scrutiny of science or accord with the lived experience of gay people, and that causes untold psychological and spiritual damage. According to the letter, we are 'guided by a vision opposed to the truth about the human person, which is fully disclosed in the mystery of Christ'. We 'reflect, even if not entirely consciously, a materialistic ideology which denies the transcendent nature of the human person as well as the supernatural vocation of every individual'.

First of all, gay people of faith are not opposed to the truth. By accepting the truth of our sexuality, we are set free from a life of isolation, emotional torment and debilitating yearning. Neither are gay people of faith opposed to the truth of the teaching of Jesus and the apostles. We love the Gospel and thank God for the presence of Christ upon the earth. What we do oppose is the church's obsessive and myopic view of sex, and we are not alone in this. Many straight people of faith don't buy the church's sexuality teaching and have stopped listening. Finally, gay Christians in no way deny the reality of the transcendence of the human person as well as God's invitational calling to every soul. These are the very things we stand for in opposing the church's teaching on this matter. In fact, most gay people of faith, just like their straight counterparts, believe that answering the call of God is much more important than which gender we love. An important part of being Christian is abandoning materialism and acquisitiveness for the life of the Spirit. Gay Catholics walk this road as much as any straight Catholic. But the church does not want us to talk this way. It is supremely uncomfortable with us using this kind of language. We should wash out our mouths with soap for daring to speak the language of spirituality when everything within us is supposed to be intrinsically ordered towards moral evil. Gay people of faith reject this utterly. It is not of God.

Section 10 of the Ratzinger letter is particularly loathsome. It begins in this way: 'It is deplorable that homosexual persons have been and are the object of violent malice in speech or in action. Such treatment deserves condemnation from the Church's pastors wherever it occurs.' Now you might be wondering what I could possibly object to in that statement. Was I not denouncing gay hate crimes earlier in the book? Yes, but it is what the text goes on to say that makes me believe that the Church is being disingenuous at best and inciting violence and aggression at worst. Here is the text. It is only two sentences, but what two sentences.

> But the proper reaction to crimes committed against homosexual persons should not be to claim that the homosexual condition is not disordered. When such a claim is made and when homosexual activity is consequently condoned, or when civil legislation is introduced to protect behavior to which no one has any conceivable right, neither the Church nor society at large should be surprised when other distorted notions and practices gain ground, and irrational and violent reactions increase.

Friends, this is hate speech. Let me paraphrase the second sentence for you: 'When some people say that homosexuality is perfectly normal and they accept gay people for who they are, or when government authorities enact laws to protect gay people from discrimination, neither the church nor society in general *should be surprised* when twisted bigots come out of the woodwork and start assaulting gay and lesbian people.' For me, this is almost too shocking to write about.

I am simply incredulous that the then Cardinal Ratzinger could be capable of such venom. 'Well, you gays shouldn't be surprised if you get beaten up. After all, you are different.' 'Well, you gays shouldn't be surprised if you get bashed. After all, you have no right, according to God, and we speak for God, to live your life that way.' 'Well, you gays shouldn't be surprised when thugs assault you. After all, you're asking for it when you live in that manner.'

This is the mentality of the bully. Allow me an analogy. 'Well, don't be surprised if the kid gets bashed up. After all, he wears glasses and he goes to the library when all the other boys are heading off to the rugby field. What can you expect? He's asking for it. What does he think he's doing anyway, acting like that? This is a sporting school. We love our sport here. He really just doesn't fit in. If he gets a few knocks, you really shouldn't be surprised.' The Ratzinger letter gives tacit approval to the conceptual connection between violence and homosexuality. It cannot be read any other way.

When read as a whole, Section 10 has a 'nudge nudge' feel about it. It talks about condemnation of violence but also suggests that the idea of gay people living out their natural sexuality is asking for violence and, when it occurs, we really shouldn't be surprised. In fact we should probably expect it. Few twisted bigots probably read Vatican documents, but there are always some and this stuff has a way of filtering through to the less educated and aggressively homophobic, who are thus given a green light for aggression and violence. I cannot tell you how much I deplore this section. 'Yes your Honour, I did bash the daylights out of the poof, but what can you expect? Even the Pope says that you shouldn't be surprised.' The Catholic Church needs to repent and ask for God's forgiveness for printing such an abomination, given as it is in God's name, and to renounce such hatred.

Section 15 of the Ratzinger letter suggests that gay people who are Catholic, while submitting themselves to the teachings of the church, should avail themselves of the sacraments in order to be able to manage the burden of their disorder as they go through life. They should especially avail themselves 'of the frequent and sincere use of the sacrament of Reconciliation', more familiarly known as confession. Gay people are invited to be kept in a perpetual state of sin consciousness. 'Whoops, there's a thought that's totally concordant with my natural biological and psychological orientation. Off to confession I go, miserable sinner that I am, always rejecting God.' This is an abhorrent image, dehumanising, patronising and emotionally manipulative. Both gay and straight Catholics are right to reject it.

Section 17 rather gets under my skin because it misrepresents my profession of clinical and counselling psychology. It starts by warning the bishops that they had better teach this doctrine: this 'important question' needs to be 'communicated fully to all the faithful'. It then asks the bishops to develop 'appropriate forms of pastoral care for homosexual persons', which would include 'the assistance of the psychological, sociological and medical sciences, in full accord with the teaching of the Church'. The great and glaring problem with this statement, which the CDF just ignores, is that the psychological, sociological and medical sciences all disagree with the church's teaching.

I would remind the church that there is such a thing as the ethical treatment of patients and clients. If I taught official Catholic attitudes to gay and lesbian sexuality to my clients, I would be in direct violation of the code of practice for the ethical treatment of gay and lesbian clientele of the Australian Psychological Society and would be deviating from the ethical standards of every other psychological association in the Western world. I would be knowingly misinforming the public. If I insisted on telling gay people that they were intrinsically disordered and inclined towards moral evil, I would more than likely be drummed out of the profession and struck off the register.

This letter is erroneous on so many levels. It is wilfully ignorant, nasty in its tone, inflexible, judgemental, unforgiving, ham-fisted and even violent. There is no sense of ambivalence here. The CDF is sure that it is right. There is no place for discovery or inquiry or openness, let alone dialogue. It is dogmatic in every way without strictly being a dogma. It is as fundamentalist in its own self-belief as any of the evangelical fundamentalists are in their conscious literalist interpretations of the Bible.

The Considerations 1992

Six years after the Ratzinger letter, the CDF had the Vatican's diplomatic representative to the United States distribute an unsigned document to the American bishops. 'Some Considerations Concerning the Response to Legislative Proposals on the Non-Discrimination of Homosexual Persons' was in effect a confidential briefing paper to the bishops about how they should respond to civil legislative proposals and judicial enactments that would offer gay and lesbian people protection from discrimination. Its original form spoke to a number of specific American proposals. The Considerations became public knowledge through a leak to the New Ways Ministry, of Jeannine Gramick and Robert Nugent fame – a ministry dedicated to justice for gay and lesbian Catholics and all Christian homosexuals. Just over a week later, the Vatican reissued a revised document minus direct references to specific proposals.

The Considerations has an unmistakably belligerent tone. It takes the fight to society, to the bishops and to gay people, without reservation, openness or compassion. It means business. There are two sections after a foreword. Section I merely reiterates and quotes liberally from the Ratzinger letter. Section II, consisting of paragraphs 10 to 16, is called Applications.

Here is the foreword to the document:

Recently, legislation has been proposed in various places which would make discrimination on the basis of sexual orientation illegal. In some cities, municipal authorities have made public housing, otherwise reserved for families, available to homosexual (and unmarried heterosexual) couples. Such initiatives, even where they seem more directed toward support of basic civil rights than condonement of homosexual activity or a homosexual lifestyle, may in fact have a negative impact on the family and society. Such things as the adoption of children, the employment of teachers, the housing needs of genuine families, landlords' legitimate concerns in screening potential tenants, for example, are often implicated.

While it would be impossible to anticipate every eventuality in respect to legislative proposals in this area, these observations will try to identify some principles and distinctions of a general nature which should be taken into consideration by the conscientious legislator, voter, or church authority who is confronted with such issues.

Note that the final sentence opens the Considerations up to a greater audience than just the bishops for whom it was originally intended. Now it refers to all conscientious (read Catholic) legislators and voters, as well as the bishops and priests. The foreword gives away the thesis of the document: allowing legislative protections in the area of public housing for gay and lesbian people 'may in fact have a negative impact on the family and society'. Further it implies that gay families are not 'genuine families' and that prejudiced landlords can discriminate. When you read that, you know what you're in for. Buckle up, it's going to be a bumpy ride.

Paragraph 10 states that, in respect to non-discrimination, 'sexual orientation' does not constitute a quality comparable to race or ethnic background. Section 14 later adds gender and age to the list. Unlike these, says the CDF, quoting itself, homosexual orientation is an objective disorder and evokes moral concern. 'Orientation,' it says, 'is not of the same kind as race or ethnicity because it's a sickness. We don't have to worry about discriminating against gay people.'

Paragraph 11 says it is just to discriminate against gay and lesbian people in some areas: adoption, foster care, employing teachers or athletic coaches and in the military. No gays here, thank you very much. They are to be excluded. And yet, we know, from real evidence,[21] that gay people can be wonderful parents and foster parents with no more harm to children than caring straight parents; that they are brilliant teachers and coaches; and that the military is replete with gay people, not just non-commissioned personnel but also the highest ranking officers.

Paragraph 12 is particularly odious. The rights of gay people are 'not absolute' but 'can be legitimately limited for objectively disordered external conduct'. And this is not only permissible, but 'obligatory'. No room for ambiguity here: you actually *should* discriminate against gay people. As examples where this occurs, gay people are then compared to the 'physically or mentally ill' and to 'contagious diseases'.

According to Paragraph 13, 'there is no right to homosexuality'. As a result, any discrimination against gay or lesbian people because of their orientation should not be grounds for litigation or, in their words, 'should not form the basis for judicial claims'. This goes against the rule of law as applied in many Western countries, where such discrimination is illegal.

Paragraph 14 takes care of the gay people who decide to stay in the church, deny their orientation, live the life-lie and lead 'chaste lives'. Legislative discrimination won't bother these people because no one will know that they are gay.

Paragraph 15 deals with the entitlements of gay partners should legislative protections for gay people be enacted. Such legislation, says the Considerations, does not defend and promote family life. God forbid, it might even protect homosexual acts. As has happened elsewhere around the world, the Australian government enacted such protections in 2008. It removed same-sex discriminatory sections in all legislation and gave gay relationships of certain longevity the same legal status, rights and privileges as apply to straight de facto couples. This is precisely the kind of legislation that the CDF is trying to stop.

Finally, Paragraph 16 says that church institutions have to speak out against 'adverse legislation' for the common good. Remaining neutral and quiet is not an option. I think the fact that the CDF has to order its own constituency to toe the official line tells us something. Could it be that not all the church thinks as the CDF does? Could it be that various people ignore or defy the CDF's teaching and go against the Magisterium? The very specific and strenuous nature of these directives seems to indicate a certain measure of non-compliance on the part of various bishops and priests. Catholic lay people will do and think as they wish in order to survive in the 21st-century church, but priests, bishops and religious have to be educated, reminded and ordered to preach and teach the official position.

By writing in this offensive and pugnacious way, the CDF, in a sense, 'out' themselves as being altogether too evangelical and funda-mentalist about this topic – as though they're engaged in an all or nothing fight to the finish with those who would change the church and its culture. It reminds me of Hamlet's mother Gertrude observing the play within the play: 'The lady doth protest too much, methinks.' And the zealotry of this teaching also reminds me of the reaction formation defence mechanism in strongly homophobic individuals discussed in an earlier chapter.

The church's 'fists-flying' attitude in the Ratzinger letter and the Considerations suggests that they have something to hide and that they must not, they cannot, let these so-called materialistic, ungodly gay people have a part in their church. There is too much zeal here; the lexis chosen is too forceful and 'out there' for this not to mean something deeper. Could the reason be that should the church change, then its whole gay culture and character might be on show, naked before the world and thus shown to be as hypocritical as it is? More on this topic a little further on.

As Mark Jordan has noted,[22] reactions to the Considerations were, if anything, more shocked and more outraged than in 1986. In their book, *Voices of Hope*, Jeannine Gramick and Robert Nugent report a number of personal reactions, one of which, found in a newspaper article, is from Thomas Gumbleton, auxiliary bishop of Detroit, who described the document as 'clearly based on an ignorance of the nature of homosexuality' and 'totally in conflict with gospel values'.[23] Jordan also reports that other bishops tried to distance themselves from the Considerations by emphasising the lack of a signed author. I wish there were more brave souls like Bishop Gumbleton.

The church's problem

The problem that the Catholic church faces in its views on homosexuality is its own authority. It is entirely caught up in its own mythology, an unassailable edifice that stops all movement forward or revision of the past. However, I do note that the church has managed to do precisely this in the last few years over the status of limbo, that exquisitely bizarre Catholic teaching that had unbaptised babies going to a place of peace and paradise – limbo – but not to heaven. Limbo came into being as a result of some twisted ecclesiastical casuistry. Well, after some more modern Magisterial casuistry, limbo has been abolished. Even the church realised that the concept didn't hold water. The church now needs to do exactly the same thing with their teaching on gay and lesbian sexuality. They are wrong and they know they are wrong. But how to change a doctrinal statement? Too much is at stake for them. Start changing doctrine, let alone dogma, and the whole edifice could come crashing down.

Openly gay priest and theologian James Alison speaks of a killing perpetrated by the church:

> Since in the original order of creation, male and female were made complementary to each other and told to multiply, it is manifest that any other form of coupling is intrinsically disordered and must of its nature be a partaker of original sin, not of the order of renewed creation. …
>
> I am not alone in understanding that this moral package, which seems an expression of Christian orthodoxy, is very much at work in what has killed us. However many caveats are put

into it concerning the distinction between acts and orientation, this package grinds down on us and says: 'as you are, you are not really part of creation. … Your longings, desiring, seeking after flourishing and sense of what is natural, however they be pruned and refined through experiences of partnership and love, have absolutely no relation with creation. For you creation is a word whose meaning you simply cannot and do not know from experience. Since everything most heartfelt that you take to be natural is intrinsically disordered, it is only by a complete rejection of your very hearts that you may come to know something of what is meant by creation. Until such a time as this happens, limp along, holding fast with your minds to the objective truth about a creation which can have no subjective resonance for you, and when you are dead, you will enter into the Creator's glory.'[24]

Here Alison's irony provides for us in a nutshell the Church's invitation to the Christian life for gay and lesbian people. Deny your very self for the rest of your life. Live the life-lie. Do not accept your orientation. Stay in the closet and say nothing. Struggle through life carrying this burden we have imposed on you, accepting that this is God's will for you. Suffering might even make you holy. Go to confession frequently to confess your sin. And after you're dead, you can enjoy God's presence then. This approach eviscerates Jesus' words, 'Come to me, all of you who are weary and loaded down with burdens, and I will give you rest. Place my yoke on you and learn from me, because I am gentle and humble, and you will find rest for your souls because my yoke is pleasant, and my burden is light.'[25] Dear reader, there is nothing pleasant or light in the Church's invitation.

The clerical closet

The greatest fear the Catholic church faces today, greater even than its fear of clerical marriage, is the well-known and obvious fact that so many of its priests and bishops have been and are gay themselves. It is the worst kept secret in the church today. As John Shelby Spong notes,

For two thousand years the church has had gay clergy in numbers far beyond what most people have dared to imagine. They have occupied every position in every ecclesiastical hierarchy. They have assisted in the fashioning of the doctrine, discipline, worship, and ecclesiastical dress of the church. When celibacy was mandated as the only proper lifestyle for the ordained, in the twelfth century, the doors were opened for gay males to find in the church's priesthood a legitimizing place where their single status would be turned from a liability to a virtue and where their lives could experience creativity and community. If gay people were excised from the ordained ministry throughout the church's history, enormous gaps would appear, perhaps as much as 80 percent in certain periods of history.[26]

Although the church has refused to do so to date, it needs to face facts and be open about the tens of thousands of gay priests, bishops and religious the world over, and for the church to continue to pretend otherwise makes it look utterly fatuous. Mark Jordan puts it well:

The most important theological facts about Catholicism and homo-sexuality are not the bureaucratic words that Catholic authorities speak. The truly significant facts concern the homosexuality of the Catholic church itself – of members of its priesthood and its clerical culture, of its rituals and spiritual traditions.[27]

Estimates of the numbers of gay priests in the church vary owing to the difficulties imposed by collecting the data. In the American church, you can read survey results that go from around 10 to 58 per cent.[28] In his controversial book, *The Changing Face of the Priesthood*, Donald Cozzens,[29] a highly respected, heterosexual seminary rector and professor of pastoral theology, estimates the number to be approximately 50 per cent of all priests. He quotes studies citing from a range of 23 to 58 per cent, and 48.5 to 55.1 per cent of seminarians. Internet searches easily pull up results that include personal accounts by priests, some named, some anonymous, who are aware that 25 per cent of their local colleagues and about 55 per cent of seminarians are gay. After two decades of counselling clergy, Richard Sipe, a 20-year monk turned psychotherapist and researcher into clerical sexuality, estimated that 30 per cent of priests were gay. He predicted that by 2010, half of the American clergy would be gay.[30]

As Cozzens writes in Chapter 7 of his book,

As a matter of practice, if not policy, many dioceses and religious congregations are open to ordaining gay men if they demonstrate a commitment to celibate living. They tend to be men who are nurturing, intelligent, talented, and sensitive – qualities especially suited to ministry. Often they excel as liturgists and homilists. Without question, gay priests minister creatively and effectively at every level of pastoral leadership.[31]

Cozzens' line, that 'the priesthood is, or is becoming, a gay profession',[32] has become infamous among conservative clerics and Catholics who oppose such a notion. Rome basically wants to bar as many gay men as it can and weed them out, preferably before they get ordained.[33] Other more thoughtful voices suggest that gay priests, though not 'outing' themselves to the public, thereby destroying their careers and vocations, should probably 'out' themselves to themselves, learn to be comfortable in their own sexuality and introduce themselves to other gay priests for support and encouragement.

I am afraid that this topic is far too big for me to treat here, and in truth, I am not a historian and so could not do it justice anyway. But we do know that the church has always had gay priests and religious. I have been taught by them at school in the past myself and I know them in the present in my adult life.

The presence of gay men and women in the ranks of the Catholic clergy ties in very closely with one of the principal points I wish to make in this chapter. It concerns hypocrisy. Not that I think gay priests and religious are necessarily hypocrites – far from it. Most of them are incredibly courageous souls who toil in the owner's vineyard against all odds and who, battle-weary and crestfallen at the intransigence of the church hierarchy, must sometimes wonder whether it is all worth it. These are good souls and they have my immense admiration.

Yet there are other secretly gay priests, who, closeted and full of self-loathing, really do believe the teachings of the church: that they are pathological, that their sexual self, which they cannot annihilate but only deny, inclines them towards moral evil, that they are perverts and that their body and their desire are fleshly and need to be 'crucified with Christ'. Some go out to a gay bar clandestinely, pick up a guy online or meet up with another man for casual sex, then, full of rage and self-disgust, return to their pulpits, spitting fury and judgement, to berate the faithful over the immorality of the times and the lusts of the flesh. In my opinion, these men have no right to be in the priesthood. They make a mockery of real spirituality. They are as guilty as the Scribes and Pharisees of Jesus' time in their hypocrisy. I would urge these men to either get some help and learn to love themselves, or, if that is not possible or indeed refused, to leave the priesthood altogether and stop projecting their self-hatred onto their parishioners, who deserve better.

The Vatican can mandate that there will be no more gay priests, or only gay priests who hate their sexuality and commit to lifelong celibacy, but this will not work. Two things come to mind.

The first is that human nature is human nature. There is no getting away from it. Just ask the straight priests who have struggled with celibacy their entire ordained lives. Their desire does not go away. We are created as embodied, sexualised, sensualised creatures of flesh and blood. And from what I understand of God, He wants us to love our selves and to value the possibility of his indwelling Spirit in our fleshly imperfect lives, spirit, soul *and* body.

The second notion here is that there should be no division between the body and the spirit. They are inextricably linked and intertwined. To enforce a celibate priesthood is to enforce a false dichotomy between the body and the spirit. The great thrust of scripture and the life of the Spirit constantly invite us to enter fully into our humanity and become all that we can be – 'to have life and to have it abundantly'. Unfortunately, for many centuries, the Catholic church has given the impression that our bodies and our human desire are the enemy of all that is good and all that is of God. Priests deserve a better go than this.[34]

Conclusions

The Catholic church is in grave error in its teaching on the issue of homosexuality and is harming people of faith. Its teaching is cruel, torturous, unnecessary and is based on erroneous suppositions. As Mark Jordan writes,

We need to identify deceits about homosexuality [in the Church's documents] without being deceived by them. So we cannot engage the documents 'on their own terms'. We cannot politely accept their categories, their rules of evidence, their patterns of argument. The categories, the rules, and the patterns enact much of the documents' forceful homophobia.[35]

He is suggesting that Catholicism is homophobic not just in content but in form. I am angry at the church for doing this and at the arrogant way in which it presents itself on these matters. This is the kind of hubris that Jesus railed against in the Pharisees (Matthew 23: 13, 4): 'You shut the Kingdom of heaven in men's faces. You yourselves do not enter nor will you let those trying to' and 'they tie up heavy loads and put them on men's shoulders, but they themselves are not willing to lift a finger to move them'. Jesus was repudiating the Pharisees' need for religious power bases, and the kind of piety that misses the deep point of spirituality. He was trying to rid his own Jewish tradition of these excesses, so it is unlikely that he would be comfortable with the same excesses in the Christian church.

These words are probably the most forceful that Jesus ever spoke in the record. They are an unequivocal dismissal of hypocrisy, ostentation, indoctrination, coercion, encumbrance and fake religious experience. His whole mission on the earth was to teach a better way to be with God and each other and to live a life that exemplified that better way. The more one reads the Gospel, the more one becomes convinced that Jesus and 'big religion' were not on the best of terms.

This is why these CDF documents make me, and many others, so angry. In Jordan's words, they are 'so carelessly offensive, so casually violent, that they provoke many readers to fury. Rage is indeed an appropriate index to the rhetorical intensity of some of the documents. Any weaker reaction would be a misreading.'[36]

Mark Jordan is correct in this. The Vatican documents are hate speech and they should be called hate speech, openly, forcefully, unashamedly and angrily. They misrepresent gay people repeatedly as selfish, bitter, sterile, hedonistic, narcissistic, pathological and in-clined towards moral evil. This is a caricature of a gay person. This is not reality, nor a description of the richness and profundity that is the lived life in this world. Anger is the right reaction to such hate speech but anger, on its own and left unchecked, only does the bearer harm and achieves little. It becomes self-consuming. There is a time to be angry and a time to let anger go so that we may be rid of its venom. We are then free to adopt some other response, which looks to the future not the past. I fervently hope that the Catholic church will change and grow; that those in the church who have the power to bring about change can do so without being destroyed in the process.

I am not against the Catholic church per se, nor do I wish its downfall. However, I, and millions of others like me, long for the church to present the Gospel in less mediaeval ways, which speak to the heart of modern women and men who know and understand their own hearts before God much better than the church does. We want a church that is closer to the Way that Jesus talked about and lived; we want a church that is not homophobic and violent but values the incredible contribution that gay people make; we want a church that is not patriarchal but values the incalculable contribution of women, and one that is not monarchical and does not treat its people as pawns on a board. This means that gay Catholics who choose not to leave the church must stand up and be counted if the church is to change. It may not do much in the short term, but the voice cannot die away; the message of dissent must be there. It is the great confession: 'I am Catholic and I am gay and you cannot, you will not, exclude me from God.'

The effect of church doctrine on everyday Catholics

In 1997, a young gay man named Nicholas Holloway asked the legitimate question, 'Given the Catholic church's teaching on gay and lesbian people, is it possible for an openly gay Catholic to receive communion at Mass?' Holloway decided to put the question to the test soon after and was twice refused the Eucharist, once in London, by Cardinal Basil Hume, and once in Melbourne, by then Archbishop George Pell. He had written to both cathedrals to inform them of who he was and his sexual orientation and that he would be attending Mass reverently and quietly the following Sunday, but wearing a rainbow sash to mark himself as an openly gay Christian man. The actions of the two clerical princes were unambiguous and decisive.

The following year, on Pentecost Sunday, a group of 70 people, mostly gay, but straight supporters as well, including family members, were all refused communion by George Pell at St Patrick's Cathedral in Melbourne after they wore the rainbow sash during Mass. Thus was born the Rainbow Sash Movement,[37] which directly challenged the church's teaching on sexuality issues and raised the consciousness of the issue among Catholics and the public in general. Since then it has spread throughout the world, quietly calling the church to dialogue and to change. It is not marked by loud declamations or megaphone advocacy but on a Gandhi-like non-violent protest against the reigning order. The presence of the rainbow sash merely acknowledges the gay or lesbian sexual orientation of the wearer, an orientation that the church's own teaching states is not a sin.

Two things strike me about the actions of the church when the Rainbow Sash people attend Mass. First, I simply cannot imagine Jesus refusing them the Eucharist. His practice of open commensality or 'freely eating at table' with others was one of his principal teaching methods. It was also one of the main ways he loved to be with people. Apostles, followers, ne'er-do-wells, women, men, children, corrupt officials, Roman collaborators, the sick, prostitutes – Jesus was there, sharing a meal and a glass of wine, enjoying their company and conversing. George Pell's miserable approach could not be in starker contrast. All men and women who seek something of God should be welcome at His table.

Second, the Rainbow Sash people are merely attending Mass. They are not engaging in sexual activity and so, even by the church's own warped definitions, they are not engaging in 'immoral behaviour'. Since their sexuality is not a sin, according to the teaching Magisterium, why are they being refused communion? If they don't wear the sash, they can participate, even though they are still gay. It seems that identifying yourself as having a gay sexual orientation is the crux of the matter. Stay closeted, don't tell anyone and don't make waves, and you're welcome. Acknowledge you are gay and be open about it and you're not. What the church wants here is the denial of self.

There is the strong sense here that the church believes gay people should be ashamed. If you are open about your gay sexuality, then that gives the signal that you are not ashamed and you should be, according to the hierarchy's thinking. I believe the church is incredibly uncomfortable with the thought that out gay people *are* comfortable with their sexuality.

Rejecting the church's teachings

Since the time of the ancient Roman law courts it has been a principle of law in many jurisdictions that silence means consent – *Qui tacet consentit* - and while there are plenty of exceptions to this rule, it would appear that it is perfectly germane in this case. As James Alison writes,

> If I do not object to a movement in my group, I consent to it. If I consent because I believe in it, all well and good. But if I consent by my silence because unwilling to face the consequences of being in the minority where I strongly suspect the truth to lie, then I am very probably a coward and a hypocrite.[38]

If, like me, you do not believe the teachings are acceptable, then a very different kind of reaction is called for. Silence will not do. Really there are only two options: you can either leave the church or stay in the church openly.

The leavers

Congratulations and commiserations to all who have left the church. You have my unreserved respect and admiration. It cannot have been easy and I know you must miss it from time to time. No one should blame you or judge you harshly. You can no longer, in all conscience, tolerate the kinds of things being said, preached and written within the Catholic church about gay people. If you are gay yourself, you probably feel attacked and find the whole thing very disturbing, if not downright wicked and intolerable. You cannot see yourself participating in the life of a church that is so blatantly homophobic and nasty. You know you are not intrinsically inclined toward moral evil and you know that the teaching is doing untold damage to people's lives, Catholic and non-Catholic alike, and you feel you can no longer tolerate it nor align yourself to such an institution. For you, the good parts of the church are now outweighed by the bad bits. It is beyond your ability to sit serenely in the pew and not have this hate speech ruin your quiet times of reflection with God.

Other reasons also crowd in upon you: the misogyny in the church, the massive power imbalances between the genders in the church hierarchy, the centuries-old history of violence, duplicity and corruption, the worldwide clerical child abuse scandal and the hierarchy's subsequent cover-ups, the monarchical trappings, the reticence to clearly educate about intolerant biblical passages, and the church's refusal to change. These things, heaped upon the gay doctrines, are now enough to drive you away. I congratulate you on your personal integrity, but I offer my commiserations too.

I am sure you feel cheated that the church is so stuck in the past that it cannot even look after one of its own, and that makes you feel both hurt and angry. I know that you must miss the Mass and sacraments, and that it feels as though the church in which you grew up, and loved, has deserted you. This is terrifyingly sad. You will have to grieve for a while, even in the midst of your anger and resentment and pain, but healthy grief does not last forever.

So take heart too. God is bigger than the church and He does not forget you. You can still connect with Him – at home, at the beach, in the lives of other people, even in the café or on the dance floor. If you miss the fellowship of believing people, you can also visit or join other churches – ones that value gay people. To leave can be excruciating, but it is also a movement towards authenticity. It is an act of profound faith.

The out stayers

To those who decide to remain in the church I also offer my admiration and commiserations. You have not made an easy choice. Many gay and even straight people will not understand your making it, and some will even criticise you for being complicit, for lacking personal integrity or being intellectually dishonest. Some will say that, by staying, you are colluding in your own oppression. I don't agree. At least I don't agree provided that you speak up. You have made an important choice to stand your ground. This is a bold decision, just as courageous, perhaps even more so, than leaving the church.

I understand, too, why you have made this decision. In essence it is about ownership. Allow me to give an analogy that may help to elucidate why gay people might choose to stay in a homophobic church. It is not exact but it is close.

Over the decades, Australians have wrestled with their past as regards our country's indigenous people, the oldest known surviving civilisation on planet earth. These Aboriginals and Torres Strait Islanders were dispossessed of their ancestral lands by colonising Europeans over 200 years ago. Still sacred, these lands were theirs; they had lived there for tens of millennia. When Captain James Cook first planted a British flag on Australian soil, he did so under the coloniser's doctrine that this was Terra Nullius, an empty land.

However, in 1982, Murray Islander Eddie Mabo and some colleagues challenged this by taking a state government to the High Court of Australia and winning a ten-year landmark case that recognised Aboriginal and Torres Strait Islanders' ownership of their ancestral lands. Eddie Mabo knew that the continent was not empty at European settlement, no matter what the English law declared, and he knew that many of the Aboriginal nations could demonstrate the court's requirement of unbroken connection to their respective lands since the Europeans had arrived.

There is some resonance here for gay Catholics. Like me, most of you were born into a Catholic home, raised in a Catholic family, educated in Catholic schools, perhaps by the nuns in primary school and the brothers in high school, introduced to the sacraments of the church at a young age, participated in class Masses, went on school retreats, attended Sunday Mass regularly as you grew older, and were present at the liturgies for baptisms and funerals of family members and friends. You know the prayers, are familiar with all the rites of the yearly liturgical cycle. You know the local clergy, priests and religious, and enjoy the solidarity of being Catholic. You might have been an altar server as a child, as I was. You pray and walk with God and try to follow the Way of Jesus in the manner of your life. You have felt this way since your childhood, in fact for decades. But now, because you unashamedly acknowledge that you are gay, and have been from the beginning, the officials say that you cannot be part of the church.

The incredulity and the sense of injustice sometimes overpower you. But, like Eddie Mabo before the High Court, you decide to stay and to fight against overwhelming odds. You say, 'This will not do. This is my church too. It always has been my church. These old men do not own it and cannot tell me how to live my life and my faith. Those days are gone. I have a stake in this church and I will not let them exclude me. I will not let them tell me that I am outside of God. I am a Catholic person too and I will remain so in this the church I have known all my life. I am Catholic, they cannot, they will not exclude me from God.'

As Australian gay contemplative Michael Kelly suggests,

There is a way of remaining in the Church that is defiant, that proclaims the right to a place and a voice, that refuses to surrender to the bigots this complex and rich phenomenon called 'Church'. Being part of the Church means being part of a people, a culture, a network of values, ideals, rituals, traditions, symbols, stories, history, music, art and literature as rich as any that human civilisation has produced. It means being at home in an ancient and worldwide tradition, and also intimately involved in a local community where many enduring and intimate relationships have developed.[39]

Then there are the more socially conscious reasons to remain. Gay Catholics who choose to stay also believe that the church has much to offer a world bent on consumerism, acquisitiveness, greed and the abuse of power, but also as an alternative to feel-good religion. Catholicism retains a deep and mature understanding of the Way that Jesus taught and lived, a Way that attempts to offer us an authentic vision of what spirituality can be; divinity in humanity – selfless, loving, compassionate, practical and intimate, both with God and with our fellow human beings. And this can remain very relevant and meaningful to the gay Catholic person.

Finally, there are the spiritual reasons for staying. These concern the nature of someone's relationship with God. For some, there is a powerfully conscious sense of the abiding presence of God. For others, it is a matter of a quiet sense of call, more invitational. For still others, it is the working out of faith in their daily life among communities of people. It is God in the ordinariness of every day. Gay Catholics tend to be very down-to-earth people. You cannot go through the stages of gay identity formation as an adolescent, come out to a befuddled world and a disapproving church, and not have some sense of who you are, your place in the world and the kinds of beliefs and causes to which you might align yourself.

Staying non-silently and openly is the only truly authentic way to be Catholic and it is not an easy path. You need to be open in your sexuality and out of the closet. An open life may be as much as you can handle, depending on your temperament, personality and gifts. You need to witness by your lived experience that you do not accept the church's teachings in this matter. You might invite a partner along to Mass, or worship together if both are involved in the church. Perhaps you might introduce your partner to the priest after Mass or to the local parishioners or simply come out to various people in the parish. This simple activity is a powerful witness to the church, its clergy and its people that you are who you are.

Perhaps, though, you are gifted with levels of confidence and speaking ability that mean you can openly discuss the gay issue and to advocate. Again, this is a brave thing to do: there will always be bigots in any parish and they may take you on publicly. You will need to be thick-skinned to say what needs to be said, without sinking to the language or style of your opponents. You must, as Ephesians 4: 15 says, offer them nothing but 'speaking the truth in love' so they can accuse you of nothing. You will more than likely find supporters among the straight parishioners, although that will depend on the parish. If you know of a gay priest in your local diocese, it might be a good idea to seek him out. He may be able to offer you spiritual encouragement and solace. In all of this, though, it is essential that you protect yourself and don't put yourself into situations that you can't handle or that will damage you emotionally.

Final Thoughts

I am going to start this chapter on a note of declaration. Don't worry, it's not the Seper Declaration – it's my own. I want to remind you that we started this book by looking at epistemology, that branch of philosophy which investigates the origin, nature, methods and limits of human knowledge. In Chapter 2, I suggested that a more scientific, evidence-based way of investigating and discussing complex issues is preferable to relying on literal interpretations of ancient undeviating texts or appeals to institutional authority.

And so to my declaration. I am going to take as truth that being gay or lesbian is neither sick nor sinful. Gay and lesbian people are as much beloved children of God as any heterosexual person. They have every right to approach God, to walk after His ways, to engage with a spiritual search by way of Christian thought, and to be accepted and valued in the church, free from prejudice, discrimination, abuse and violence. In a nutshell, my declaration is this: you can be gay *and* Christian. And you can be this in a healthy, flourishing self.

The integrity of the self

We need to remember, though, that the self is not inviolable. It can be damaged. Some parts of the Christian church spend considerable time and energy on condemning and rejecting gay people, and threatening them with separation from God and even eternal damnation. This is damaging, especially to the young.

In a 2008 paper that investigated this kind of damage, a group of Australian psychologists noted that 'Religious discourse based on homophobic beliefs may be particularly dangerous for same sex attracted young people because it claims territory beyond the physical world and the people in it to the loss of God's love in a damned afterlife.'[1] Young adolescents are particularly prone to social processes, particularly those that emphasise the importance of belonging to the group. If you've ever watched teenagers together, you will know exactly how powerful these 'in-group/out-group' forces can be. During the teenage years and early 20s, belonging to the group is typically more important than parents, schoolwork, career, the household chores, the dog – just about everything. To be placed in the out-group is almost the worst thing that can happen.

So for the church to arbitrarily exclude a young gay person is particularly cruel. Because they are inexperienced and emotionally immature, most young gay people of faith suffer enormously as a result of such action – and through absolutely no fault of their own. They suffer because of their positive desire for authenticity and their refusal to accede to the church's attitude to and treatment of gay people. Some older gay people can probably handle themselves against such onslaught, but the younger ones almost inevitably leave. Can you blame them?

The Australian researchers conducted a quantitative analysis of data that had been collected as part of a larger national survey on the sexuality, health and wellbeing of 14–21-year-old same sex-attracted young Australians. There were 1747 participants, which is a really good-sized sample. Of these, 119, about 6.8 per cent, mentioned religious issues in their responses to a number of open-ended questions regarding their well-being. Three important questions were asked of the whole sample:

▼ questions concerning feelings about sexuality

▼ questions concerning feelings about life

▼ questions concerning the propensity to self-harm.

The raw results are illuminating, as the researchers were able to compare these 119 young people (who did mention religion) with the other 1628 participants (who didn't mention religion).

The first question was about feelings concerning being same sex attracted. Participants could respond: 'Great', 'Pretty good', 'OK', 'Pretty bad' or 'Really bad.' Of the 119, 66.4 per cent said 'Great' or 'Pretty good', while the percentage for those who didn't mention religion was 76.7 per cent in these two categories – a significant difference. Of those who mentioned religion, 9.2 per cent answered 'Pretty bad' or 'Really bad', compared with only 4.3 per cent of those who did not mention religion. If you're young, gay and a person of faith, you are more likely to feel less positive about your sexuality than if you are not a person of faith.

The second question asked the young people to rate how they felt about life as a whole. They were given a seven-point scale where '1' meant 'Terrible' and '7' meant 'Extremely happy'. For the 119, the mean or average score was 4.7, while those who did not mention religion scored an average 5.1. Again, a statistically significant difference. The religious ones scored lower than the rest. A young gay person of faith is more likely to feel that life generally is more negative than his or her non-religious counterpart.

The third question asked the young people whether they had thought of or actually succeeded in harming themselves as a direct result of other people's homophobia. Of those who mentioned religion, 52.2 per cent answered yes; in the other group the percentage was 34.7 per cent – another statistically significant difference. The results of this study are an indictment on the church for not only *not* looking after its young people, but also for actually harming them and causing them terrible pain.

Dividing practices

The adolescent world is filled with alcohol and drugs, and young gay people rejected by their church sometimes turn to them for solace. They are also much more prone to clinical levels of depression and self-hatred. The norm for most of the 119 in the sub-sample was rejection of their sexuality by the church and their fellow Christians. In every single case, there were negative health outcomes, including suicide attempts. In Chapter 6, I discussed the notion of internalised homophobia, that process by which gay people who have grown up in an intolerant, even aggressive world, introject, or project inwards, the non-acceptance and hatred they encounter. French philosopher Michel Foucault provides a way for us to understand how this process works. He describes a mechanism that he calls *dividing practices*, by which individuals who are different are separated, first from the group, and then from themselves.

In our context, the dividing from the group would go like this. The church condemns homosexuality outright and states that if you are gay, you must deny your very self, stay constantly in a sin consciousness by frequenting the confessional or asking God to forgive you, and remain celibate for life. This is because you are different. The second step, the dividing from the self, works this way. Certain susceptible gay and lesbian individuals who accept unquestioningly a literal interpretation of the Scriptures or church doctrine introject this teaching and accede to the notion that 'I am different'. Over time, this notion develops into 'I am sinful' or 'I am evil' and there ensues a dividing of the self – the gay self in opposition to the Christian self. This results in cognitive dissonance, the presence of two mutually exclusive positions held in tension at the same time. It's a mental and emotional tug of war.

Cognitive dissonance

Cognitive dissonance is not a new concept. The theory was first proposed in 1957 by a researcher named Leon Festinger,[2] who suggested that a state of psychological tension is generated when an individual has two or more thoughts, attitudes or beliefs that are competing and are therefore incompatible. Such dissonance also causes such an uncomfortable physical state that the individual tries to reduce the tension. The severity of the tension depends on how much importance you place on each of the competing thoughts. In Festinger's view, an individual could choose a number of ways to reduce the tension, for example:

▼ changing one or other of the incompatible cognitions

▼ changing the behaviour that creates the dissonance

▼ changing the social environment that reinforces the dissonance

▼ searching for extra evidence to augment one side or the other, or

▼ derogating, or disparaging, the source of one of the cognitions.

To change one or other of the incompatible cognitions, a gay person would have to alter what he or she thought of either being gay or being Christian. Now, given that gay and lesbian identity formation is a long and complicated process, changing the way one feels about being gay is probably not the most desirable option. Changing the way of thinking about God and faith is possible because it is the method I myself chose to reduce the dissonance, so I know it works. I changed how I looked at Christianity, at faith. This reduced the dissonance within me so that being gay and being Christian were no longer incompatible for me.

The second method is to change the behaviour that creates the dissonance. Since they are invariably in churches with highly entrenched positions that are unlikely to change, this avenue is not open to gay people of faith. The only way it could work would be for the gay person to return or partially return to the closet, a response I would discourage. The only real solution is for the gay person to leave the church, which is precisely what most do. It is for this reason that Festinger's third suggestion, changing the environment that causes the dissonance, will not work either.

The fourth suggestion, augmenting one side or the other with extra evidence, is really related to the first. Because of the impasse I had reached, I was forced to change my cognitions about God and the church. I did this partly by gaining extra information: new learning that enabled me to weigh up the countervailing arguments. I read and read. I talked to others who had gone before me. I meditated constantly and also invited the Spirit of God to be part of my thoughts and journey. Eventually, I had enough evidence to be able to safely and confidently change my position. After almost two decades, I am more convinced than ever that I made the right choices. I would not return to my old view of God for anything.

Finally, Festinger's fifth suggestion is to derogate the source of one of the cognitions. You might think that this is what I have done here when writing about my views on the church. Actually, I don't think so. Where I am harsh on the church, I believe that it deserves it. I am not going out of my way to speak about the church in a derogatory manner because I hate it or think it should cease or because I like church-bashing. But change the church must. And if strong words must be spoken from time to time, then let them be spoken. Lives are at stake and so is the reputation of the Gospel. I want to look after both. For some, it may be that leaving the church angrily and berating it for its hypocrisy is the only way for them to be able to move on after being so hurt. I cannot blame them for this. But I do hope that some time in the future, they will remember the message of Jesus and not conflate the manmade rules of powerful religious institutions with the power of being in flow with the Spirit of God.

In 1996 Kimberly Mahaffy published a very interesting paper that examined the nature of cognitive dissonance in a group of Christian lesbians who were active in the life of their various churches.[3] She characterised the locus, or position, of each dissonance as one of three possibilities:

▼ internal, that is, caused by one's own thoughts and beliefs;

▼ external, that is, caused by church or others' rules, regulations, or views of acceptable behaviour; or

▼ non-existent, where there was no dissonance at all.

A series of open-ended questions was answered by 163 participants, members of various churches ranging from middle of the road evangelical to strongly conservative evangelical to liberal non-Catholic and Catholic. While 27 per cent placed themselves in the non-existent camp, nearly three-quarters of the sample reported some level of cognitive dissonance.

Using the magic of some quite sophisticated statistical analysis, Mahaffy was able to pinpoint a number of very interesting predictive factors. First, she looked at what predicted internal dissonance and found that only one factor existed: evangelical identity before coming out. By viewing the theology of the various churches on a spectrum, with arch-evangelical conservatism down one end and liberal/Catholic at the other, Mahaffy was able to analyse the group in terms of what predicted their dissonance. Using the non-existent dissonance group as the comparison, she found that for every unit of increasing evangelical identity, the odds of internal dissonance grew by 42 per cent. This is a remarkable result and a very strong one. The more theologically conservative you are in your religious attitudes as a gay person, the greater the internal tug of war you will experience.

Second, Mahaffy wanted to examine what predicted external dissonance. Again using the non-existent camp as a comparison, she found that for every unit of increasing evangelical identity, the odds of external dissonance grew by 16 per cent. Although the result is not as strong as that found in the internal group, it is still a notable finding. Put simply, if you are gay and Christian, the more evangelically conservative you are, the more your cognitive dissonance as a result of other people's attitudes will increase.

Both these findings are interesting in that they provide evidence for my long-held belief, based on personal experience, that it is harder to integrate a gay or lesbian orientation in a non-Catholic, Bible-believing church than it is within the Catholic church. This has everything to do with attitudes to scripture on both sides of the denominational divide, as well as day-to-day life as a member in the local church.

On the whole, Catholics tend not to talk about the priest's homily or go near too much theology as they stand around chatting on the church steps after Mass. They are more likely to talk about secular things such as the weather, business or the family. Evangelicals, more used to using the Bible in their personal devotion, are not averse to discussing elements of the pastor's sermon or teaching, the liturgy used in the service or even some theological point. Pentecostal groups pray with each other openly and discuss such things as a matter of course, before and after services and in mid-week prayer or Bible-study meetings. That kind of culture, combined with a conscious literalist approach to biblical interpretation, concretes in a rejecting ethos towards gay people at the local church level. In contrast, the rejection of gay people in the Catholic Church appears to be much more on a hierarchical level. It comes from Rome and is, perhaps, a little less visible in the local parish.

Mahaffy asked each of her participants how they managed to resolve the amount of tension caused by the incompatible cognitions. She identified three resolutions in these women: change the beliefs, leave the church or live with the tension. Over half changed their beliefs about God and the church rather than leave or learn to live with the tension. This was most associated with the internal dissonance group. In contrast, the external dissonance group was more strongly associated with living with the tension or leaving the church.

Identity integration

There is another method of resolving cognitive dissonance between the gay self and the Christian self, although I do not recommend it. This is known as *compartmentalisation*. It amounts to this: 'I'm gay and I'm Christian. But I don't bring my Christianity into my gay lifestyle and I don't bring my gay lifestyle into my Christianity. I leave the church out of my private life and I leave my private life out of the church.' This is not an easy option. It requires the use of significant amounts of psychological energy and a strict, rigorous mind that never allows the separation to slip. I don't recommend this approach because it lacks authenticity and perpetuates an exhausting and unsatisfying game-playing ritual.

So what is the ultimate answer for such individuals beyond the kinds of options proposed by Festinger? Really, there is only one acceptable answer: identity integration. Practising gay Christians must somehow navigate their way through this complicated psychological terrain and integrate the two identities: sexual (I am gay) and religious (I am Christian). Researchers Eric Rodriguez and Suzanne Ouellette put it this way:

> Identity conflict can be alleviated when gay men and lesbians integrate their religious beliefs and their homosexuality into a single, new, workable understanding of the self…. Such people have no self-imposed walls between their homosexuality and their religious beliefs, and perceive societally-imposed barriers as surmountable. This creates a new, complex and yet coherent identity: gay or lesbian Christian.[4]

Rodriguez and Ouellette investigated the identity integration of a sample of 40 gay and lesbian members of a gay church, the Metropolitan Community Church in New York (MCC/NY). Their working hypothesis was that a forum that accepted and valued both gay and lesbian lifestyles and the Gospel message would enhance the likelihood of identity integration. So, if full identity integration is possible, then theoretically it should be able to happen in a gay church with a gay minister. The researchers wanted to know specifically what kinds of factors helped members of this church to achieve such integration.

In their first study, published in 1999,[5] they identified a number of such factors:

▼ The use of inclusive and gender-neutral language.

▼ The use of the historical-critical method of biblical interpretation.

▼ The structure of the liturgy enabled members to recognise that the church itself had integrated both gay sexual orientation and Christianity in its services.

▼ The preaching of its lesbian pastor provided positive ways for gay men and lesbians to think about themselves as gay Christians.

▼ The transparent struggle that belongs to every moral group to provide a safe, positive and inclusive atmosphere for one particular group of people without excluding others.

In the second study, published in 2000,[6] the researchers further refined their hypothesis to investigate the importance of involvement, suggesting that the more involved participants were in the MCC/NY, the greater the identity integration would be. The 40 participants in the study were asked a number of questions, one of which was: 'Today, do you feel that you have combined together your sexual orientation and your religious beliefs?' A quarter reported that they had not fully integrated their sexual and Christian identities and just under three quarters, 72.5 per cent, reported that they had managed to do this. Mostly, the latter were church members; the other group were casual though regular visitors. And, right in line with the researchers' hypothesis, there were statistically significant differences between the 'fully' and 'not fully' groups with regard to involvement.

There was a strong relationship between 'fully integrated' and higher role involvement, higher worship service attendance and higher ministry and activity attendance. Religious identity can be defined as the management of personal religious experience. It is both an internal psychological phenomenon and a social phenomenon. Integration between sexual identity and religious identity is possible for gay people but for the most part it is, as we have seen, contingent on a number of factors. If one remains a member of a local church, then the attitudes of that church are paramount to the process of integration. If one leaves the church altogether but retains a religious or spiritual identity, it is also possible to achieve integration, but this, too, will depend to a degree on external input and some level of support. Whether you remain in the church or not, identity integration is the principal goal if you are gay and follow the Way of Jesus.

The Way of Jesus

In John's Gospel, we read one of the most famous sayings that Jesus ever uttered. In Chapter 14: 6, he says, 'I am the way, the truth and the life. No one comes to the Father except through me.' Of course, conservative Christians of all persuasions have used this verse to offer evidence for the exclusivity of Christianity. 'You can't go anywhere near God if you don't become a Christian first, and that would be becoming a Christian according to our method and teaching.' I would like to offer an alternative reading here.

Mark is the earliest Gospel. It was written around the year 70 CE, just 40 or so years after Jesus. In fact, Matthew and Luke both used it as their principal source. Mark is not the Gospel of messiahship, glory and wonderful statements about Jesus. Rather, it has two principal themes: the kingdom of God and the Way. It even begins with a verse quoting one of the prophets on the latter subject: 'I will send my messenger ahead of you, who will prepare your way'. The Greek word used here is *hodos* and it appears often throughout the Gospel. However, it is not always translated as 'way' in English: sometimes it is given as 'path' or 'road'.[7]

In Acts 9: 2, for the first time in the Bible, we read of Christianity itself being called the Way. I am drawn to this description: it was one of Jesus' key themes and, as you have probably noticed, I have used it regularly throughout this book. From a metaphorical perspective, the word 'way' for me has a number of different meanings:

▼ a journey

▼ a method, manner, technique or style

▼ a direction, a path, the answer to being lost.

Each of these indicates the part that Jesus plays in our lives as his followers. I want to take a brief look at each as they have much to say about our achieving full identity integration.

The journey

The Way of Jesus is a journey. In fact, I believe all spiritual paths can be characterised as journeys. We begin this life in our mother's womb, are born into the world, travel through it as children and then as adults and ultimately leave it again when we die. It is no wonder that religious teachers of all faiths across time have described this process as a journey. Gay or straight, we progress, we make mistakes, we find some wisdom, but there is much we do not know and much we do not understand.

In the first chapter of Mark we read of Jesus walking on the lakeshore at Galilee and calling the disciples to journey with him. He comes across Simon and Andrew, absorbed in their own lives, and says, 'Come follow me'. Further on he sees the two brothers, James and John, and 'without delay' calls them too. Jesus invites his disciples to walk with him throughout his own journey. And, over their three years together, Jesus shares their lives intimately as they walk their own paths.

And Jesus calls to us, too, to walk in his company. This journey with Jesus is a great comfort to many people. It is a different way of starting and ending each day. It is a consciousness that as I go through my day, as I go through my life, I can be connected to God through his Spirit. There is a closeness, an intimacy, in journeying with Jesus as my friend and mentor. I believe all gay and lesbian people can develop their sexual identity while being a companion of Jesus. God loves us as much as any straight person and desires us to enter into the fullness of our humanity in the same way. God can be part of your journey, both the journey of sexual identity formation and the much bigger journey, living your life as a gay person. There is nothing to stop us from accepting his invitation. It is a journey of contact and connection with our loving God.

A method

The Way of Jesus is also a different method by which to live our lives and live out our faith. Jesus came to teach us that there is a different way to approach God, through relationship and intimacy. It is a way of love, of forgiveness, of compassion, of humility, of inclusivity. In fact, in his own time Jesus became infamous for his willingness to be with all types of people. No one was excluded. When we act as Jesus did, we are following God's way. This is what I believe Jesus meant when he said, 'No one can come to the Father except through me.' There is no other way to be in tune with God than by acting His way: through relationship, love, forgiveness, compassion, humility and inclusivity – being with and supporting the marginalised and the ordinary, those who do not possess great wealth or power, the vast majority of humanity. Jesus rejected no one at all. This is the Way of God and it is also the Way to God. Jesus showed us the Way by living the Way.

It is not the way of power, wealth, possessions and success; nor is it the church's traditional view of the sacred and righteous. Jesus was crucified precisely because he offended the religious leaders of his time and they manipulated the situation so that powerful Rome would execute him. It wasn't the Jews who killed Jesus, it was big religion collaborating with imperial power. Big religion, which did not understand that its rules were made for humanity, not humanity for the rules. Big religion, which did not understand that connection with God was about intimacy and relationship, not regulation and ritual. Big religion, which did not understand the importance of justice and fairness to the people. It was big religion that Jesus attacked vociferously in Matthew 23 when he described the religious leaders, the teachers of the law, as hypocrites, wicked, corrupt, selfish, ostent-atious, manipulative, pedantic, foolish, misguided, false, snakes and vipers. This Matthean account has no truck with the idea that it was always a 'gentle Jesus meek and mild'. Not even the Roman occupation of Judaea and the various political machinations of Herod could bring Jesus to this kind of anger. But where Jesus did get riled up, it was always over big religion and he didn't mince words.

Gay and lesbian Christians, having grown up in a straight world that is often heterosexist and homophobic, know what it feels like to be in a minority, to feel marginalised, to be on the receiving end of everything that Jesus is not: judgement, blame, unfairness, discrimination and exclusion. We know how difficult this is, and how painful. Gay people are well placed to follow Jesus. We are able to offer empathy and to stand with our neighbour in an often harsh and critical world in ways that straight people perhaps cannot.

A direction

Finally, the Way can be characterised as a path or a direction. When we are lost or confused, our greatest need is to find the path that takes us in a direction and gives us a destination far from loss and confusion. Jesus' way is such a path. It is about connection with the Spirit of God in daily life, a way to treat our fellow human beings, our brothers and sisters, a way to be ethical and just in our dealings, and a way to enter the fullness of our own humanity. It is a wonderful way of life for gay and lesbian people who have integrated their religious and sexual identities. I find this very attractive as a pathway though life.

The images of God

However, the traditional images of God taught by the church through-out the ages no longer make sense, and gay people have been badly burned by them. These images either state or imply that God is stern and punitive – usually an ancient, bearded, humourless judge-like figure, quick to anger, who needs to be propitiated in order for us to come anywhere near Him. Jesus' God is vastly different. As a consequence of Jesus' life and teaching, the way that all human beings relate to God has changed forever. Jesus presented new ways of envisioning God, and I want to make a few of them explicit.

God is personal

When I say that God is personal, I mean to distinguish my belief from some of the New Age suggestions that God is merely a force for good in the universe, a little like gravitational or electro-magnetic force. So many people have said to me that they don't believe in God, but that they do believe in *something*. This most often seems to be some kind of neutral, non-human, impersonal force, neither benevolent nor malevolent. Some people talk about God as 'the Universe' itself, or 'nature' or even 'existence'. Although I am drawn to the language describing God as existence – after all His ancient unspeakable name is said to be 'I Am Who I Am' – I do not see Jesus characterising God as a non-person.

Rather, Jesus portrays God as an aspect of his own character and indeed he himself as an aspect of God's own character. There is a person in and through all this. I believe that God is nothing like a human being, but cannot be less than a human being. And perhaps the greatest of human attributes is our consciousness. This gives us personality and idiosyncratic attributes; it makes us recognisable and consistent to others. Jesus shows us a personal God, a recognisable and consistent personality to whom we can relate.

God is love

This sounds like the greatest cliché of all. We've heard this one before so many times, haven't we? But this one small thought expresses such a wealth of meaning. Even the ancient people of Israel and the early Christians, who by our standards lived in a barbaric world, knew and wrote that the one and only God, the prime mover and agent of the universe, is a God whose nature, whose very essence, is love.

The people who consult me sometimes say that they are isolated and alone, that no one seems to care what they do, where they go, whether they live or die. Before I met my partner, everything I did was done alone as a non-partnered individual. I would go out for dinner or meetings or church gatherings and come home to an empty house. I lived this way for many lonely years. After I met my partner, one of the best things was that somebody else cared. These days, if I get home late from work, there is somebody who cares enough to be thinking, 'I wonder where he is? I hope he's okay.' When I am out in the garden on a hot summer's day, it feels wonderful when my partner brings me out a glass of ice-cold water. The water is refreshing, certainly, but it pales beside the fact that my partner has been thinking of my needs and cares enough to do that for me. It is the best feeling in the world.

This is how Jesus changed our view of God. He is not some distant pompous deity, uncaring and nonchalant about all human activity, but a person who deeply cares and who is deeply interested. In the infinite and exquisite wonder of God loving us, we can find it difficult to get our heads around the whole thing. James Alison takes it down a peg or two and suggests that we just try accepting that God *likes* us. Don't worry just for now about God loving you. Just go with God likes you. For me, this idea has been a great blessing. As I go about my daily work, it feels great to think that God not only loves me but actually likes me. To get a sense of this, think of yourself and your own best friend. It's easy to be in their company. You really like being around them. It feels safe, it feels close, there's a shared history, there's trust and reliability, there's companionship, food, fun and laughter. God likes you.

God is a loving father

There is no doubt in my mind, after a lifetime of reading and studying the Bible, that Jesus' pre-eminent characterisation of God is as a loving father. Now before we go any further, I want to say that I believe this and all other characterisations of God found in the Bible are metaphor. Human language is incapable of describing God, much less defining Him. I do not believe that God is even male, but is beyond human sex and gender. But Jesus does speak of God as his, and our, father – and a loving, caring father who desires only the best for His children.

Now I admit that there are some pretty lousy fathers out there and it is harder for the children of such men to identify with Jesus' vision. Still, although many earthly fathers are far from perfect, the good dads are not bad comparisons for what Jesus was trying to show us about God. First, fathers are protectors of their families. They will protect us in any way they can from harm done to us by others or by ourselves through our own sometimes less than wise choices. Second, a good father loves his children and wants only the best for them. He wants his children to succeed in life and develop into responsible, respectful adults who are capable of living life well. He wants his children to grow up and enjoy each of life's stages in the best possible way. He wants to share in his children's lives so that they can have a rich store of positive memories: of being held, played with, laughed with, learned with, run with and discovered with; there should be memories, too, of discussing, questioning and understanding, of loving and companionship.

The distress experienced by deeply wounded adults is very often caused by unmet childhood needs. Schema therapy, developed by Jeffrey Young, calls these early maladaptive schemas or EMS. Of the 18 EMS that have so far been identified, emotional deprivation is the one that seems to cause the most pain and difficulty later in life. It is where the child is deprived of emotional contact or presence from its parent or parents, sometimes called benign neglect. The child is not beaten or assaulted in any way; he or she is just ignored, invisible. The three areas of emotional deprivation we talk about are:

1. nurturance – the deprivation of affection or caring

2. empathy – the deprivation of listening or understanding

3. protection – the deprivation of strength or guidance from others.[8]

Deprivation in one or all of these areas sets up a way of dealing with the world that is maladaptive and repetitive in adulthood. Emotional deprivation is the direct opposite of the vision of God that Jesus tried to show us. He is not a God who is distant, uncaring and cold, but a God who is like a loving father. He wants to give his children the sense that they are loved and cared for and wanted. He wants to give them the sense that He is always on their side. He will always encourage and reassure them in times of self-doubt or confusion. In short, He wants the child to know that, as their dad,[9] He will always be there for them. He provides full nurturance, empathy and protection. I am blessed enough to have such an earthly dad, so it is relatively easy for me to know that if my own father can accept, love and value me the way I am, then surely the same is not beyond the capacity of God, who *is* love.

Jesus' best known parable, 'the prodigal son' in the 15th chapter of the Gospel of Luke, gives us a wonderful glimpse of God the way Jesus saw Him, as loving father. Many homilies about this story emphasise the son, but on this occasion, let's take a closer look at the character of the father.

In verse 20 it says that 'while he [the son] was still a long way off, his father saw him and was filled with compassion for him; he ran to his son, threw his arms around him and kissed him'. There is the sense here that the father was out looking for him or, at the very least, keeping a watchful eye out. The father is not filled with thoughts of retribution, duty, justice, or payment of debt or obligation. No, he forgets all that and is just filled with compassion. He runs towards his son. After the embrace and kisses and no doubt lots of tears from both of them, the son wants to list all the rotten things he has done and starts to beg forgiveness of his father. Now note what the father says in response to all this 'I'm so unworthy' and 'I'm not fit to be called your son' stuff – absolutely nothing. He shows no interest whatsoever and doesn't even bother addressing it. Instead he orders the servants to prepare a feast because he is so ecstatic that his son is home again, safe and sound, and close to him. This is the relational God as loving father that Jesus disclosed to us.

What Jesus did was to bring God close. He taught that the Kingdom of God was 'near us', 'at hand', even 'within us'. Jesus' Way makes God near and present. Jesus teaches that God is not interested in the old ways of sacrifice and propitiation, of codes and regulation. What He is interested in is you and me.

During his earthly life, Jesus emulated the nature of God in all he did and said. So when Jesus shares life with his disciples and includes all who come to him, that is what God is like. That is how God acts. To say that God is a loving and intimate presence for everyone in the world *except* gay people is a pernicious lie. God can no more go against His own nature than a gay person can become straight. God loves and includes gay people just as much as straight people.

It is impossible to believe that God would be so perverse as to reject a group of people because they are biologically and psychologically oriented to same-sex attraction. To accept such a proposition is to accept that, when faced with a gay individual, God becomes cold, rejecting, emotionally distant, pedantic about the keeping of rules and regulations and somehow reverts to the old stern, punitive judge. In short, it would mean that gay people cause God to change His nature. I don't think so!

Jesus and homosexuality

The fundamentalists, both Catholic and evangelical/Pentecostal, would have us believe that being gay is a deal breaker with God. If you're an out gay person, then you're not acceptable. Have you ever wondered, if the whole gay thing is of such magnitude to God and is of such fundamental importance theologically and morally, why it is that Jesus never dealt with the whole vexed matter explicitly? I can think of only one good answer to such a question. I don't think same-sex attracted people were an issue for Jesus, vexed or otherwise.

He would certainly have known such people existed. After all, he lived in Roman-occupied Palestine. The Romans permitted such sexual activity and understood that it was part of the way human sexuality manifested itself. They had unwritten codes of conduct regarding their own citizenry and same-sex sexual behaviour and their writings are replete with same-sex activity and relationships. Some very famous Roman people were known to have same-sex lovers. The nearest big town to Nazareth was Sepphoris, probably less than an hour's walk away, and Jesus no doubt spent a lot of time there growing up and would have encountered same-sex attracted people. The same thing probably applied when he was older and living in Capernaum. It does not take a great stretch of the imagination to believe that there were same-sex attracted Jews living around him. Jesus didn't live some holy, sanitised, cloistered life. He plied his trade as a joiner in the real world, so it is not impossible that he knew some gay people personally. I can only think that he didn't talk about this explicitly because it didn't much matter to him. If it were a burning issue, like some of the other things that he *did* teach about and where he challenged religious authority, surely we would have some record of it in the Gospel accounts.

Homosexuality is not like some of the other 'issues' that some people say Jesus never spoke about – embryonic stem cell research, nuclear energy, global warming, political systems. These are of a different order to homosexuality because they did not exist in his time. But homosexuality did exist in Jesus' time and was not uncommon. And yet, Jesus didn't pinpoint it as something that he had to speak about, teach about, do something special over or attend some special event about. There is no special Jesus moment regarding homosexuality equivalent to the Sermon on the Mount, the wedding feast at Cana or the raising of Lazarus. No, in fact, it is quite the opposite; there is nothing. Same-sex sexual activity and same-sex relationships were not on Jesus' agenda as an issue that had to be fixed, changed, dealt with or even mentioned. Victor Furnish, Professor of New Testament at a number of theological institutions, suggests that, given this total absence of reference in the Gospels, Jesus had nothing distinctive to say on the subject, nor was the issue a salient one for the early church,[10] among whose members were the authors of the four Gospels, covering some 60 or so years after Jesus' earthly life. This makes up almost the whole first century.

Thus, the notion of 'homosexuality as issue' appears to be discounted, but, as a plausible conjecture, I believe that there is one account in the Gospels in which it is credible to suggest that Jesus is dealing with what is quite possibly a same-sex loving relationship. I am perfectly happy to concede that I may be wrong here, but I am equally confident in saying that what you are about to read is entirely plausible and totally consistent with our knowledge of the ancient world, and of the actual text of the Gospels. In this account, Jesus does not say anything about homosexuality, or teach about it in any way, but we should take especial notice of his actions.

In the Gospels of Matthew (8: 5–13) and Luke (7: 1–9), we read about the Roman centurion who asked Jesus to heal his servant. The two narratives differ slightly in their recounting of the story. In Matthew, the centurion himself comes to Jesus to ask for help, while in Luke he sends some 'elders of the Jews' to ask him. Jesus is so impressed by this man that he speaks glowingly of him in the following superlative, 'I have not found anyone in Israel with such great faith' (Matthew 8: 10). There is a real distinction in Jesus' mind between the faith of this Gentile Roman, a soldier, a foreigner and an occupier no less, and the faith promulgated by the official Jewish teachers and authorities. At the end of the account the young servant is healed by Jesus of a condition that would otherwise have killed him. Let's take a closer look at some of the background to this event.

As a centurion, this man was the commander of 100 men. He therefore had a certain measure of authority and since the Roman legions were renowned for their discipline, he would have been deeply respected by his troops. In both versions the centurion says, 'For I myself am a man under authority, with soldiers under me. I tell this one "Go", and he goes; and that one "Come", and he comes. I say to my servant, "Do this", and he does it' (Matthew 8: 9). Apparently, this centurion, unusually, was somewhat of a benefactor to Capernaum. The version in Luke has the messengers tell Jesus, 'This man deserves to have you do this, because he loves our nation and has built our synagogue' (Luke 7: 4–5).

The next thing to understand is that most Roman campaigns lasted for a number of years, so soldiers, centurions and even generals were often away from home, hearth and family for extended periods of time. It was not uncommon for certain Roman soldiers or leaders who were so inclined, to have sexual relations with a young male slave who might be part of their personal retinue. In such circumstances, such sexual behaviour was probably mostly just physical. From time to time, though, Roman centurions, leaders and even generals would fall in love with their servants and grow to care for them greatly.[11] It is a distinct possibility that this is what occurred between our centurion and his very ill young servant.

In both accounts, the English word 'servant' is used – four times in each. In some instances, the Gospel writer uses the word, in other places the centurion himself speaks about his servant. In the ancient Greek in which these passages were written, two entirely distinct words are used for this single English word 'servant'. The common Greek word for a slave or a servant, transliterated into English, is *doulos*. Both Gospels use this word when the writer himself is telling the story, but the centurion himself uses a different word altogether, *pais*, which signifies 'a child', 'a servant', 'a son' or 'a young man'. It refers to someone young and is always a term of great endearment from an adult. Webster's original dictionary translated *pais* as 'a dear one', 'a lover' or 'a sweetheart'. The centurion refers only to this particular servant as *pais*; all the others he refers to as *doulos*. Exactly the same distinction is made in Luke's account. In both Gospel accounts, there is something very special about this young man. The Gospel of Luke adds one more detail that we don't get in Matthew. In Luke 7: 2, in the NIV, we read, 'There [in Capernaum] a centurion's servant, *whom his master valued highly,* was sick and about to die.' It is interesting to examine the Greek for the italicised phrase. Many versions translate it as 'who was dear to him'. Here is the original Greek and a literal English translation:

os	*en*	*auto*	*entimos*
who	was	to him	dear
			highly regarded
			precious

We can tell that the centurion was not talking about his son, because both Luke and Matthew have this young man listed as one of the servants, the *douloi*. However, Luke says that this young man was *entimos* to the centurion. So what does this mean? Does it mean valuable? Given that the centurion was wealthy – after all, he had built the town's synagogue – he could easily have gone off to the traders to buy a new servant should the young man die, so reading *entimos* this way is not a reliable interpretation, especially in the light of the centurion's use of the word *pais*. Could it mean 'highly regarded' as a clever and useful slave? Probably not, since he is described as young and would not have been highly experienced. Finally, *entimos* could mean precious in the sense of an emotional bond, and I think this is the most likely meaning, given the nature of the words used. *Entimos* is generally rendered 'dear' or 'precious', both literally and emotionally, just as we use the word 'dear' in two ways today. In the rough Roman military world there would not be many tears shed over the death of a slave, unless there were something very special about him. This young man and his master were probably lovers. This centurion was most assuredly not the first Roman soldier to have had a young male lover, but he does appear to be the only one mentioned in the Christian Bible.

Now we need to take a look at how Jesus deals with this situation. First, as we have seen, he is astonished at the centurion's faith. Second, he commends the centurion with that amazingly generous 'I haven't come across faith like this anywhere in Israel' superlative that I cited earlier. Thirdly, he agrees to go to his house to heal the young man. There is no exclusion here. If we accept for now that my interpretation of the account is true, then nowhere does Jesus appear to be astonished or shocked or scandalised by this man's personal life. Quite the contrary; Jesus remains composed and in emotional equilibrium throughout the whole encounter. Like the Gospel writers reporting the event decades later, he focuses on the man's faith and understanding of the Kingdom of God, not on any sexual behaviour or status. So, going out on a limb, but, I think, a safe enough one, I would suggest that Jesus was not disturbed by same-sex attraction, which is probably why he never said anything about it.

Sexual desire and authentic spirituality

Let me briefly say something about the relationship between sexual desire and spiritual life. The first thing to note is that, as we saw in Chapter 11, sexuality and spirituality are not incompatible or mutually exclusive. You don't have to make a choice between the sacred and the carnal. The traditional church teaching is that the carnal, which just means 'of or pertaining to the body' (from the Latin, *carnalis,* for body or flesh), is sinful, dirty and needs to be repudiated. Typically it is compared with the spiritual and characterised as inferior in every way. It is even described as being anti-God.

Yet sexual desire in all its manifestations, from soft tenderness to the heat of passionate 'grunt-type' sex, and everything in between, is a part of how God has designed us. It is an essential part of our humanity and fundamental to our existence. After the imperative to survive, our sexual drive is probably the strongest and most elemental. If anything is *contra naturam*, against nature, it is the willing abnegation of the self as a sexual being. And we do this to great insult to the human psyche. This is surely not what God intends for us.

Second, it is important to know that you can be sexual *and* be spiritual. In fact, I think that each can be a part of the other. Why do I believe this? Because I believe the essential message of Jesus, that he came to give us life so that we may have it more abundantly. And sex is part of life.

Abundant life means entering fully into one's humanity. It is to be willing to engage with our humanity (plural) and my humanity (singular), connecting with the vastness of the human race in all of its manifestations, its strengths, weaknesses and potentialities, but also, to live an authentic personal life where self-engagement with my own personality, temperament, intellect, body and sexuality is evolving and valued. This is spiritual. Let me repeat Daniel Helminiak's words: 'acknowledgement of truth, any acknowledgement of truth, is a spiritual act'. My desire and my sexual identity make up the very fabric of my humanity. As a gay person, my authentic sexuality is same-sex directed and this is part of the very foundation of who I am. This is how it needs to be; an acknowledgement of my fundamental sexual desire; something to be valued, esteemed and developed. Such an acknowledgement goes to the very heart of what it means to enter fully into our humanity for gay people, or to use Jesus' words, to have abundant living.

Authentic spirituality is the recognition that there is something other than us. Spirituality comes before religion. It is the elemental force of human nature, the drive to reach out to that which is beyond. Religion, with its focus on transcendence, can offer quite specific ways to do this, but it is not the only way. Every time I stretch myself to know or understand something new and fresh, I engage in a spiritual act. Every time I move out of my comfort zone to attempt something unfamiliar, I engage in a spiritual act. Every time I learn something that I did not know before, I engage in the spiritual life. Every time I love someone or reach out to another person, I undertake a spiritual act. These things take me beyond myself.

When I fall in love, or commit myself to a relationship, I move beyond myself. As a gay man, when I make love to my partner, I do so in full acceptance of myself, having made the journey of gay identity formation to self-acceptance – a vast spiritual act in itself. I reach beyond to my partner and accept him in ways that only sexual love can express; it is a connection that can be profoundly spiritual yet is utterly human.

Just as our temperament and personality as well as our intelligence and education colour the way we see the world, so, for those of us who are gay, with a fully realised gay self-identity, does our sexual orientation. Such self-awareness and self-acceptance is to be encouraged and admired for it is in this engagement with our sexuality and our 'gay' way of viewing the world that we seek to enter our full humanity. This is spiritual. It is entering in to who I am and what I can become. If I am following the Way of Jesus, I can do this with him as my companion, pointing me to the Spirit of God.

If you're gay and you've never done so before, take some time out to thank God for being gay, to thank God for allowing you this wonderful, different view of what life can be about. Take a moment to think about how incredible it has been for you to walk the road of gay identity formation and, in so doing, to become involved in the great questions of life, like, who am I? what is this all about? what purpose is there in all this? among many others, and to do all this in your late teens, 20s and 30s, perhaps decades before straight people typically do so. Start to think of your own spiritual journey of constant learning, stretching, becoming, all through the eyes of being a gay person.

Some logical questions

I want to take a brief moment before finishing off to refer to a couple of thoughts that I think are also important. You see, certain beliefs demand certain logical consequences about the nature of God, and so for me, most of the statements from the Christian church pertaining to gay sexuality imply certain things about God, things that are not consistent with the loving, relational God of whom Jesus spoke. So let me just specify a few of these for you.

How does the traditional church explain the presence of gay and lesbian people? Where do we come from? Given that the church has always viewed God as creator, then does it not follow that gay people were created also, since we are definitely here? If that is the case, then the traditional teaching is very obviously false. If what God creates is good, and the author of the great creation myth in Genesis tells us this no less than seven times, then gay people are to be seen as good too. Or are only gay people exempt from God's good creative act? This demands an answer. As Psalm 139 says,

For You formed my inward parts;
You wove me in my mother's womb.
I will give thanks to You, for I am fearfully and
    wonderfully made;
Wonderful are Your works,
And my soul knows it very well.
My frame was not hidden from You,
When I was made in secret,
And skilfully wrought in the depths of the earth;
Your eyes have seen my unformed substance;
And in Your book were all written
The days that were ordained for me,
When as yet there was not one of them.

Does this beautiful language refer only to heterosexual people? Gays need not apply?

But then some traditionalists suggest that gay people are a result of sin in the world. They appear to be saying that God's creative act is spoiled in some people, so that their existence is not good. This doesn't say much about the wonder of God's creation, does it? In fact, it seems that God's creation is pretty easily spoiled, given the number of gay and lesbian people there are and have been throughout history. It also says much about the willingness of the people who say such things to be comfortable judging other people's hearts – an action expressly forbidden by Jesus.

This position also suggests that God is prepared to allow approximately 5 per cent of the human population to be born gay, and then to judge them and find them wanting. Can this be true? Does God act that way? It doesn't seem very fair, given that no one chooses to be gay. This is hardly a picture of a God of justice, or of the loving God that Jesus showed us. This picture of God also suggests, disturbingly, that He is capricious, toying with gay people's lives. Is He, after all, a copy of the image at the end of King Lear: 'As flies to wanton boys are we to the gods. They kill us for their sport'?

Of course, the traditionalists would counter and say that God *did* create all humanity as good, but in our sinfulness and selfishness, we gay people turned our backs on Him and chose instead a life that is forever against Him. But we no more reject God than anyone else does who is seeking to follow Jesus. Moreover, this 'gays-are-sinners' position is based on outdated, erroneous and literal interpretations of Scriptural passages that can only be applied to us by bigots or those who are just plain ignorant. These old judgemental and patently prejudiced interpretations simply cannot bear the scrutiny of modern scholarship as applied to 21st century gay and lesbian people who are not involved in cultic sexual worship or cruel and disrespectful sexual practices.

This particular view of God is simply not consistent with the God Jesus himself spoke about. And the millions of people who used to belong to the church and have since walked away, have done so very largely because the church insisted on that older view of God: a short-fused judge quick to punish, who needs a blood sacrifice in order to be paid off if we are to be in his good books. There are copious amounts of good theology out there that frames this conversation in different language. You ministers of the church need to engage with it.

To the clergy

Finally, a word to all the clergy, priests, religious, ministers, youth pastors, choir leaders, church leaders and others in positions of authority within the church who have been open-minded enough to stay with me over the course of this book. I want to take a moment to remind you that, as much as anyone else, gay and lesbian people need the direction, purpose and meaning in their lives that Christian faith brings. If you are straight, please understand that they are the same as you in almost every way, except for the direction of their physical and emotional attraction. Their orientation is part of their being. It is not an added extra. It is not something they can choose today and eschew tomorrow. It cannot be erased, denied or prayed away any more than your own sexuality can be. They do not need to repent of it, much less deny it. The loving God to whom Jesus introduced us does not call gay people to do any of that. Such a life is misery beyond compare. God is not into torturing His children – and neither should you be.

It is no use in theologising something that is not theology. We can theologise that the world is the centre of the universe, as implied and understood by the scriptures, as we all used to hundreds of years ago, but none of that changes the fact that it is not. We have learned better. We can theologise that the world is only 6000 years old, as we used to, but none of that will change the fact that it is not. We have learned better. Today we understand that God and science are not mutually exclusive and that we have been able to accommodate newer understandings of the world we live in, from the perspectives of both science and biblical studies. And, for Catholic clergy, we need to do the same with church teaching.

I call on you to do exactly the same concerning human sexuality. I am not asking you to accept the disrespectful or the harmful, but I am asking you to accept the fact that approximately 95 per cent of the human population is heterosexually oriented and approximately 5 per cent is homosexually oriented. It is also a fact that sexuality is not something that is chosen individually. No amount of theologising will make it otherwise. We have learned better.

So you need to stop blaming gay people for their sexuality and accept that our modern epistemology has taught us something newer and more truthful. You need to stop trying to put God into an older framework where He must reject and punish His gay and lesbian children. This is *not* what God is about. Modernity has wiped away for all time a perverse dark ages mentality that sex is dirty, that everyone should be straight and that those of us who are not are sick and sinful. There have always been gay people. Christianity has not erased same-sex attraction from the earth in 2000 years, and it never will. There will always be gay people. You need to start accepting them for who they are and help them in accepting themselves.

One of the wonderful movements in the church today is the acceptance by ordinary people of gay and lesbian brothers and sisters in the community of faith. Some churches experience the great benefit of these people ministering to them as part of the liturgy. Let's recall the amazing account in the Book of Acts, chapters 10 and 11, about Peter in the household of Cornelius. Let me go to the punch-line first and then backtrack. If God is already blessing gay people, then who are you to deny them?

When, in a vision, God tells Peter to eat unclean animals, he is horrified. His response, 'Surely not, Lord! I have never eaten anything impure or unclean,' resonates with dogma, religious rule and intransigence. Yet God's message to him on that rooftop is clarion clear: 'There is no exclusion in me. My invitation is to all.' Peter's religious rules and regulations didn't mean a jot in the light that God had already acted by blessing the Gentile people in Cornelius' household, contrary to the religious rules of the time. This single act, perhaps more than any other outside of Jesus' own work, irrevocably changed the face and direction of Christianity. And it was God who initiated it. His invitation to relationship is open to everyone.

I have been privileged to walk in the Way of Jesus as a gay man for over 20 years. I have never once felt that God has abandoned me in any way, let alone rejected me. On the contrary, my experience of God now is closer than it has ever been. I love the fact that we don't know it all, that we can enter into that search for meaning with Jesus as our companion. Some of those I know who are closest to God are gay people. Let not the church reject those whom God accepts.

I urge you, men and women leaders of the church, to stop asking the impossible of gay people. Stop asking them to deny themselves. Stop telling them to repent. Stop perpetuating a sin consciousness within them. Don't lay this guilt trip of 'love the sinner but hate the sin' stuff on them. It is grossly unfair. Start accepting that God created them too. Start to celebrate their dignity and wonderful attributes. Start to acknowledge that they can bring great gifts into the family of God. Start valuing them. Start standing up for them. Start to get acquainted with more recent scholarship in biblical studies and theology. Speak out. You've got a great conversation but you need to have it in a different way.

To my gay and lesbian brothers and sisters

Well, this certainly has been a journey, hasn't it? Thank you for staying with me to the end. I have tried to help you understand that it is not only okay to be gay and Christian, but that it is wonderful to be gay and Christian. You don't need me to tell you how rewarding and satisfying it is to be a follower of the Way of Jesus. Many of you have probably experienced that deep and abiding feeling, the sense that following Jesus speaks right to our hearts.

But it is a call to live in a way that is entirely different from the rest of the world's power structures and values; a call into minority status. It is a call to emulate Jesus in our life, to include everyone, to allow others to lean on us, to understand that the Spirit of God is still upon the earth breathing His life in and through us. It is a permanent call to love. You remember the words in John 13: 34-35, 'A new commandment, I give to you: Love one another. *As I have loved you*, so you must love one another.' And *how* did Jesus love us? He loved us to the point of emptying Himself. Such a life is not easy. But it is the Way of Jesus.

The Way of Jesus is not the same thing as the institutional church. Very often you can find the Spirit of God in the church, but sometimes you cannot. One of my cancer patients spoke to me three weeks before his death about his love for the great Renaissance artists. With tears in his eyes he described a beautiful, full-sized replica of Michelangelo's Pietà in St Mary's Cathedral in Sydney. But then he said that he felt closest to God out under the trees in Hyde Park: 'That's my cathedral. That's my cathedral.' Your relationship with God is not contingent on church membership or acceptance by church authorities. If it were, then none of us would be in relationship with God. It's not a happy thing to say, but it is the truth. The Christian church has been hopelessly wrong about us ever since it started talking about us. So it's important to know that your relationship with and to God is between you and God, not between you and God as mediated by the institutional church. No, our living and moving in the Spirit of God is bound only to our acceptance of God's open invitation to all.

Being gay can be a great blessing in so many ways. There is a 'family' of gay people with whom we can feel at home. We love our fun, our laughter, our meeting up with each other, our stories, our conversation and our shared histories of identity formation. This can build such a strong bond. But our minority sexuality status also allows us to see through the so-called normality of the straight world, where the gender order is accepted as being natural, where alpha males so often run the world, where success is measured in how much money you've got, where acquisitiveness is expected, where governments spin their way out of trouble and don't deal with the real needs of the people, and where church seems to spiral further and further away from meeting people's spiritual hunger.

Our minority status gives eyes to see and ears to hear. Using a different kind of language, gay people can play a prophetic role within the world and the church. They can bring their strength and wisdom to the Christian life in a unique way. I refer to Michael Kelly for a few of the following points.[12]

Through our lives and loves, as citizens, community members, members of local neighbourhoods, working in our professions and occupations, we can be a witness to the church that we are here, that the church cannot merely wish away our sexual orientation and that our lives have the same normality and needs as those of the straight world – and that our lives and loves are to be valued, celebrated and nurtured. Living well as a gay person rejects imposed shame utterly.

Second, as gay Christians, we can also show the gay world what is life-affirming, positive and nurturing to people. We can offer alternative ways to young gay people who, like their straight counterparts, sometimes look to drugs and alcohol as a way to numb the pain or to experience the freedom of youth. We may be able to offer a different voice that can assist with the longing for togetherness, connectivity and companionship in a less destructive way. We may also be able to offer a greater understanding of the family of humanity as distinct from biological family. Jesus spoke about this in the Gospels (Mark 3: 32–34).

We can also offer the church a new way of looking at human desire, sexuality and sensuality – and by that I mean *all* human desire and its expressions. We can help to bring the church's views out of the dark ages and show it that there is nothing to fear in desire, in touch, in lovemaking (for all kinds of reasons), and that none of this is ungodly, or profane, or non-spiritual. The church has much to learn from us here, and much to make up for.

Gay Christians are expert in understanding the lived experience, and when we combine that self-awareness with our faith, this can be a powerful gift to the church. With so much theologising and theorising in the seminaries, houses of formation and Bible colleges, the world of the lived experience has much to say to the church in correcting, in refining and in organising thought to help ask the right questions. It is in the messiness of human life that the Spirit lives with us.

We can help the church let go of its inflexibility, its rigidity, its sometimes dictatorial control over the lives of its people. We know that there are many imponderables, many grey areas, and that 'the search' and 'the quest' are grand metaphors for the Christian life, a life lived in the chaos of an often cruel world, in the darkness, fear and despair that life sometimes brings, and in the ineradicable mystery that is being human.

As a minority, gay people know what it is like to be marginalised. We can help to remind the church of other marginalised people and to never let it forget that it was among such people that Jesus mostly lived his life. There is great humanity and wisdom in the marginalised. Gay Christians can augment the church's already strong sense of social justice.

Further, many gay people are very creative and tend to be well represented in the arts. With our creativity and sense of humour, we can bring our gifts and talents to the church's music, art, literature, devotions and its liturgies. We can offer the church much that is beautiful and much that is fun.

Finally, we can offer a great deal in the way of Christian leadership. Our call to the pastoral life of the church is as obvious as it is historic. There have always been gay priests, bishops, ministers and preachers, and since some more enlightened churches are now ordaining women as local ministers and bishops, there will obviously be an increase in lesbian leadership too. Perhaps through our recognition that so many people need healing and wholeness, and our acknowledgement that our own personal journey has so often been a difficult one, as mostly the journeys of the marginalised are, we can offer empathy, comfort, solace, wisdom and empowerment to the people of God in a different way than straight pastors.

Being gay is great. We can sometimes lose sight of that, can't we? Especially when or if we've been fighting church authorities, or even worse, when we've been at war with ourselves over our faith and our sexuality. Never forget, God loves you. Jesus came to the earth to show you the Way, just as he did for everybody else. And that Way is not about denying who you are, your intrinsic self. Please know and understand that the God of love accepts you, though many in the church may reject you. You are greatly loved. (He even likes you.)

Certainly, I want the church to change and yes, I would like the church to read this book, but most of all, it is for you. I want you to learn to be comfortable in your sexuality and comfortable in your faith. I want you to be able to successfully walk the road of sexual and religious identity integration. Both science and modern biblical and theological scholarship support you in this endeavour. And it is only blind prejudice and tradition that would repudiate it.

You must not allow any church authority figure to demean you or reject you, especially if he or she is doing it in God's name. Such behaviour is reprehensible and should be named as such. Don't let the church frighten you or cajole you back into the closet to live the life-lie. You know where that leads. Instead, you must gather around you like-minded gay people of faith: if there are none in your church, then you need to find some in other groups. Don't be alone. Don't stay isolated. Reach out to the family of gay people of faith. They are out there. You just need to find them.

An ending

I want to finish with a personal story. My own journey has been long and often very difficult. I have been involved with the church and with faith my entire life, even in those years when I placed God on the shelf in order to get some help regarding my own sexuality. After Easter, the two disciples walking on the Emmaus road were companions of Jesus, only they didn't know it. Sometimes Jesus walks our journey with us and we don't recognise him. I believe that God has been with me the whole time and has never left me for a second.

My story took me through a childish faith of pre-critical naïveté and then into a minor seminary for three years living in a monastery as a committed Catholic, to a revelation of God in the mainstream Protestant churches with their Bibles, their music and their individual appropriation of the Gospel message, to Pentecostal renewal and the gifts of the spirit, to being one of the founders of an independent charismatic church,[13] all the while denying the sexuality in which God had brought me into this world and, as a result, living in torment and loneliness. Then I lost all my friends and social support, and put God to one side while I began to learn to accept myself, like myself and even love myself, only to have God burst back into my consciousness as though He had never left. And studying psychology and working with people in need has helped me how to better understand human nature and behaviour and to hone my skills of thinking and analysis. I'm quite sure it's helped me understand myself better too. What a journey it's been. It took me a long time to find out I was okay. So there you have it: an ex-Catholic, ex-Protestant, Christian gay psychologist telling you that you're okay too.

Your own journey may be as long as mine or less meandering, but I hope and pray you find the place where your sexuality is a blessing and not a curse and where you understand deep within yourself that the Way of Jesus is for you, not against you. May God's richest blessings be upon you now and in all the journeyings of your life. And may you revel in your sexuality, as straight people get to do, and in your faith.

Don't ever think, even for a moment, that your sexuality separates you from God. I finish with a text from the Bible. It is from St Paul to the Romans (8: 38–39). In it, he is trying to get people to understand that there is *absolutely nothing at all* that can separate us from God's love. It is powerful language and it is meant for you too. God loves you and celebrates the day when his 'good' creative act made you and brought you into His world gay.

> For I am convinced that neither death, nor life, nor angels, nor rulers, nor things present, nor things to come, nor powers, nor anything above, nor anything below, nor anything else in all creation can separate us from the love of God that is ours in Christ Jesus, our Lord.

Notes

Foreword

1. Leviticus 20: 13.
2. M.D. Kirby (2011), 'The Sodomy Offence: England's Least Lovely Criminal Law Export?', *Journal of Commonwealth Criminal Law*, 1, p. 22.
3. Crimes Act 1900 (NSW), SS.79-81 ('Unnatural Offences').
4. Read, for example, Gary Gibbs (2005), *Homosexuality – Return to Sodom*, Roseville, CA: Amazing Facts Inc.; E.G. White (2001), *The Great Controversy Between Christ and Satan*, Pilgrim Books, 2nd ed.
5. Alfred Kinsey et al (1948), *Sexual Behaviour in the Human Male*, Philadelphia: W.B. Saunders; A. Kinsey et al (1953), *Sexual Behaviour in the Human Female*, Philadelphia: W.B. Saunders.
6. Leesha McKenny, 'Same-sex marriage will lead to polygamy, says Jensen', *Sydney Morning Herald*, 11 June 2011, p. 5.
7. Ibid.
8. The Roman Catholic Church in Sydney is reportedly no different. See L. McKenny, 'Catholic church that opens its arms to gays divides parishioners', *Sydney Morning Herald*, 4 June 2011, p. 3.
9. For a fuller report, A.M. Potts, 'Same-sex marriage "inevitable"', *Sydney Star Observer*, 8 June 2011, p. 1.
10. Including the story of my own life. See A.J. Brown (2011), *Michael Kirby: Paradoxes/Principles*, Sydney: Federation Press, pp. 84ff.
11. United Nations, High Level Meeting in the General Assembly on HIV/Aids, *Declaration of Commitment*, adopted 10 June 2011.
12. United Nations, Human Rights Council, 'Resolution on Sexual Orientation and Gender Identity', Geneva, 17 June 2011.
13. Earlier on 7 June 2011 at the Forty-First General Assembly of the Organisation of American States, all of the countries of the Americas and the Caribbean adopted a resolution condemning discrimination against people on the grounds of sexual orientation and gender identity. They did so despite lobbying by the Holy See.
14. Gary Bouma (2007), *Australian Soul: Religion and Spirituality in Twenty-First Century Australia*, Cambridge: Cambridge University Press; reviewed in *Sociology of Religion* (2009), p. 496.
15. There are other writers in the same genre, including Steven Ogden (2011), *Love Upside Down*, Winchester: O Books; Steven Ogden (2009), *I Met God In Bermuda – Faith in the 21st Century*, Winchester: O Books; Anthony W. Bartlett (2011), *Virtually Christian*, Winchester: O Books.

16. On 21 June 2011, it was reported by AFP that the Anglican Church in the United Kingdom would 'update its rules' to allow celibate openly homosexual clergy to be consecrated as bishops. See 'Choosing Bishops – The Equality Act 2010', reported in *The Australian*, 21 June 2011, p. 9.

Chapter 2

1. Epistemology. (n.d.). *Dictionary.com Unabridged (v 1.1)*. Retrieved December 21, 2007, from Dictionary.com website: http://dictionary.reference.com/browse/epistemology

2. Being omniscient, surely God would have known, even before He created him, that Adam was going to need a partner and created them both at the same time? The text reads as though God only just came to this realisation after all the animals marched past Adam and 'no suitable helper was found' (Genesis 2.20). Had God thought that perhaps there might have been a suitable helper among the animals? Had He been unsure and needed to have them march past just to make certain? I say this not to be satirical about God – far from it – but to indicate that the text itself suggests metaphor rather than literalism. Otherwise we are left with a non-omniscient God figure in the story.

3. Using http://www.ibiblio.org/lunarbin/worldpop and retrieved on 14 June 2010, this figure was derived by taking 5 per cent (the estimate of how many gay and lesbian people there at any given time statistically) of the world population calculated for this day using the logarithmic equation on this website.

Chapter 4

1. A.M. Johnson, C.H. Mercer, B. Erens et al. (2001), 'Sexual behaviour in Britain: Partnerships, practices and HIV risk behaviours', *The Lancet*, 358, pp.1835–42; B. Erens, S. McManus, A. Prescott et al. (2003), *National Survey of sexual attitudes and lifestyles II. Reference tables and summary reports*, London: National Centre for Social Research; B. Traeen, H. Stigum and D. Sorensen (2002), 'Sexual diversity among urban Norwegians', *Journal of Sex Research*, 39, pp. 249–58; N. Dickson, C. Paul and P. Herbison (2003), 'Same-sex attraction in a birth cohort: Prevalence and persistence in early adulthood', *Social Science and Medicine*, 56, pp. 1607–15.

2. G. Wilson and Q. Rahman (2005), *Born Gay. The Psychobiology of Sex Orientation*, London: Peter Owen.

3. R.C. Lewontin, S. Rose and L.J. Kamin (1984), *Not in Our Genes: Biology, ideology, and human nature*. New York: Pantheon.

4. J.P. De Cecco and J.P. Elia (1993), *If you seduce a straight person,*

can you make them gay?: Issues in biological essentialism versus social constructionism in gay and lesbian identities, New York: Haworth Press, p. 7.

5. Ibid., p. 8.

Chapter 5

1. Wilson and Rahman, *Born Gay*.
2. R.C. Pillard and J.D. Weinrich (1986), 'Evidence of familial nature of male homosexuality', *Archives of General Psychiatry*, 43, pp. 808–12.
3. R.C. Pillard and J.M. Bailey (1998), 'Human sexual orientation has a heritable component', *Human Biology*, 70, pp. 347–65.
4. J.M. Bailey et al. (1999), 'A family history study of male sexual orientation using three independent samples', *Behavior Genetics*, 29, pp. 79–86.
5. J.M. Bailey and B.A. Benishay (1993), 'Familial aggregation of female sexual orientation', *American Journal of Psychiatry*, 150, pp. 272–7; A.M.L. Pattatucci and D.H. Hamer (1995), 'Development and familiarity of sexual orientation in females', *Behavior Genetics*, 25, pp. 407–20.
6. J.M. Bailey and R.C. Pillard (1991), 'A genetic study of male sexual orientation', *Archives of General Psychiatry*, 48, pp. 1089–1096.
7. E.L. Whitam, M. Diamond and J. Martin (1993), 'Homosexual orientation in twins: A report on 61 pairs and 3 sets of triplets', *Archives of Sexual Behavior*, 22, pp. 187–206.
8. J.M. Bailey and A.P. Bell (1993), 'Familiarity of female and male homosexuality', *Behavior Genetics*, 23, pp. 313–22.
9. K.M. Kirk, J.M. Bailey, M.P. Dunne and N.G. Martin, N. G. (2000), 'Measurement models for sexual orientation in a community twin sample', *Behavior Genetics*, 30, pp. 345–56.
10. D.H. Hamer, S. Hu, V.L. Magnuson, N. Hu and A.M.L. Pattatucci (1993), 'A linkage between DNA markers on the X chromosome and male sexual orientation', *Science*, 261, pp. 321–7.
11. S. Hu et al. (1995), 'Linkage between sexual orientation and chromosome Xq28 in males but not in females', *Nature Genetics*, 11, pp. 248–56.
12. A.R. Sanders et al (1998), Poster presentation 149, annual meeting of American Psychiatric Association, Toronto, Canada.
13. R. Blanchard and A.F. Bogaert (1996), *American Journal of Psychiatry*, 153, pp. 27–31.
14. D.A. Puts, C.L. Jordan and S.M. Breedlove (2006), 'O brother, where art thou? The fraternal birth-order effect on male sexual orientation', *Proceedings of the National Academy of Sciences*, 103, pp. 10531–2.
15. Wilson and Rahman, *Born Gay*, p. 108.

16. D.F. Swaab and M.A. Hofman (1990), 'An enlarged suprachiasmatic nucleus in homosexual men', *Brain Research*, 537, pp. 141–8.

17. S. LeVay (1991), 'A difference in hypothalamic structure between heterosexual and homosexual men', *Science*, 253, pp. 1034–47.

18. W. Byrne et al. (2001), 'The interstitial nuclei of the human anterior hypothalamus: An investigation of variation with sex, sexual orientation and HIV status', *Hormones and Behavior*, 40, pp. 86–92.

Chapter 6

1. A.C. Kinsey, W.B. Pomeroy and C.E. Martin (1948), *Sexual Behavior in the Human Male*, Philadelphia: W.B. Saunders.

2. http://abcnews.go.com/2020/Story?id = 277685&page = 4

3. The Kinsey profile is not the only formulation proposed for identification of orientation. There are other methods, notably, the Klein Sexual Orientation Grid (KSOG) where seven factors are investigated: sexual attraction, sexual behaviour, sexual fantasies, emotional preference, social preference, self-identification, hetero/gay lifestyle: F. Klein, B. Sepekoff and T.J. Wolf (1985), 'Sexual orientation: A multi-variable dynamic process', *Journal of Homosexuality*, 11, 1/2, pp. 35–49.

4. R. Stevens (ed.) (1996), *Understanding the Self*, The Open University, UK: Sage Publications.

5. Bisexuality is another orientation, whose actual existence has been debated in research circles. It is another topic altogether and far too complicated to discuss in a mere footnote.

6. With one exception: most straight male teens find it quite important from time to time to ensure that their peers know that they are straight. Because being gay is still relatively unacceptable in many teen circles, various serial demonstrations of straight orientation, either in word or deed, are commonplace. In other words, while it is not so important to prove that you're straight when you're a teenager, it is important if the occasion should arise to prove that you're not gay.

7. Every year I teach counselling skills for sexual issues to medical students at my local university. In the role-play training, I invariably have to remind students to enquire after their patient's partner's name before they start using gender-specific pronouns: most just assume the partner is of the opposite sex. In real life, this is not always the case.

8. V.C. Cass (1984), ' Homosexual identity: A concept in need of definition, in J. P. De Cecco and M. G. Shively (eds), *Bisexual and Homosexual Identities : Critical theoretical issues*, New York: Haworth Press.

9. M.J. Eliason (1996), 'Identity formation for lesbians, bisexual and gay persons: Beyond a "minoritizing" view', *Journal of Homosexuality*, 30, 3, pp. 31–58.

Chapter 7

1. A. Marshall (1995), *Together Forever?*, London: Pan Books.

Chapter 8

1. J. Boswell (1980), *Christianity, Social Tolerance and Homosexuality*, Chicago: University of Chicago Press.

2. R. Trumbach (1991), 'London's sapphist: From three sexes to four genders in the making of modern culture', in J. Epstein and K. Straub (eds), *Body Guards: The culture and politics of gender ambiguity*, pp. 112–41, London: Routledge.

3. E. Jones (1957), *Sigmund Freud: Life and work*, (Vol. 3), pp. 208–09, London: Hogarth.

4. J. C. Gonsiorek (1991), 'The empirical basis for the demise of the illness model of homosexuality' in J. C. Gonsiorek and J. D. Weinrich (eds), *Homosexuality: Research implications for public policy*, pp. 115–36, California: Sage Publications.

5. Western Psychological Services products web page: http://portal.wpspublish.com/portal/page?_pageid = 53,69421&_dad = portal&_schema = PORTAL

6. E. Hooker (1957), 'The Adjustment of the Male Overt Homosexual', *Journal of Projective Techniques*, 21, pp. 18–31.

7. 'Reflections of a 40 year exploration: A scientific view on homosexuality', comments by Evelyn Hooker on receiving an award from the American Psychological Association in 1992. http://psyweb2.ucdavis.edu/rainbow/html/hooker_address.html

8. Gonsiorek, 'The empirical basis for the demise of the illness model of homosexuality'.

9. R.B. Dean and H. Richardson (1964), 'Analysis of MMPI profiles of forty college-educated overt male homosexuals', *Journal of Consulting Psychology*, 28, 6, pp. 483–6.

10. R.K. Turner, H. Pielmaier, S. James and A. Orwin (1974), 'Personality characteristics of male homosexuals referred for aversion therapy: A comparative study', *British Journal of Psychology*, 125, pp. 447–9.

11. W.G. Miller (1963), 'Characteristics of homosexually-involved incarcerated females', *Journal of Consulting Psychology*, 27, p. 227; E.L. Ohlson and M. Wilson (1974), 'Differentiating female homosexuals from female heterosexuals by use of the MMPI', *Journal of Sex Research*, 10, pp. 308–15.

12. M. Siegelman (1972b), 'Adjustment of male homosexuals and heterosexuals', *Archives of Sexual Behavior*, 2, pp. 9–25.

13. M. Siegelman (1978), 'Psychological adjustment of homosexual and heterosexual men: A cross-national replication', *Archives of Sexual Behavior*, 7, 1, pp. 1–11.

14. M. Siegelman (1972a), 'Adjustment of homosexual and heterosexual women', *British Journal of Psychiatry*, 120, pp. 477–81.

15. M. Siegelman (1979), 'Adjustment of homosexual and heterosexual women: A cross-national replication', *Archives of Sexual Behavior*, 8, 2, pp. 121–5.

16. D.C. Haldeman (1991), 'Sexual orientation conversion therapy for gay men and lesbians: A scientific examination' in Gonsiorek and Weinrich (eds), *Homosexuality: Research implications for public policy*, pp. 149–60.

17. If you doubt the point, take a look at the literature on the placebo response and how research has shown that there is an increasingly greater placebo effect beginning with a lay person, then a nurse, then a doctor, then a doctor in a white coat. Authority figures like medicos can be powerfully influential to the ignorant, the naïve, the uneducated, the vulnerable or the desperate.

18. G.C. Davison (1991), 'Constructionism and morality in therapy for homosexuality', in Gonsiorek and Weinrich (eds), *Homosexuality: Research implications for public policy*, pp. 137–48.

19. Haldeman, 'Sexual orientation conversion therapy', pp. 149–50.

20. You can go to the following website to view the text of the Position Statement of the American Psychological Association on reparative therapy: http://www.apa.org/pi/sexual.html

21. APS webpage: http://www.psychology.org.au/Assets/Files/Gay_lesbian_ethical_guidelines.pdf

22. http://www.apa.org/pi/lgbc/publications/therapeutic-response.pdf

23. L. Birk (1980), 'The myth of classical homosexuality: Views of a behavioral psychotherapist', in J. Marmor (ed.), *Homosexual behavior: A modern reappraisal*, New York: Basic Books.

24. Haldeman, 'Sexual orientation conversion therapy', p. 155.

25. T. Erzen (2006), *Straight to Jesus: Sexual and Christian conversion in the ex-gay movement*, University of California Press: London, p. 3.

26. Haldeman, 'Sexual orientation conversion therapy', p. 159.

Chapter 9

1. On 8 July 2008 the Anglican Synod in Britain voted overwhelmingly to allow women to be bishops. A thousand other clergy immediately stated that they might leave the church over the issue. On the same evening, the Vatican released a statement: 'We learned with regret the news of the vote of the Church of

England that opens the way to the introduction of legislation that would lead to the ordination of women bishops'. The decision would be 'a new obstacle to reconciliation between the Catholic Church and the Church of England'.

2. M.J. Borg (2001), *Reading the Bible Again for the First Time: Taking the Bible seriously but not literally*, HarperCollins: San Francisco.
3. I.G. Barbour (2000), *When Science Meets Religion*, New York: HarperCollins, p. 11.
4. Borg, *Reading the Bible*, p. 9.
5. P. Kennedy (2006), *A Modern Introduction to Theology: New questions for old beliefs*, New York: I. B. Taurus & Co. Ltd, p.133.
6. Ibid., pp. 133–4.
7. Borg, *Reading the Bible*, p. 7.
8. Kennedy, *A Modern Introduction to Theology*, pp. 133–4.
9. Borg, *Reading the Bible*, p.14.
10. J.S. Spong (1998), *Why Christianity Must Change or Die*, San Francisco: HarperCollins, p.xix.
11. http://www.gordonconwell.edu/ockenga/globalchristianity/wce.php
12. Borg, *Reading the Bible*, pp. 22–3.
13. Kennedy, *A Modern Introduction to Theology*, p. 129.
14. Borg, *Reading the Bible*, p. 38.
15. Ibid., p. 39.
16. Ibid., p. 38
17. J.H. Ellens (2006), *Sex in The Bible*, Westport: Praeger Publishers, p. 11.
18. Ibid., p. 12.
19. Ibid., p. 35.
20. Ibid., p. 41.
21. Ibid., p. 7.
22. *Confessions*, Book 3, Chapter 1.
23. J. Mc Manners (2001), *The Oxford illustrated history of Christianity*, New York: Oxford University Press.
24. Ibid., p. 69.
25. Given Jerome's homosexual sexual identity, was his attitude to the body and sexuality a Freudian 'reaction formation', the defence mechanism that drives an individual into the exact opposite behaviour to that which he is really feeling? I think a good case can be made for such a view.
26. Ellens, *Sex in The Bible*, p. 9.

Chapter 10

1. Ellens, *Sex in The Bible*, p. 106.
2. New International Version Study Bible (1985), Zondervan Corporation.
3. Ellens, *Sex in The Bible*, p. 108.

4. A. Kosnik et al. (1977), *Human Sexuality*, p. 191, cited in Ellens, *Sex in The Bible*, p. 117.

5. D.A. Helminiak (2000), *What the Bible Really Says About Homosexuality*, New Mexico: Alamo Square Press, pp. 49–50.

6. http://www.foxnews.com/story/0,2933,324966,00.html accessed 1 October 2008.

7. Ellens, *Sex in The Bible*, p. 110.

8. I am indebted to Helminiak for reminding me of it.

9. Helminiak, *What the Bible Really Says*, p. 53.

10. Ibid.

11. Ibid., p. 79.

12. B.J. Brooten (1996), *Love Between Women: Early Christian Responses to Female Homoeroticism*, Chicago/London: University of Chicago Press.

13. Can you imagine how the Jews would have felt about their holy, separate and distinct calling when they heard Paul's thoughts on this topic? No more distinction between Jew and Gentile, religious boundaries gone, males and females equal before God in every way, thousands of years of tribalism wiped away. For Paul, being in Christ is homogenising. This is revolutionary stuff, utterly radical, both in Paul's time and our own. We haven't quite realised it yet, have we? Although I don't always agree with Paul, he was certainly not a conservative peddling stability. This 'new creation' theme comes through again and again in his writings.

14. For a more exhaustive list of over 50 translations, see http://www.robandhans.com/religion/Malakoi-Arsenokoitai.html

15. Helminiak, *What the Bible Really Says*, p. 109.

16. Ibid., p. 111.

17. I am indebted to the scholarship of Justin Cannon from the GALIP website: http://www.gaychurch.org/Gay_and_Christian_YES/the_bible_christianity_and_homosexuality_justin_cannon.htm

18. http://www.searchgodsword.org/

19. Helminiak, *What the Bible Really Says*, p. 115.

20. Always find a psychologist who is a member of the professional association.

21. The church hierarchy spared him the ignominy of confessing the 'sin of homosexuality' while his wife and daughters watched in the congregation. Adultery would do.
A. Venn-Brown (2004), *A Life of Unlearning*, Sydney: New Holland Publishers.

Chapter 11

1. From this point on in this chapter, when I refer to the church, I am referring to the Roman Catholic church.

2. Of course, some of these religious have fallen foul of the Roman curia. A good example are the many priests, brothers and nuns who took up the mantle of liberation theology in the South American nations and, in defiance of Rome, actively worked to help feed, clothe and educate people to work against corrupt fascist governments. Pope John Paul II did not approve, spoke out against their activities and even castigated some of them in public.

3. Vatican II, Dogmatic Constitution on Divine Revelation, n. 11.

4. R.P. McBrien (1981), *Catholicism*. Oak Grove, Minneapolis: Winston Press Inc., p. 64.

5. Ibid., p. 66.

6. An award-winning documentary has been made of her life and struggle, *In Good Conscience: Sister Jeannine Gramick's Journey of Faith*, directed by Emmy Award winner Barbara Rick. New Ways Ministry continues to this day; its website: http://www.newwaysministry.org/

7. There is a third that we will briefly examine but by the time it was published in 1992, the church had well and truly formulated its position and the damage had already been done.

8. *Humanae Vitae*, Section 8.

9. Ibid., Section 9.

10. Ibid., Section 14.

11. *Sunday Telegraph*, 8 February 2008, Body and Soul Section, p. 5.

12. That's not good news for virtually every teenaged male on the planet.

13. http://www.vatican.va/roman_curia/congregations/cfaith/documents/rc_con_cfaith_doc_19751229_persona-humana_en.html

14. Note that I said the church hierarchy's attitude, not necessarily that of the clergy themselves. You can investigate for yourself if you wish the enormous change in clergy attitudes to marriage and celibacy over the last 30 years or so. Single status and celibacy were not there from the beginning. They were imposed in the 12th century. The apostles had wives and celibacy is not a part of the Tradition, but is only tradition.

15. http://www.vatican.va/roman_curia/congregations/cfaith/documents/rc_con_cfaith_doc_19861001_homosexual-persons_en.html

16. http://www.nhm.uio.no/againstnature/gayanimals.html

17. The same points can be made of many plants and fungi as well as single-celled organisms that reproduce asexually rather than sexually. This is not the usual pattern. And what about the male sea horse, which receives the eggs and undergoes pregnancy and gives birth? Not exactly typical, is it? Or what about the *Turritopsis nutricula* jellyfish, which not only reproduces asexually,

but appears to be immortal, reverting to a pupa stage after each adult phase and then indefinitely regenerating? Do we say then that these creatures are against nature because they are in the minority and do things differently? Not in the least. We accept that they are a normal variant of biological life. Atypical is not pathological.

18. J. Alison (2001), *Faith Beyond Resentment*, London: Darton, Longman & Todd, p. 203.

19. YAHWEH is the Hebrew for God's own name. Jews do not speak it out loud. It is best translated as 'I am who I am'. Thus, God's name represents pure being. 'I am' is the simplest and most profound thing you can say of anyone.

20. Alison, *Faith Beyond Resentment*, pp. 202–03.

21. See APS Document: Lesbian Gay Bisexual and Transgender (LGBT) Parented Families http://www.psychology.org.au/Assets/Files/LGBT-Families-Lit-Review.pdf

22. M.D. Jordan (2000), *The Silence of Sodom*, Chicago: University of Chicago Press.

23. J. Gramick and R. Nugent (eds) (1995), *Voices of Hope: A Collection of Positive Catholic Writings on Gay and Lesbian Issues*, New York: Center for Homophobia Education.

24. Alison, *Faith Beyond Resentment*, pp. 97–9.

25. Matthew 11: 28–30.

26. J.S. Spong (1988). *Living in Sin? A Bishop Rethinks Human Sexuality*, New York: HarperCollins, pp. 86–7.

27. Jordan, *The Silence of Sodom*, p. 6.

28. http://www.religioustolerance.org/hom_rcc.htm
http://www.religioustolerance.org/hom_rcc.htm#cozz

29. D.B. Cozzens (2000), *The Changing Face of the Priesthood: A Reflection on the Priest's Crisis of Soul*, Collegeville, Minnesota: The Order of St Benedict, Inc.

30. I think the Vatican might have something to say about that, as it has since released binding declarations on the non-admission of gay men to the priesthood and into seminaries.

31. Cozzens, *Changing Face*, pp. 99–100.

32. Ibid., p. 107.

33. Two documents from the Congregation of Catholic Education show how this is to be achieved. The first is the *Criteria for Discernment of Vocations with Regard to Persons with Homosexual Tendencies in View of Their Admission to the Seminary and to Holy Orders*: http://www.vatican.va/roman_curia/congregations/ccatheduc/documents/rc_con_ccatheduc_doc_20051104_istruzione_en.html The second is the *Guidelines for the Use of Psychology in the Admission and Formation of Candidates for the Priesthood*:

http://www.vatican.va/roman_curia/congregations/ccatheduc/documents/rc_con_ccatheduc_doc_20080628_orientamenti_en.html

34. It is absolutely essential that the reader understand that I am *not* talking about priests, straight or gay, who abuse children. Such men have no place in the ministry and should be reported to the police the moment any crime comes to light. Paedophilia is an extremely serious disorder. It is also a crime – against children, against society, and, when it is perpetrated by priests (or ministers of other Christian denominations), against the Gospel and against God. The ripping asunder of trust by such clerics is an especially bitter experience.

    I also believe this scandal, and subsequent episcopal cover-ups, have further diminished the moral authority of the Catholic church. Even more people have stopped listening and spiritual behavioural bifurcation is winning the day.

35. Jordan, *The Silence of Sodom*, pp. 22–3.
36. Ibid., p. 23.
37. http://www.rainbowsash.com/
38. Alison, *Faith Beyond Resentment*, pp. 192–3.
39. M.B. Kelly (2007), *Seduced By Grace: Contemporary Spirituality, Gay Experience and Christian Faith*, Melbourne: Clouds of Magellan Publishing, p. 90.

Chapter 12

1. L. Hillier, A. Mitchell and H. Mulcare (2008), '"I couldn't do both at the same time": Same sex attracted youth and the negotiation of religious discourse', *Gay & Lesbian Issues and Psychology Review*, 4, 2, pp. 80–93, 80.
2. L. Festinger (1957), *A Theory of Cognitive Dissonance*, Stanford: Stanford University Press.
3. K.A. Mahaffy (1996), 'Cognitive dissonance and its resolution: A study of lesbian Christians', *Journal for the Scientific Study of Religion*, 35, 4, pp. 392–402.
4. E.M. Rodriguez and S.C. Ouellette (2000), 'Gay and Lesbian Christians: Homosexual and Religious Identity Integration in the Members and Participants of a Gay-Positive Church', *Journal for the Scientific Study of Religion*, 39, 3, pp. 334–5.
5. E.M. Rodriguez and S.C. Ouellette (1999), 'The Metropolitan Community Church of New York: A gay and lesbian community', *The Community Psychologist*, 32, 3, pp. 24–9.
6. Rodriguez and Ouellette, 'Gay and Lesbian Christians'.
7. M.J. Borg and J.D. Crossan (2006), *The Last Week: The Day-by-Day Account of Jesus's Final Week in Jerusalem*, New York: HarperSanFrancisco.

8. J.E. Young, J. S. Klosko and M.E. Weishaar (2003), *Schema Therapy: A Practitioner's Guide*, New York: Guilford Press.

9. This term 'dad' or possibly even 'daddy' or 'papa' is used by Jesus in the Garden of Gethsemane, as recounted in Mark 14: 36 where he uses the word 'Abba': 'He kept repeating, "Abba! Father! All things are possible for you. Take this cup away from me. Yet not what I want but what you want."'The Bible Dictionary refers to Abba as an address to a father that connotes warm affection and filial confidence. It is a kinship term of emotional closeness.

10. V.P. Furnish (1994), 'The Bible and Homosexuality: Reading the Texts in Context', in J. S. Siker (ed.), *Homosexuality in the Church: Both Sides of the Debate*, pp. 18–35, Louisville Kentucky: Westminster John Knox Press.

11. The most famous of these relationships in the ancient world was that between the emperor Hadrian no less and his young lover Antinous. Although it is unlikely Antinous was a slave, he was certainly not Roman and was taken into the imperial household where he was probably a page of some sort. In his late teens or early 20s he took the eye of the emperor and the two became devoted lovers over a period of ten years until his untimely death by drowning in the Nile River. Hadrian grieved for Antinous until his own death aged 62 in 138 CE.

12. Kelly, *Seduced By Grace*.

13. I even stood as a parliamentary candidate in a New South Wales election for Fred Nile's Call to Australia party. Just over 1000 people voted for me. Oh dear, if only they knew! The Call to Australia Party, as it was then known, is a Christian Bible-based political party with a strong anti-gay agenda.

Index

abomination 123, 132, 133, 134–6, 153
Abraham 125–8
adikia 144
Alison, James 178–9, 186–7, 194, 212
American Psychiatric Association 83–5, 95, 169
American Psychological Association 85, 88, 89, 95, 98
andrapodistai 151
Anglican 20, 22, 32, 108–9, 155, 232n.16, 236n.1
Anglican Communion 26
animal kingdom 177–8
APA *see* American Psychiatric Association
APS *see* Australian Psychological Society
arsenokoitai 146–52
aschemosyne 143–4
asebeia 144
atimia 143
Attitude magazine 15
Australian Psychological Society 96

Barbour, Ian 107, 113
bdelygma 136
Bible, the: 'cherry picking' 152–3; methods of interpretation 115–18, 125; place in Catholicism 160; place in Christianity 106–9
biological determinism, theory of *see* biological essentialism
biological essentialism, theory of 46–7

birth control *see* contraception
bisexuality 45, 61, 234n.5
Blair, Tony 15
Borg, Marcus 36, 106–11, 115, 116–17
Boswell, John 81, 141, 149
Brokeback Mountain (film) 39, 131
Brooten, Bernadette 142

Cass, Vivienne 67–9
Catholicism: and doctrine 162; and Tradition 160–2; ordinary Catholics more liberal minded 15, 158–9, 205; sources of authority 159–63
CDF *see* Congregation for the Doctrine of the Faith
celibacy 22, 104, 122, 172, 176, 188, 190, 239n.14
closet, the *see* life lie
cognitive dissonance 25, 68, 70, 202–5, 206
coming out 70, 71–80; examples of 77–8; in an evangelical church 154; to parents 76–8
Congregation for the Doctrine of the Faith 162, 163, 167–86
Considerations 1992, The 182–6
contraception 111, 158–9
conversion therapy *see* reparative therapy
Council of Trent 160
counselling *see* psychological therapy
Countryman, L. William 141, 149–50

Cozzens, David 188, 189
creation science *see* creationism
creationism 32, 33, 36

deliverance 23–4, 155
depersonalisation 40
Diagnostic and Statistical Manual
of Mental Disorders 83–5, 169
doulos 218
DSM *see* Diagnostic and
Statistical Manual of Mental
Disorders

early maladaptive schemas
213–14
Ellens, J. Harold 118, 119, 120,
122, 124, 129, 134–5
EMS *see* early maladaptive
schemas
entimos 218–19
epilepsy 35–6
epistemology 29, 36, 224
erophobia 166
Erzen, Tanya 102, 103
ex-gay ministry 95, 100–4
exorcism 35 *see also*
deliverance

fasting 23
femininity 82, 103
Festinger, Leon 202–3
Foucault, Michel 202
fraternal birth order 55
Freud, Sigmund 62, 82–3
fundamentalism 108–11, 113;
decline of 111–13
Furnish, Victor 216

Galileo 33
gay people: as percentage of the
population 44–6; diversity 41;
in popular culture 39
gay priests 187–90
Gestalt therapy 26
Glasspool, Mary 26

God: as omniscient 126, 232n.2;
Jesus' new way of envisioning
211–15; traditional images of
211
Gramick, Sister Jeannine 18, 162,
183, 186, 239n.6
Gumbleton, Thomas 186

Haldeman, Douglas 95, 96, 97,
98, 103–4
Helminiak, Daniel 131, 135, 136,
137–8, 141, 145–6, 148, 149,
152, 220
heresy 33
HIV-Aids 139, 145
hodos 208
holiness code 133–7, 140, 142,
144, 150, 153
Holloway, Nicholas 192
homophobia: and violence 41;
as reaction formation 62;
displaced 75–6; in the Middle
Ages 81; internalised 74, 75
homosexual (as heteronormative
term) 17
Hooker, Dr Evelyn 85–9
hospitality 126–30
Humanae Vitae 158, 159, 161,
163–5, 176
Hume, Cardinal Basil 192
hypothalamus 54, 55–6

identity integration 206–8
impurity *see* uncleanness
Inquisition 33
interpenetrative approach, the 47

Jesus as healer 34–5
Jordan, Mark 185–6, 188, 190–1

Kelly, Michael 197, 227
Kennedy, Philip 110, 115
Kinsey, Alfred 44, 58–9
Kinsey profile 62–3, 234n.3
Kirby, Michael 16

language, the importance of 17, 43–4, 114, 134, 160, 207
Ledger, Heath 131, 132
Letter to the Bishops of the Catholic Church on the Pastoral Care of Homosexual Persons *see* Ratzinger Letter 1986, The
liberalism 107, 109
life lie, the 72–4, 75–7, 103, 146, 184, 187
literalism 31, 108–12, 138 *see also* fundamentalism
Lot 125, 126, 128–9

Mabo, Eddie 196
Mahaffy, Kimberly 204–5
malakoi 146–9
Marist Brothers 22
marriage, Catholic view of 163–5
masculinity 62, 82, 83, 97, 103, 148–9
masturbation 60, 149, 168
MCC/NY *see* Metropolitan Community Church New York
mental illness 35
metaphor 72, 108, 109, 117–18, 142, 208, 213, 228, 232n.2
Metropolitan Community Church New York 206–7
modernity *see* worldview, modern
Morrissey, Dr Gabrielle 166

New Ways Ministry 162, 183, 239n.6
Nugent, Father Robert 162, 183, 186

Ouellette, Suzanne 206

pais 218
para physin 141–3
Pell, Cardinal George 103, 192–3

Persona Humana see Seper Declaration, The 1975
Pertot, Dr Sandra 24–5
perversion 83, 140, 145
plethysmography 61–2
PNA theory *see* pre-natal androgen theory
Pope Benedict XVI 174 *see also* Ratzinger, Cardinal Joseph
Pope John Paul II 33, 174, 239n.2
Pope John XXIII 159
Pope Paul VI 158, 159, 167
pornoi 151
pre-natal androgen theory 53–5
psychiatry 82–5, 86, 88, 90, 95, 96, 97, 99
psychological therapy 24–5
purity *see* uncleanness

Rainbow Sash Movement, The 192–3
Ratzinger, Cardinal Joseph 174, 181
Ratzinger Letter 1986, The 174–82
Redemptorist order 21
reparative therapy 95–104, 236n.20
research methodologies 89–92
Robinson, Gene 26
Rodriguez, Eric 206–7

Satan 23
schema therapy 213
scientific method 31
scripture *see* Bible, the
self, the 64–5
self-labelling 60
Seper Declaration, The 1975 167–74
Septuagint 132, 136, 150
sex in the Bible 118–22
sexual identity 20, 64–70, 76, 101, 172, 220

sexual orientation 40, 44, 46–8;
    Cass model of development
    67–70; versus sexual preference
    66; ways of determining 60–1
sexual preference *see* sexual
    orientation
Shepard, Matthew 40–1
siblings, study of 50
Sipe, Richard 188
Sisters of Loretto 162
slavery 43, 153, 217–19,
    242n.11
social constructionism, theory of
    46–7
Sodom 125–31
Some Considerations Concerning
    the Response to Legislative
    Proposals on the Non-
    Discrimination of Homosexual
    Persons *see* Considerations
    1992, The
speaking in tongues 23
Spong, John Shelby 113, 170,
    187–8
St Augustine 120–1, 166
St Jerome 121–2, 166, 237n.25
St Paul 116, 120, 122, 139–46,
    148, 150, 151, 153, 176
suicide 24, 104, 201

Sydney Gay and Lesbian Mardi
    Gras 38

toevah 134–6
translation 114, 135, 136, 147–8
twins *see* siblings

uncleanness 136–8, 140, 142,
    144, 146, 153, 225
Uniting Church 23, 109
unnatural acts 141–3, 146, 220

Vatican II 159–61
Venn-Brown, Anthony 154

Way of Jesus, the 208–11, 221,
    226
Westboro Baptist Church 131–2
worldview: classical 30; modern
    30–2

X-chromosome linkage 52
Xq28 region 52–3

Young, Jeffrey 213
young people, attitudes to sex
    among 200–1

zimah 135

Index of
Biblical References

Old Testament

Genesis 18: 1–33 *125–8*
Genesis 19: 1–11 *124, 125–31*
Genesis 2: 18 *32*

Leviticus *118–19, 123, 132–4*
Leviticus 18: 1–3 *133*
Leviticus 18: 22–4 *124, 132, 136*
Leviticus 20:13 *124, 132, 137–8*

Deuteronomy 7: 25 *134*
Deuteronomy 12: 29–31 *134*
Deuteronomy 13: 14 *134*
Deuteronomy 17: 4 *134*
Deuteronomy 18: 9 *134*
Deuteronomy 23: 17–18 *135*
Deuteronomy 27: 15 *134*

Judges 19 *129–30*

1 Kings 14: 24 *135*
1 Kings 15: 12 *135*

2 Kings 16: 3 *134*

2 Kings 21: 2 *134*
2 Kings 23: 13 *134*

2 Chronicles 33: 2 *134*

Psalm 139: 13–16 *222*

Song of Songs *119*

Isaiah 1: 10–17 *130*

Jeremiah 16: 18 *134*
Jeremiah 23: 14 *130*

Ezekiel 14: 6 *134*
Ezekiel 16: 48–50 *130*
Ezekiel 5: 9 *134*
Ezekiel 5: 11 *134*

Zephaniah 2: 8–11 *130*

Malachi 2: 11 *134*

New Testament

Matthew 8: 5–13 *217–19*
Matthew 10: 5–16 *130*
Matthew 11: 8 *148*
Matthew 11: 28–30 *187*
Matthew 23 *191, 210*

Mark 1: 2 *208*
Mark 14: 36 *242n9*

Mark 1: 16 *209*
Mark 1: 19 *209*
Mark 3: 32–4 *227*
Mark 5: 1–20 *34–5*
Mark 9: 17–29 *35*

Luke 7: 1–9 *217–19*
Luke 15: 11–32 *214–15*

Luke 24: 13–16 *229*

John 10: 10 *26, 37*
John 13: 34–5 *226*
John 14: 6 *208*

Acts 9: 2 *208*
Acts 10 *225*
Acts 11: 1–18 *225*

Romans 1 *139–46*
Romans 1: 18–32 *124, 139–40*
Romans 1: 26 *141, 143*
Romans 1: 27 *143, 145–6*

Romans 2: 14 *141*

Romans 2: 27 *141*
Romans 8: 38–9 *230*
Romans 9: 21 *143*
Romans 11: 24 *142*
Romans 13: 13–14 *120*

1 Corinthians 6: 9–10 *124, 146–52*
1 Corinthians 11: 14 *141, 143*
1 Corinthians 12: 23 *143*
1 Corinthians 15: 3 *161*

Galatians 2: 15 *141*
Galatians 3: 26–8 *145*

1 Timothy 1: 10 *124, 146–52*